Building Value

Building Value

The Business *of* Venture Capital

Simon Barnes

WILEY

This edition first published 2025
© 2025 by Simon Barnes. All rights reserved

All rights reserved, including rights for text and data mining and training of artificial intelligence technologies or similar technologies. No part of this publication may be reproduced, stored in a retrieval system, or transmitted, in any form or by any means, electronic, mechanical, photocopying, recording or otherwise, except as permitted by law. Advice on how to obtain permission to reuse material from this title is available at http://www.wiley.com/go/permissions.

The right of Simon Barnes to be identified as the author of this work has been asserted in accordance with law.

Registered Office(s)
John Wiley & Sons, Inc., 111 River Street, Hoboken, NJ 07030, USA
John Wiley & Sons Ltd, New Era House, 8 Oldlands Way, Bognor Regis, West Sussex, PO22 9NQ

For details of our global editorial offices, customer services, and more information about Wiley products visit us at www.wiley.com.

Wiley also publishes its books in a variety of electronic formats and by print-on-demand. Some content that appears in standard print versions of this book may not be available in other formats.

Trademarks: Wiley and the Wiley logo are trademarks or registered trademarks of John Wiley & Sons, Inc. and/or its affiliates in the United States and other countries and may not be used without written permission. All other trademarks are the property of their respective owners. John Wiley & Sons, Inc. is not associated with any product or vendor mentioned in this book.

Limit of Liability/Disclaimer of Warranty: While the publisher and authors have used their best efforts in preparing this work, they make no representations or warranties with respect to the accuracy or completeness of the contents of this work and specifically disclaim all warranties, including without limitation any implied warranties of merchantability or fitness for a particular purpose. No warranty may be created or extended by sales representatives, written sales materials or promotional statements for this work. This work is sold with the understanding that the publisher is not engaged in rendering professional services. The advice and strategies contained herein may not be suitable for your situation. You should consult with a specialist where appropriate. The fact that an organization, website, or product is referred to in this work as a citation and/or potential source of further information does not mean that the publisher and authors endorse the information or services the organization, website, or product may provide or recommendations it may make. Further, readers should be aware that websites listed in this work may have changed or disappeared between when this work was written and when it is read. Neither the publisher nor authors shall be liable for any loss of profit or any other commercial damages, including but not limited to special, incidental, consequential, or other damages.

Library of Congress Cataloging-in-Publication Data

Names: Barnes, Simon, 1969- author.
Title: Building value: The business of venture capital / Simon Barnes.
Description: Hoboken, NJ: John Wiley & Sons, 2025. | Includes bibliographical references and index.
  | Summary: "This book, rooted in Simon Barnes' MBA courses on venture capital and his 25 years of industry experience, offers a practical insider's perspective on venture capital. Aimed at first-time entrepreneurs and young VCs, it emphasizes that entrepreneurial finance is more about aligning interests and behaviors than numbers. The book includes four case studies, model term sheets, and examples illustrating share structures and deal negotiations, providing valuable insights into the venture capital process. It advocates for mutual understanding between entrepreneurs and VCs to create deals that build value with minimal conflict" – Provided by publisher.
Identifiers: LCCN 2024038847 | ISBN 9781394231898 (hardback) | ISBN 9781394231904 (epub) |
  ISBN 9781394231911 (ebook)
Subjects: LCSH: Venture capital.
Classification: LCC HG4751 .B357 2025 | DDC 658.15/224–dc23/eng/20241017
LC record available at https://lccn.loc.gov/2024038847

Cover image: *Thick fog covering Golden Gate Bridge.* © Radoslaw Lecyk/Shutterstock

Cover design by Wiley

Set in 11/14pt AvenirLTStd by Lumina Datamatics

SKY10092384_112824

Contents

About the Author		vii
Acknowledgements		ix
Chapter 1	Why Do Start-ups Raise Capital?	1
Chapter 2	Equity and the Art of Milestone-Based Financing	13
Chapter 3	A History Lesson	43
Chapter 4	Business Models	59
Chapter 5	A Day in the Life	85
Chapter 6	Valuation	111
Chapter 7	Inside the Deal	149
Chapter 8	Raising the Next Round	201
Chapter 9	Towards the Exit	245
Chapter 10	Building Value: The Business of Venture Capital	281
Case Study Solutions		293

About the Author

Simon Barnes has worked in and around the venture capital industry since 1998, first with the London office of Atlas Venture, where he experienced the dotcom boom and subsequent bust first-hand. He spent time on the faculty of Imperial College Business School, London, co-authoring *Raising Venture Capital* before co-founding Circadia Ventures in 2005 to manage early-stage venture capital funds investing in life sciences, nutrition and industrial biotechnology. He has served on the boards of directors of numerous venture capital-backed businesses in the United States, United Kingdom and European Union. He holds an MA in Natural Sciences and a PhD in Molecular Biology & Biochemistry from the University of Cambridge and an MBA from Imperial College Business School.

Acknowledgements

I would like to thank Ben Barnes for his research into the history of the venture capital industry and for his assistance in preparing and reviewing this text. Thank you to John Lyon for enjoyable discussions about entrepreneurial finance and making teaching it fun.

Chapter 1

Why Do Start-ups Raise Capital?

It might seem a strange question to ask at the beginning of a book about venture capital, where so much of the culture of the start-up industry appears to focus on 'doing the next raise'. Of course, start-ups raise capital, that's what they do, isn't it? We are sometimes led to believe that the only goal for entrepreneurs or start-up CEOs is to raise money from venture capitalists (VCs). But ask yourself a fundamental question: Why? In the old days, entrepreneurs didn't always do that, so why now? In the early part of the 20th century, companies which started small ended up being global corporations without huge amounts of capital being injected into them. With a sometimes limited number of informal backers, their management teams reinvested cash generated from hard-won sales to build companies step by step, often failing and restarting along the way. Was there a different entrepreneurial mentality necessitated by the scarcity of resources? Can we learn something important from the old ways? Reading even a small amount of literature on the history of business can be illuminating when seeking an answer to these questions.

The Ford Motor Company was a start-up once. Henry Ford began small with a few investors to form the Detroit Automobile Company. The company failed. The assets were bought out of administration by some of the investors, who allowed Ford to carry on as the Henry Ford Company. The company failed for a second time. For Henry Ford it was a case of third time lucky; the Ford Motor Company was formed with investments totalling $28,000 in 1903. The early investors in the Ford Motor Company included a successful Detroit coal merchant and the director of a well-regarded bank. These individuals were not professional VCs, they were private investors with a sense of adventure and a vision of the future. The company operated with very little resource; Henry Ford himself didn't take a salary and was adept at persuading others to work for very little. This approach, raising money where he could and stretching very limited resources, eventually led to the successful global corporation we know today. The early investments into Ford's various attempts to launch were not from modern-style venture capital funds, but piecemeal investments from a group of business owners and managers who took a chance and eventually made remarkable returns (Brinkley 2004). Tight financial control and careful business practices were the secret to Ford's early success, before the exponential growth of the Model-T powered the business to profit.

Countless other early 20th-century success stories took decades to become the global corporations they are now. Throughout history, 'start-ups' (before they were really called that) often grew slowly and organically, and sometimes independent of a financing industry that was simpler and more limited in scope than it is today.

By injecting substantial amounts of external funding, the modern venture capital industry confers upon start-ups the ability for *time travel*, accelerating through the difficult early years of product development and business model experimentation. It affords start-ups the ability to try designs and test markets and business models via trial and error or the scientific method now termed 'lean start-up', and build world-class management teams to execute aggressive growth plans, including the acquisition of smaller competitors or suppliers. Technology means that the pace of innovation is quicker than it was in Henry Ford's day, and the race to conquer unique business opportunities before others is conducted at break-neck speed. The venture capital industry provides the fuel to grow fast…

ASSET PARSIMONY

In a 1984 academic paper, Donald Hambrick and Ian MacMillan coined the term *asset parsimony*, namely 'skill at deploying the minimum assets needed to achieve the desired business results' (Hambrick and MacMillan 1984). Their paper focused on return on investment (ROI) and pointed out that investing heavily in assets upfront, without understanding the risks and the payoff, can rapidly pave the way to the bankruptcy court. This is not a complicated concept, and most will agree that it is intuitive to most experienced managers, but it is surprising how few entrepreneurs (and VCs) adhere to this business philosophy today.

Raising finance for start-ups is a time-consuming and expensive process. More favourable conditions for raising finance are best achieved by having a compelling investment opportunity, supported by evidence of technical progress and a scalable business model, before approaching investors. Demonstrating an ability to make sales, strike deals or at least generate interest from potential customers (often referred to as 'traction') is a key aspect of convincing investors that this is more than 'an idea'. In other words, it's 'best foot forward' before attempting to raise capital. Entrepreneurs should go as far as they can before attempting to raise money for the first time; maximise the utility of assets at hand; and beg, borrow and salvage until the business is ready and sufficiently attractive to raise investment on the most favourable terms.

This thought process should be nailed to the wall of every fledgling start-up business – achieve as much as you can and deliver tangible value before engaging with the investment community as this will enable you to raise more capital, on better terms and with less time and energy.

In recent years, asset parsimony seems to have been forgotten by entrepreneurs. The culture within the technology-based entrepreneurial community seems to have been the opposite – raise as much money as you can, as fast as you can, on as little progress as possible and invest heavily upfront. This has been possible for some entrepreneurs in the tech industry as venture capital markets have been awash with capital for extended periods between 2012 and 2022 – technology markets have been hot and venture capital funds swollen by historically low global interest rates. This is discussed in more detail later in the book, but for now the key lesson is that during times of plentiful venture capital, the 'culture' of start-ups shifts to fashionably large funding rounds and away from the *grit* of the hard-bitten entrepreneur who understands what it means to survive tough times.

THE BEST TIME TO RAISE MONEY IS WHEN YOU DON'T NEED TO

Seemingly paradoxical to the concept of asset parsimony, experienced entrepreneurs know that *the best time to raise money is when you don't need to*. The asset parsimony approach has one flaw: it assumes a steady supply of investment capital on constant, stable terms that do not change. For start-ups especially, this is not true. Market conditions in general can change overnight, but sentiment towards a particular sector in venture capital can disappear even faster – in the blink of an eye. There is no point frugally and methodically working to achieve proof of concept, and then going out to raise capital just as the financing climate turns sour.

Getting the timing right, therefore, plays a huge role in raising capital. Experienced entrepreneurs are constantly alert to the possibility of external investment, because the most favourable terms are achieved when they don't really need the money. When the bank balance is healthy, entrepreneurs have the luxury of walking away from an investment offer, and that makes investors more eager to invest, driving up the price of the deal. It is easier to negotiate price when you don't need investment urgently…

Putting aside negotiation tactics, experienced entrepreneurs usually think very carefully before turning down investment offers, even when they are not looking for funding. They are also open to accepting more investment than they are asking for in their business plan or pitch. It is usually the case that early-stage ventures run into delays – be they technical challenges or commercial hurdles – and having a cash buffer for unforeseen events can be a life saver for the company.

In conclusion, the seemingly paradoxical 'go as far as you can on as little as possible' and 'raise money when you don't need it' is not a paradox at all. Entrepreneurs need to respect asset parsimony with the knowledge that many a failed entrepreneur has turned down external investment for fear of dilution, and then gone bust when the climate changes. Balancing these twin pressures of making progress in a changing financing climate is a core skill for entrepreneurs. There is no universal solution to balancing this risk, just an awareness of the issue and an acknowledgement of one fundamental truth – a company that runs out of cash is bankrupt. So, the overriding force in all of this is making sure the company is funded and sometimes that means raising investment when you can.

Take money when you can get it, but respect asset parsimony.

CROSSING THE VALLEYS OF DEATH

Revisiting our initial question, 'Why do start-ups raise capital?', it is reasonable to assume that new ventures generally spend money before they earn it. Investment in research and development, hiring personnel and embarking on expensive marketing campaigns all occur before the company has generated revenue. These activities result in cash flowing out of the company, sometimes for an extended period, before the first revenues are generated.

If we view this as a cumulative cash-flow chart (see Figure 1.1) we arrive at a generic picture, the so-called 'Valley of Death', a well-known concept in the field of entrepreneurial finance. For any given start-up, cash declines as the business invests in R&D, product development and so on, until sales begin and revenue (and subsequently cash) starts to climb. The point at which cash flow turns positive marks the lowest point in the Valley of Death, the

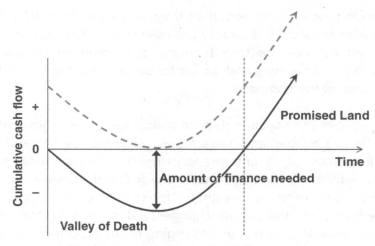

Figure 1.1 Financing the journey to the Promised Land.
The total amount of finance required for the company to reach the Promised Land is the distance between the curve and the x-axis; in other words, the lowest point in the cumulative cash flow (bank balance). Raising capital shifts the curve upwards so that it never crosses into negative values and keeps the company solvent, illustrated by the dashed line. The capital raised by an entrepreneurial team should be based on this logic with a buffer for delays and not, as is often the case, a simple desire to raise as large an amount as possible...

most negative 'bank balance' the business will experience as it grows towards a profitable 'Promised Land' in which cash is generated to be used for further growth. Most start-ups fail somewhere in the Valley of Death, not because their ideas were inherently wrong, but more often because they ran out of cash before reaching the other side.

The function of the venture capital industry, and other early-stage investors, is very simply to enable start-ups to cross the Valley of Death. According to our Valley of Death cash-flow chart, the amount of capital required by the start-up ought to be dictated by the lowest point in the valley – in other words, a capital injection at the beginning that shifts the curve upwards so that the lowest point touches the x-axis and prevents the bank balance straying into negative territory.

Of course, life is never as simple as that, at least in the world of entrepreneurial finance. The Valley of Death is often shrouded in fog, making it almost impossible to see the bottom or the other side of the valley. A faint glimmer of a possible foothold to clamber out of the chasm is sometimes as good as it gets. VCs are familiar with management teams telling them that the turning point is imminent, only to find that they have not reached the bottom at all, and in fact they are only half-way down, or some seismic shift has made the valley deeper, wider or both. In some cases, even as revenues grow and the business nears the Promised Land, new and unexpected valleys may appear from the fog. A contract is lost, a technology fails, a competitor appears or a regulator imposes new requirements on the product. This section was titled 'Crossing the Valleys of Death' (in the plural) for a reason, as entirely new valleys may open before the management team's eyes (see Figure 1.2). Plans are revised, budgets revisited and, inevitably, fresh funding is required to cross the newly appeared valley. So, it goes on…

A close colleague and friend, Professor John Lyon, describes 'the uncertainty of entrepreneurial finance' as the third certainty in life, alongside death and taxes'. This is a lesson well remembered by all who have travelled through the multiple Valleys of Death, and even more so by those who never made it out. This reinforces our earlier conclusion about respecting asset parsimony but taking money when you can get it – entrepreneurial teams never really know what is around the next corner and an unexpected adverse

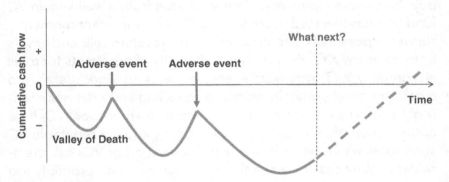

Figure 1.2   There are multiple Valleys of Death.
To the surprise of entrepreneurial teams and investors alike, just as things are picking up there is a setback, perhaps technical, perhaps commercial and sometimes people related. This can plunge the business into a second or third Valley of Death. They may end up bumping along the floor of a very wide and seemingly endless valley. This presents the entrepreneurial team with a never-ending question: how much to raise? Balancing a financial safety net or financial buffer with the dilution of raising too much capital is an ongoing debate in all entrepreneurial management teams.

event can spell the end of the business, or at the very least a requirement for new finance in distressed circumstances.

Wise entrepreneurs raise more than they need in anticipation of setbacks that will almost certainly come...

IS IT JUST THE MONEY?

Ask an experienced entrepreneur why they raised venture capital, and they will tell you it's not just about crossing the Valleys of Death or speed to market. It is not simply 'the money'. It is about what else the VCs bring: credibility, networks, experience, reputation and (importantly) access to further capital and financial services such as investment banks and the best accountancy and law firms. They serve as guides within the financial ecosystem and can help start-ups avoid the blind alleys that lie along the way to reaching a profitable outcome. The venture capital industry calls this *money plus* and this may be the *real* reason why start-ups *should* raise money, perhaps even if they don't need to.

The credibility associated with raising capital from a highly reputable VC can make a considerable difference to the fortunes of an otherwise unknown start-up (see Figure 1.3). Start-ups effectively buy themselves *legitimacy*. A press release from a well-known VC fund that has invested in company XYZ is an important moment – suddenly, potential customers and suppliers return calls and emails from company XYZ; the number and quality of applicants for roles at company XYZ increases; everyone wants to work there. And most importantly, other investors come calling and what was previously a drought of financial interest turns into a monsoon. VCs hate nothing more than missing an opportunity, and if a reputable VC announces an investment, the first question other VCs ask themselves is 'Why didn't we see that?'. At that point it's probably too late for them to invest in the current financing round but they will certainly be aiming at the front of the line for the next round of financing when it occurs.

Reputation is everything in the world of entrepreneurial finance. Research has shown that entrepreneurs will accept less favourable

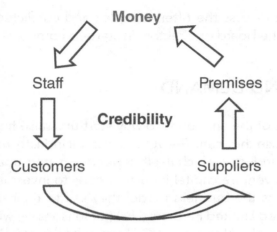

Figure 1.3 The credibility carousel.
Raising money is not just about crossing multiple Valleys of Death. It is about acquiring credibility via the backing of reputable investors. Raising capital from a well-known and well-regarded VC can enable a start-up to benefit from the halo effect of their reputation. Prior to raising money, the start-up suffers from the liability of newness in which it is difficult to gain customers and suppliers, rent premises and hire staff. Sue Birley, a Distinguished Professor on the MBA programme at Imperial College London's Management School taught many years ago that money is often the ingredient that breaks the 'credibility carousel'. This is a lesson that has been borne out time and again, and reputable money is best of all...

investment terms (a lower price per share) to raise capital from a VC with a particularly strong reputation. For the reasons above, entrepreneurs will *trade* precious equity in their start-up for the non-monetary value that such VCs bring via their reputation and track record. This is often referred to as 'paying for association', and a number of researchers have attempted to measure how much additional equity entrepreneurs will give up just to get a really well-known VC on board. We should not read too much into the precise quantification of this trade-off – it will vary from industry to industry, across regions and over time – but it is safe to conclude that entrepreneurs expect extra value, or 'money plus', from highly reputable VCs and are prepared to surrender additional equity in return.

Do VCs really add the value they claim and for which entrepreneurs are prepared to 'pay for association'? That is a question we will deal with in more detail later in this book – opinions are split within the entrepreneurial community and there is research to support arguments for and against. Later chapters will refer to this question and discuss the often complex and conflicted role that VCs play on the board of directors in start-up companies.

SUPPLY AND DEMAND

The final part of the answer as to why start-ups raise finance is, of course, because they can. The venture capital industry has evolved into a global industry, which itself depends on start-ups as its raw material. The venture capital industry *needs* to invest in start-ups because that is the business model they sell to their own share-holders, termed Limited Partners (LPs) (for reasons we will examine later in this book). Numerous VCs have raised increasingly large funds and there is pressure to invest the money they have raised. They look aggressively for 'deal flow' (opportunities) to deploy their capital into, and there is competition to find the best deals and generate the best returns for their LPs.

The delicate balance between the *supply* of venture capital and the *demand* from start-ups creates a finely tuned global innovation engine. When this global innovation engine is in balance, it has the potential to operate at high speed, generating wealth and providing solutions to some of society's biggest problems, some of which we didn't even know we had. When supply and demand is out of balance, it may lead to catastrophe as over-egged venture-backed companies or entire sectors fail to deliver. The peaks and troughs observed on the NASDAQ index since 1994 (see Figure 1.4) illustrate clearly how market sentiment towards technology and science-based companies rises and falls with alarming frequency – a proxy for the returns generated by the venture capital industry.

Any economist will confirm that supply and demand is a fundamental economic truth and many market phenomena may be explained this way. Venture capital is no different. There are periods of time, such as the decade following the financial crisis of 2008–2009, in which quantitative easing by central banks around the world fuelled the expansion of the venture capital industry as investors sought returns in riskier assets, which led to increased supplies of venture capital seeking opportunities. The demand for venture capital

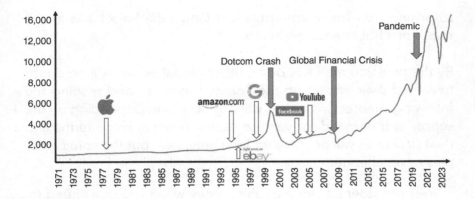

Figure 1.4 The NASDAQ is a good proxy for the state of the venture capital market.
From the inception of the NASDAQ index, the value of stocks for technology-based businesses has shown remarkable growth but it has been a bumpy ride. The approximate dates for the launch of several well-known companies are marked, as are three key global events in the financial world: the dotcom crash of 2000, the financial crisis of 2009 and the COVID-19 pandemic. Entrepreneurial teams raising capital faced a very different financial climate depending on timing...

arguably failed to keep up, at least with the same quality, and eventually 2022 saw a sharp reversal as VCs turned off the taps, leaving an unsatisfied demand for venture capital following an overinflated entrepreneurial bubble.

SUMMARY OF CHAPTER 1

This opening chapter has attempted to provide an overview of the entrepreneurial financing environment from the perspective of both entrepreneurs and VCs. It has focused on crossing the Valleys of Death and the principles of 'money plus' – in other words, seeking additional value from investors who back growing businesses.

Entrepreneurs should not raise money for the sake of it; this is not the goal, it is the means to reach the goal – a profitable enterprise. Although we now live in a world with a large and sophisticated venture capital industry to fuel the global innovation engine, perhaps we can learn something from the 'old ways' when entrepreneurs built businesses in tough financing climates with precious few resources. This seems an obvious statement to make, but it is surprising how many entrepreneurs (and VCs) forget this in the frenzy of a hot financing climate.

By the time you read this book, other global events will no doubt have had their impact on the financial markets, and reading the following chapters in context will be important. Depending on the supply and demand for venture capital finance, some terms and deal structures will be more (or less) prevalent, but the core principles never change.

Respect asset parsimony, raise money when you don't need to, raise more than you think you need and raise with money plus as your priority.

REFERENCES

Brinkley, D. (2004). *Wheels for the World: Henry Ford, His Company and a Century of Progress, 1903–2003.* New York: Penguin Random House.
Hambrick, D.C. and MacMillan, I.C. (1984). SMR forum: Asset parsimony – managing assets to manage profits. *Sloan Management Review* 25 (2): 67–74.

Chapter 2

Equity and the Art of Milestone-Based Financing

In the previous chapter, we examined some of the basic character-istics of the world of entrepreneurial finance, beginning with the question 'Why do start-ups raise capital?' We explored the idea of asset parsimony and how the changing fortunes of the financial climate will impact the ability of entrepreneurs to raise finance and cross multiple Valleys of Death.

In the current chapter, we will examine the key principles underpin-ning the entrepreneurial financing journey, the forms and sources of investment entrepreneurs might access and the way in which the venture capital industry views its own world. Only by understanding the business model of venture capital funds and the fund managers who operate them can entrepreneurial teams navigate the financ-ing journey with optimal results. Key to this is understanding the

THE EQUITY PIE

Ask any class of undergraduate students where entrepreneurial start-ups should raise finance and one of the first answers will usually be 'get a loan from a bank'. Banks do not, however, make loans to high-risk companies with unproven technologies, business models and management teams. Small businesses such as shops, local services and cash-generating ventures seeking to expand and open a new branch based upon a track record of solid financial results may access bank loans (think of a reputable and successful hairdresser opening a second branch in a neighbouring town) but pioneering entrepreneurs seeking to change the world cannot usually persuade a bank to back a high-risk, unproven idea with a loan.

Such entrepreneurs, aiming to disrupt markets and build big businesses, are faced with a simple solution: raise equity finance. Entrepreneurial teams need to sell a share of their start-up company to investors who are prepared to back it at great risk. Such investors must be prepared to lose their entire investment in the start-up if it fails but hope to share in enormous returns if it succeeds. This is the business of venture capital in a nutshell and equity is its currency.

Just as the shares of established companies are traded on various stock exchanges around the world, changing hands readily via intermediary market-making stockbrokers, so too can shares in start-ups be sold. Selling equity simply means selling a portion of ownership (or shares) in the company, and the first question which springs to mind is how much? What portion of the equity pie (i.e. how many shares) must the founders of the business sell to raise the finance they need to build it and what conditions are attached to that sale?

How big a portion of the equity pie is sold, and at what price, is the subject of Chapter 6, where we examine valuation (or pricing) of venture capital deals. For now, it is enough to say that the valuation of start-ups is more *art* than science. Formal valuation methodologies do not work very well for high-risk, early-stage ventures and the valuation is determined by the market: how much investors are prepared to pay for a piece of the company based on their views of the risks and returns and the supply and demand for venture capital. But what constitutes the market for shares in start-ups and who are the participants? Who buys and sells equity in start-ups and how do these transactions occur? What is the process and how are the deals structured? These are all issues that we will address throughout this book, and the aim is to unpick the activities of the venture capital industry from the perspective of both entrepreneurial teams and the VCs who back them.

Equity is the currency of entrepreneurial finance; the question is, who are the buyers?

PRIVATE EQUITY AND VENTURE CAPITAL

When shares are sold directly by a privately owned company to a buyer, we call this 'private equity'; a private contract to sell shares as opposed to 'public equity' for larger corporations, in which shares are traded daily on a stock market. The venture capital industry is essentially a subset of the private equity industry, and the question is often asked, therefore, what is the real difference between private equity and venture capital, as the terms are sometimes used interchangeably? The answer is that whereas VCs specialise in buying equity in start-up and early-stage companies, the wider private equity industry usually focuses on established businesses with revenues and cash flows, and often uses debt alongside equity as part of its financing mix.

It is important to note here that starting a company is not the only route to owning one. Some entrepreneurs buy pre-existing companies, sometimes when the current owners retire and often to turn them around or combine them with other assets. When managers buy the company they currently work for, we term this activity a *management buyout* and when they buy external target companies, we refer to this as a *management buy-in*. Both are important routes to ownership supported by private equity funds but are beyond the scope of this book.

The goal of private equity is often to turn around underperforming companies, unlocking the value within their assets and exploring new markets and geographies with a proven business model. There is often a lot of financial engineering and the use of debt to leverage the assets of the target company. Venture capital, on the other hand, focuses entirely on start-ups and early-stage companies, where almost everything is unproven. VCs are taking a holistic view of the opportunity, there is almost no financial engineering – it is pure equity. Although we will explore preferred shares and preference shares used by VCs later in this book, the share instruments and financial structures used in venture capital are relatively simple compared to private equity, and indeed VCs and private equity fund managers often appear to speak a different language. Sometimes, however, private equity funds overlap with venture capital funds when growing ventures become sufficiently cash-generative for the private equity industry to step in and take a stake, often with a specific exit goal in mind.

Figure 2.1 shows the relationship between private equity and venture capital. It is worth noting that buyouts use a combination of equity and debt. Management buyouts, buy-ins and very large 'leveraged buyouts' target companies with established businesses and reliable (but likely underperforming) business models. These transactions use debt because the risks are lower, and the business has sufficient free cash flow to service debt. Start-ups are different. They have little or no cash flow, and rarely have a proven product, business model or even management team. Debt is off the table and equity financing is the instrument of choice.

This book focuses on the role of the venture capital industry in investing in start-ups, but VCs are not the only source of early-stage equity finance. New ventures often find that their first capital comes from other sources, some of which are informal and very close to home. Friends and family, business angels, accelerators and incubators and crowdfunding play a role in the early steps towards building a successful company.

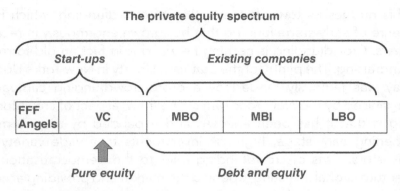

Figure 2.1 The private equity spectrum.
Venture capital forms a subset of the private equity spectrum and focuses on start-ups and early-stage ventures. Venture capital funds are generally much smaller than private equity buyout funds, which target established businesses, usually with the goal of turning around underperforming assets. Venture capital funds invest in pure equity and rarely use debt, but buyout funds are different. Management buyouts (MBOs), management buy-ins (MBIs, in which external management teams buy a company) and leveraged buyouts (LBOs, which are very large buyouts) use debt as a source of capital in their financing mix. The debt is repaid from free cash flow within the target company over several years, leaving the equity holders as the owners of a debt-free company. This is an oversimplification of a complex industry, but the key principle is that VCs, business angels and friends, family and fools (FFF) are all a subset of the wider private equity market.

FOOLS AND ANGELS

Who would be unwise enough to buy shares in a start-up with an unproven technology, business model and management team? The entrepreneurial team's extended friends and family might. In fact, the very first investment into start-ups frequently comes from those whose investment decision might go beyond the purely rational analysis of a VC; in other words, friends and family. This is often described, perhaps more accurately, as 'friends, family and fools'. This is not meant to be derogatory; sometimes humans invest in other humans because they are related, because they like them or perhaps because they just want to help someone in a quest that means something to them personally – or they feel a connection. A quick scan of websites like gofundme.com or justgiving.com will illustrate just how generous people can be with a wide variety of causes: some charitable, some personal and others blatantly commercial.

This nudges us towards the notion of crowdfunding, which is a genre of early-stage funding that has grown enormously in recent years. Crowdfunding is nothing new and is in fact an old form of fundraising. The plinth for the Statue of Liberty in New York's Upper Bay was famously funded by a proto-crowdfunding campaign organised by the *New York Times*. The 'new' aspect of crowdfunding is that it has been enabled and expanded by the internet, opening early-stage, high-risk investments to a wide variety of investors. Fans of crowdfunding refer to the democratisation of venture capital investing, opening the market and providing access to high-return deals for ordinary investors.

Critics of crowdfunding, on the other hand, talk about the extreme information asymmetry existing between the promoters of new ventures on crowdfunding platforms and the inexperienced investors who back them. Information asymmetry is discussed later in the book; it is a fundamental function of the venture capital industry to manage the information asymmetry that exists between entrepreneurs and investors. Entrepreneurs know a lot more about the risks of their business than the investors who back them. In the case of crowdfunding, there are very few if any means to manage this information asymmetry and investors are exposed directly to a wide variety of pioneering ideas that carry enormous risk. Some commentators argue that such investors rarely have the skills and experience to know what they are getting into and should proceed with extreme caution. *Buyer beware* is nowhere more evident than in the world of crowdfunding…

Business angels are dealt with in other texts, such as Richard Hargreaves's practical guide *Business Angel Investing* (Hargreaves 2021), but suffice to say they form an important component of the early-stage entrepreneurial financing journey. The term 'business angel' covers a variety of investors, from individual high-net-worth investors (the classic view being successful entrepreneurs reinvesting their great wealth and experience into new ventures) to smaller participants investing $10,000 or less. Indeed, Scott Shane, in his book *Fool's Gold*, points out that most angel investors in America are much smaller and play a less prominent role than popular views would have us believe (Shane 2008). Whether large or small, however, the key word for business angel investors is 'experience'. Just as VCs offer money plus via their experience, networks, connections and reputation, the same is true of the best business angels–whatever their quantum of investment.

Raising capital from an angel with a great track record and reputation in a particular field has value beyond the dollars they put in. It is worth highlighting the subtle difference here from a high-net-worth investor who has amassed wealth through some other means, be it investment banking, sports, fame, celebrity, inheritance or even a major lottery win. They may be able to invest in a start-up but whether they can offer the same 'money plus' as an individual who has built and sold an entrepreneurial venture is a matter for debate. The operational experiences of a successful entrepreneur turned angel is often the true value of angel investing.

The single item that binds all these angels together and sets them apart from VCs is that they are investing their own wealth. Contrast this with VCs who, as will be discussed later in Chapter 4, are professional fund managers investing other people's money with specific targets in mind and timelines to adhere to. Business angels can have more flexibility in their timelines to exit, but having no clear guidelines can have its own downsides. Sometimes angels write their own rules and that can lead to challenges later in the entrepreneurial finance journey.

It has sometimes been said that 'if they were really angels they wouldn't be where they are today'. This is a deliberately provocative comment designed to make a point – and it is this: entrepreneurial teams need to know the investors they are dealing with, how they behave and what their business model is. The venture capital business model is relatively simple to understand and almost uniform across different funds and different countries. This is not the case with business angels, who are sometimes unpredictable and occasionally present challenges for a growing business seeking to raise venture capital.

Sometimes business angels organise themselves into networks or groups with professional procedures, structures and the reputations to go with them. These business angel networks often hold regular pitching events, and lead investors within the group will nominate and sponsor start-ups through the investment process. Such groups often coordinate their investments through standard investment agreements and may have one individual (the lead investor or sponsor) who is mandated to sign documents on behalf of all the angel investors who participate in a round. This makes deal management much easier for the entrepreneurial team, who no longer must deal with multiple business angels when they need shareholder consent for major corporate decisions.

VCs find it easier to invest in companies that have raised angel finance from organised business angel networks or groups rather than individual angels. This is because the business angel networks use more recognisable terms and construct deals that neatly dovetail with later venture capital rounds. Often, smaller VCs will co-invest with established business angel groups in a cross-over round as the company transitions from the early angel rounds to larger venture capital rounds. Contrary to some commentators' views, VCs and business angels can co-exist very easily and provide a smooth transition through the funding rounds – to be discussed later in this chapter.

INCUBATORS AND ACCELERATORS

Prior to the dotcom boom it was difficult to come across something that could be described formally as an 'incubator' or an 'accelerator'. Up until that time there were informal arrangements, mostly within universities where start-ups would be housed for free, consistent with the asset parsimony concept discussed in Chapter 1; there was a mindset of beg, borrow and salvage that included free space and access to facilities provided by the parent organisation. It was investment in kind, although some universities developed spinout funds to back companies developed within their instructions and using their intellectual property. In the United Kingdom, the University of Manchester was an early proponent of the model, with the formation of the Manchester Bio Incubator at the end of the 1990s.

After 2000, a legacy of the dotcom era was the notion that an organised approach to company creation could be a lucrative business if carried out correctly. The incubator model began to spread within universities and then into the private sector. Incubators began to operate as landlords housing their own start-ups (known as spinouts), sometimes for rent payable in cash and sometimes with the expectation of equity when the business raised money from investors. They began to tack on advice, professional services and in some cases small amounts of seed funding.

Accelerators arrived a little later, and it is generally recognised that this sector began with the launch of Y Combinator in 2005 and TechStars in 2007. The industry has grown substantially and at the time of writing this book, accelerators appear to be almost ubiquitous – operated with varying degrees of success by universities, national and regional governments, groups of investors who club together behind an independent accelerator and numerous corporates as part of their open innovation strategies. Although there is an overlap in the operation of accelerators and incubators (both offer mentoring and planning, office and technical facilities, and sometimes funding), accelerators differ in their 'admissions' policy. They tend to operate like a quasi-educational programme, offering admission to companies as a cohort for a fixed period, putting them through a mentoring programme with a defined endpoint or 'graduation' rather than the tenancy approach of incubators, where the endpoint is loosely defined.

Some accelerators offer investment upon 'graduation' and others run a competition, with the winners receiving investment in cash or in kind through further mentoring services. Accelerators often charge fees for their programmes, either in cash or in kind via equity – they are in effect acting like early-stage VCs, acquiring equity in a portfolio of hand-picked start-ups that they nurture and accelerate. Accelerators may be viewed as a bridge between incubators and the external investment industry (both angels and VCs) but the overlap is now substantial, as incubators and accelerators have migrated towards each other by adopting aspects of each of their business models.

Both incubators and accelerators (and the hybrids that exist between them) are a viable and important source of finance for start-ups. They go some way to filling part of the equity gap left by VCs as they migrate to more lucrative, large fund sizes and provide a more formal source of finance than friends and family rounds.

SELLING EQUITY IS EXPENSIVE

Selling equity is an expensive business. Selling equity doesn't just mean raising money, it means selling 'upside' in the business – a substantial share of the future success. Perhaps more importantly, it means surrendering *control*. The founders' ownership is diluted when the company raises equity finance, the magnitude of their dilution being determined by the valuation (share price) of the transaction. Valuation and pricing of equity is discussed in detail in Chapter 6. Not only does this mean sharing the economic benefits of future success, it also requires an acceptance that there will be other voices to be heard in discussions about the strategic direction of the business, both via appointments to the board of directors and via shareholder vetoes (discussed in Chapter 7).

When VCs buy equity in start-ups, they usually require a seat on the board of directors, this being part of their 'money plus', delivering additional value beyond the cash investment discussed in Chapter 1. There are, however, other mechanisms through which they exert some degree of control over the businesses they invest in. The right to exercise shareholder vetoes over key decisions such as spending, board appointments and the use of preferred or preference shares to enable their rights are all aimed at exercising control beyond their simple percentage equity stake. In other words, even if the founders and shareholders surrender less than 50% of the equity ownership in return for investment from VCs, they will not be able to make decisions without the VCs' approval by virtue of board and shareholder rights. Retaining more than 50% of the equity does not mean the founders can 'outvote' their new investors. The imbalance of power is designed by VCs to address what they see as information asymmetry in favour of the founders and management team. By holding the balance of power via their board seat and shareholder veto rights, their aim is to prevent founders and management forcing decisions they are not comfortable with.

This dynamic evolves as the business grows and raises further rounds of finance, with new investors joining the shareholder register and obtaining board seats and shareholder rights. Often, shareholder rights are awarded to classes of shares such as the preferred shares sold in the first venture capital round, often termed 'Series A', or the second venture capital round, 'Series B' (see later in the chapter for a discussion of the terminology of investment rounds). By spreading shareholder veto rights among a variety of investors, the company at least avoids concentrating too much power within the hands of one substantial minority shareholder who may act in their own (possibly selfish) interests. Where these control 'balance points' lie is the subject of the shareholders agreement and is discussed in Chapter 7.

Founders must recognise, therefore, that selling equity in their start-up is not a purely financial transaction, like selling a house or selling a car; it is the beginning of a business partnership in which the partners are bound together for a period of years, through thick and thin, crisis after crisis, failure and success – until eventually they part ways at an exit event in which the VCs sell their shares. So, there is a long-term human relationship element to the venture capital investment, similar in some respects to a marriage – it's best to make sure you get along before signing on the dotted line because the relationship will be strained at moments of stress, failure and disagreement. This is why entrepreneurial finance is a people business; it is less about numbers and more about behaviour. The biggest determinant of eventual success may not relate to the number of shares held by each party but how effectively they work together to make the best business decisions (see Figure 2.2).

Early in my own venture capital career, a senior partner made a comment along the lines of 'If you don't want to have dinner with them, don't invest'. At the time, this sounded trivial to me, a flippant remark from an old-timer. Surely the decision came down to rational, objective, measurable parameters such as market size, intellectual property and proof of concept. Only in later years did I appreciate just how accurate the 'dinner' comment was. The success or failure of businesses often did not come down to rational, objective decisions, it came down to effective working relationships, rapid decision-making and an ability to disagree in a constructive manner and then get on with it. The successes came where no grudges were borne, no egos bruised after disagreements.

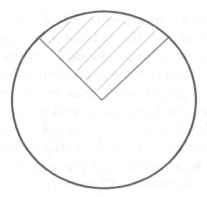

Figure 2.2 Dividing the equity pie to align interests.
Selling equity to raise investment is like selling portions of an equity pie. Doing so means surrendering a portion of success and control in return for the investment needed to build the business. How the price of the slice is determined is the subject of Chapter 6 but suffice to say there is more *art* than *science* in this process for start-ups. An important and sometimes underappreciated aspect of this is achieving 'felt fairness' for founders, investors and other shareholders at the outset. A VC who negotiates too hard and squeezes the equity ownership of founders too much is likely to find this comes back to haunt them. If important groups of shareholders believe themselves to have been unfairly treated at the outset it is likely they will exact revenge at an important moment in the future of the company – often at the *exit*, when they are required to sign over the ownership of their shares. It is essential to align interests and motivations at the beginning to deliver the best exit in the future.

A healthy 'constructive conflict' led to debate and solution. 'Destructive conflict', where lingering bad relations coloured all decision-making, led to failures. This does not mean being best friends (or even wanting to have dinner together as per the 'dinner' comment all those years ago) but getting along and having good personal chemistry made the difference in the inevitable tough times.

> *Being direct and honest without an emotional element is the key to building value.*

MILESTONES

Regardless of the perceived imbalance of control brought about by preferred shares, board seats and veto rights, the absolute percentage ownership retained by founders and management determines their economic reward when good exits are achieved. The underlying principle of founders raising equity finance should be to minimise the amount of future economic success they surrender in return for the investment they need. In other words, they need to maximise their stake in the business in the long run, over the entire length of the entrepreneurial journey from start-up all the way to exit (see Figure 2.3).

Crossing the Valleys of Death is best achieved by breaking the journey into smaller steps. Instead of attempting to raise *all* the finance required to reach the Promised Land in one financing round at the beginning, entrepreneurs generally raise a series of investment rounds at increasing share prices, based upon the principle of achieving value-adding milestones (or *value inflexion points*) prior to raising the next investment round. Raise finance, deliver valuable achievements, raise finance again and so on, until the company reaches the Promised Land. The simple concept of milestone-based financing is the key to entrepreneurial finance:

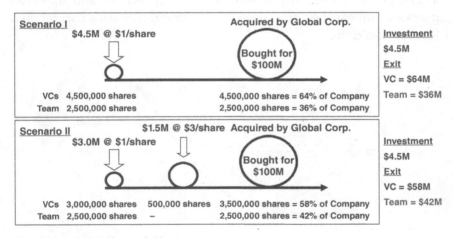

Figure 2.3 The effects of dilution.
The example shows an entrepreneurial team raising capital for their business in two scenarios, both of which raise the same total amount. The company is then bought by 'Global Corp.' for $100 million in a highly successful exit for the team and for the VCs who backed them. In both Scenarios I and II, the same amount of total investment ($4.5 million) delivers the same exit price ($100 million ignoring any transaction fees to corporate advisors and lawyers) but the share of the exit for the team versus the VCs is different. By raising their $4.5 million equity finance in two stages, in Scenario II the team has managed to retain a greater proportion of the equity (42% vs 36%), resulting in an extra $6 million of proceeds at exit. The risk the management team runs is that they are unable to raise the second round of $1.5 million in Scenario II because of a change in the financing climate or delays in their progress. This is a risk they will need to evaluate and depends on the level of risk they are willing to bear…

raise enough to hit milestones, then raise again until you don't need to raise anymore. By doing so, founders and management teams can minimise their dilution over the course of the entrepreneurial journey, with the result that they retain a greater share in the economic success at exit and the relinquishment of as little control as they can manage.

Milestone-based financing is also desirable for the VCs who invest in a business, as it mitigates their risks in backing unpredictable start-ups: invest a little, see how they do in achieving milestones, invest some more and so on (Figure 2.4). This is the mindset adopted by VCs: a step-by-step journey of increasing share prices over time to deliver an eventual return to the fund when the company is sold, or liquidity is achieved via an initial public offering (IPO) on a stock market, delivering an exit. Entrepreneurial teams need to adopt the same mindset as VCs to achieve success in raising investment: raise investment in stages based on value inflexion points, or milestones, to deliver an exit and generate a capital gain for shareholders.

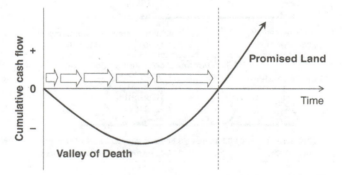

Figure 2.4 Baby steps, then strides towards success.
Minimising dilution for entrepreneurial teams means raising a series of investment rounds to achieve milestones or value inflexion points. Funding rounds typically start small to achieve some near-term milestones, often proof of concept for the innovation or the business model. Subsequent rounds tend to get bigger and bigger to fund accelerated growth, hopefully at increasing share prices to minimise dilution for existing shareholders. The outcome of this process is that the start-up raises the capital it needs, minimising dilution for the founders and management, and mitigating risk for the investors, whose confidence grows as the start-up progresses – enabling them to invest larger amounts at higher share price. The goal is to reach the Promised Land, but many venture capital-backed companies are snapped up by global corporates eager to acquire their unique technologies or skills well before the company generates a profit, or in some cases revenues.

THE VENTURE CAPITAL BUSINESS MODEL DEMANDS AN EXIT

Numerous times in the preceding paragraphs the word 'exit' has appeared, as if it is a given – a natural part of the lifecycle for start-ups. It indicates a sale of the business, or an event such as an IPO on a stock market allowing shareholders to sell all (or some) of their stake. But why is it there? Why is it needed? Why don't shareholders want to remain part of the story for ever and receive long-term dividends as a stream of income from their successful investments? If it is going well, why sell at all?

The answer lies in the venture capital business model, perhaps one of the simplest business models ever devised: buy low and sell high (Figure 2.5), or more accurately, *buy very low and sell very high* to account for the extreme risks inherent in buying equity in unproven start-ups. They simply buy cheap shares in a portfolio of risky start-ups and sell them when the start-ups have developed into successful companies. What could be simpler than that? This business model is driven by the structure of venture capital funds as fixed-life investment funds with a 10-year time horizon in which the investors in those funds, the Limited Partners (LPs), make

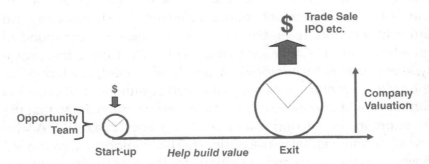

Figure 2.5   The simplest business model in the world?

The venture capital industry has an adaptation of one of the oldest business models devised by humans: buy low and sell high. In the case of venture capital, it is a case of buying equity *very* low and aiming to sell *very* high because the risks involved in buying equity in unproven start-ups are so great. There are investments where VCs might lose everything, so the potential winners have to more than compensate for the losers. The goal for VCs is simple: generate the highest capital gain on as many companies within the portfolio as possible. The possibility of selling the shares of a successful company to generate a substantial capital gain is very much at the front of VCs' minds when they choose companies to invest in.

a kind of '10-year loan' to the VCs. The structure of venture capital funds is discussed in detail in Chapter 4 but the fact that most VCs operate 10-year Limited Partnership models is the driving force behind the requirement for an exit from investments. Within the 10-year life of the fund, VCs must make their investments, help grow them in value and then sell the investments to allow the LPs to receive their returns as *capital gains*.

This business model, therefore, requires companies that raise investment from VCs to deliver an exit – a point in time at which shareholders can sell out. They are not in it for the long-term dividends, their goal is always to sell at the right moment and harvest their capital gain. Exits, and their implications for founders and VCs alike, are dealt with in detail in Chapter 9, but for now a simple recognition of the business model and the exit requirement is sufficient.

Accepting that an exit must occur is a prerequisite for founders raising capital from VCs.

THE MILESTONE-BASED JOURNEY TO EXIT

If we combine the principle of 'baby steps, then strides' to exit with the notion of investment rounds at increasing share prices, we arrive at a picture resembling Figure 2.6. Raising a first round of investment from VC A leads to a tangible milestone, a first prototype of whatever technology is under development, at which point the growing venture goes out to the market with the goal of raising further capital to achieve its next tangible milestone. Note that the investors in the second round are VC B and, again, VC A who invests further capital in the business. This is important, as it is VC B who sets the terms and conditions for the new round, including the share price, type of share, board seat rights and shareholder vetoes to which VC A signals their acceptance of the terms by investing again on the same terms.

The notion that the new, incoming investors set the terms is an important one. As external investors, they take an objective view of the business and make their offer to invest based on market

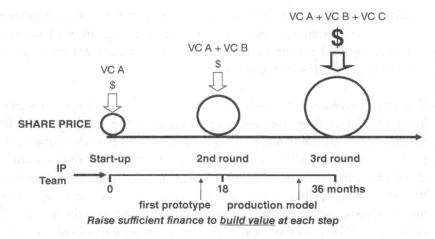

Figure 2.6 Milestone-based financing is the key to the journey.
Delivering a capital gain on paper is how VCs measure their progress towards eventually delivering an exit in the form of cash via a sale of the business or an IPO on a stock market. New, incoming investors 'price' each investment round and set the terms and conditions for which the existing investors 'signal' their agreement by investing in the new round on the same terms and conditions. Investment rounds ought to become larger in size and at higher share prices as the venture progresses, allowing the business to climb a steady valuation curve towards an eventual exit. Sometimes, when things do not go to plan, the venture may need to resort to raising a later round at a lower share price, known as a 'down round'.

conditions; they value the business based on their view of the market and impose terms they believe are consistent with the financing climate at the time and their estimates of the potential returns from their investment. As VC A is an existing shareholder in the business, they are in a conflicted position, being both a buyer and a beneficiary of the new investment round. Hence, they cannot easily set the terms of the round for fear of auditors pointing out the potential impact of such a conflict on the valuation of the existing investment. When a new investment round occurs at a higher share price than previously, all the existing shares in the business are revalued – 'marked up' to the price of the new investment round – so on paper, VC A stands to gain from a higher share price for the round and will show that valuation in their books. If VC A sets the price themselves, or in discussion with the board, it would be easy to accuse everyone involved of manipulating the share price to make it look like a better 'on paper' return than it really is, and not at all reflecting the market view of the business.

> *External investors propose the conditions for the investment round and existing investors signal their acceptance by investing alongside on the same terms, in other words 'putting their money where their mouths are'.*

If existing investors indicate that they agree with the new terms from VC B but then decline to co-invest in the new round, this sends a poor signal to VC B, who may conclude that they are overpaying for equity as VC A no longer believes in the business sufficiently to make further investments at the new, higher share price. VC A's failure to invest may simply mean they do not have the financial reserves to do so but even if that is the reason, VC B will sense a weakness in the existing investor base of the business and likely revise their valuation of the business downwards, buying shares at a lower price and giving them a higher share of the equity for the same investment.

In general, existing investors do step up to reinvest in successive financing rounds, in fact they will have made their first investment on the assumption that there will be further rounds to participate in, and they will have ensured they have the legal right to do so in the shareholders agreement to maintain their equity share. This right, but not the obligation, to invest *pro rata* in any new investment round to maintain their overall stake in the business is a central pillar of venture capital shareholder agreements – VCs always retain the right to maintain their share if they want to but they cannot be forced.

And so, this journey goes on. New investors are added at every new investment round, each successive investment round being bigger and at a higher share price than the previous one based on the company achieving some milestone or set of milestones that delivers a higher share price and a healthy upward trajectory towards exit. This ideal scenario is sometimes derailed by changes in market conditions that mean the achievement of milestones is negated by a downturn in the financing market, meaning that a new investment round must be concluded at the same share price as the previous round, or even worse at a lower share price, despite the progress. So-called 'flat rounds' or 'down rounds' are a feature of the entrepreneurial financing journey that should be avoided, if possible, but are often inevitable if the markets change for the worse. Keeping the company alive is the most important goal and if that means more dilution because of challenging conditions in the financial markets then so be it. There is no point maintaining an artificially high valuation/share price that is not supported by the market to preserve a 'return on paper' if the company fails.

THE ENTREPRENEURIAL FINANCING ECOSYSTEM

Different investors hunt for deals at different stages of the entrepreneurial financial food chain (see Figure 2.7). Seed-stage investors such as business angels and smaller venture capital funds

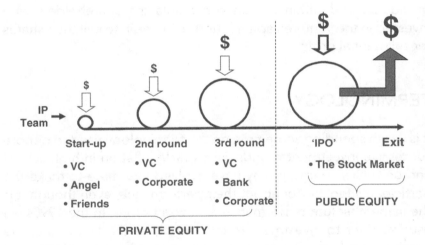

Figure 2.7 The financial food chain.
Different investors focus on different stages of the entrepreneurial finance journey. Start-ups are the hunting ground for business angels and early-stage VCs, the latter hoping to reinvest in successive rounds to an exit, the former usually focusing on protecting their early investment. Larger venture capital funds will often see their target as later equity rounds, where they can deploy larger amounts of capital. They are often prepared to pay higher share prices as the investment will have been 'de-risked' slightly by the early investors funding proof of concept and so on. When a company is sufficiently mature and stable, often generating reliable revenue streams, it might float its shares on a stock market in which shares are publicly traded. The IPO of a company is the moment at which it can begin to raise large amounts of capital for future growth and expansion. It is also the moment at which the earlier private investors can begin to think about selling their shares. Their 'exit' from the company needs to be conducted in an orderly manner to avoid a collapse in the share price, and this is managed via a lock-up period in which shares may not be sold.

focus on complete start-ups, even getting involved in writing business plans alongside the founders. For the second round of investment (sometimes referred to as Series A), larger venture capital funds will often take the lead, setting a new price and shaping a larger investment round. They specialise in the early stages of growth and will then form the link to even larger venture capital funds who might lead the Series B round, perhaps alongside corporate venture capital funds and so on. These investment rounds all exist within the realms of 'private equity' (as discussed earlier in the chapter) before the company occasionally transitions into the world of public equity via an IPO. It should be remembered that an IPO is not an exit. It is a further investment round, this time raising a large amount of equity finance from stock market investors to enable the company to continue growing. The IPO does, however, mark the point at which equity in the company becomes tradeable or 'liquid', and within certain constraints the shareholders who invested in the venture capital rounds can begin to sell their shares for substantial profit.

TERMINOLOGY

It is worth spending some time on the terminology used to denote successive investment rounds. Like grade inflation in high school and university exams, it may have evolved over time to make the participants feel better about their performance, even though it is the same absolute performance as it was before. In the 1990s we used to refer to investment rounds simply as the first round, the second round, etc. But as investment rounds became bigger and more numerous, it became fashionable to refer to small first rounds as 'seed' rounds, then 'pre-seed' rounds and ultimately in some circles the (even earlier and smaller) 'bird seed' round.

There was a cynical reason for this in some cases. It did not look good for entrepreneurial teams to market a company raising its fourth or fifth round. 'We are raising our second round' (having raised a pre-seed and a seed round) sounds a lot better than 'We are raising our fourth round'. Investors might conclude very quickly that there was something wrong if a company needed this many financing rounds and might not even look at the pitch. So, in some cases, the first round gradually evolved into the 'seed round'. It didn't count in the same way and could be regarded as experimental money rather than the proper start of the financing journey.

It also served VCs to tell their LPs they had invested in the second round of a company's financing journey (which had done a pre-seed and a seed round) rather than the fourth round. It implied that they were getting in earlier and working hard to find early deals rather than lazily backing a company that had been around for a long time. LPs like to know that the management fees they are paying to VCs are being well spent seeking out the best early-stage opportunities before anyone else. How could investing in the fourth round be the true function of the venture capital fund they had backed?

The next stage in this process was a shift from talking about the first round and second round to the 'Series A' and 'Series B'. Some will argue that Series A means something specific – the first institutional venture capital round – and Series B denotes a round where a company is generating its first reliable revenue streams. This is mostly correct, as the terminology grew out of the tech industry where companies followed an almost uniform business model and funding strategy, but it does not fit all industry sectors. Raising Series B sounds so much more positive than the fourth round. It is worth remembering this as an investor: Series B could be the second round or even the fifth round, and it is well worth knowing which it is...

EVOLUTION OF THE FUNDING GAP

As venture capital funds become more successful, they tend to migrate away from their roots. As will be explained in detail in Chapter 4, the business model of venture capital firms includes charging management fees to their investors based on the initial size of the fund they have raised. The management fee for a larger fund delivers greater and more predictable yearly revenue to the VCs. It is therefore attractive for them to raise larger funds and it is well established that this is the general direction of travel for successful VCs; they tend not to remain as specialised managers of smaller funds.

Although the management fee is only one component of a venture capital firm's revenue, managing a large fund is more attractive. At the same time, venture capital firms organised as partnerships tend not to hire investment professionals in line with the size of the fund, and the requirement to deploy larger amounts of capital per investment professional becomes a driving force. This naturally means they need to make bigger investments in companies.

The result of VCs migrating to bigger investments is that they move away from true venture capital deals towards the world of growth capital, and end up focusing on Series B and C rather than seed or Series A. This results in the evolution of an *equity gap* at the beginning of the entrepreneurial financing journey. The equity gap exists where funding rounds are too large for business angels but too small for the VCs, who have migrated downstream. The equity gap has existed and been talked about for 30 years or more; it shifts with time and across industries and varies between countries, but it is usually there in some form. It means that sometimes it is easier for entrepreneurial teams to raise (for example) $5 million than $1 million, which is too small for VCs but beyond most business angels.

Mind the gap: Larger financing rounds might be easier...

VENTURE DEBT – AN EXCEPTION?

Having said that debt is not an option for new ventures, and that equity is the currency of entrepreneurial finance, there is an exception that appears on the horizon for more established new ventures, and that is the use of venture debt. When companies have raised a series of investment rounds from reputable, well-known VCs and are generating evidence of growing revenues, there are certain specialised lenders who are prepared to make loans to them. These loans are termed 'venture debt' and have specific rights attached to them, including substantially higher interest rates than most debt products and with special rights called 'warrants' to purchase small amounts of equity in the business at discounted prices – akin to having options.

These products are useful for growing ventures aiming to extend their cash runway to reach an exit or a new equity financing round at a higher share price, thereby avoiding dilution for the existing shareholders.

Think in milestones and dream of exits. Nobody makes real money until then…

DILUTION VERSUS SECURITY

The goal of entrepreneurial teams is to raise the capital they need to execute their business plan. By raising in steps, the team minimises dilution (as shown in Figure 2.3). The decision regarding how much to raise and when is, however, an ongoing, continuous process – it never stops for the CEOs and board of directors of growing ventures. Of course, we know from Chapter 1 that 'the best time to raise money is when you don't need it' but in general this is not very helpful for planning purposes. The amount raised is, theoretically, the amount required to cross the Valleys of Death in stages linked to value-adding milestones or inflexion points. But this is an imprecise science and covers a range of scenarios. What if targets are missed (as they usually are), how much of a buffer should the management team put in place by raising more than the plan calls for? What if investors offer to invest more than the plan calls for, either because they don't believe the plan or (as sometimes happens) they want to deploy more capital from their fund because they believe the start-up can grow faster with more money? In these scenarios, should the management team accept more money 'just in case' or to 'grow twice as fast'? The downside that every management team thinks about is dilution.

Accepting more cash than may be required means selling more shares than planned. That means giving up economic upside and control to investors unnecessarily. But the question is: what if more money is required later and it is more difficult – or even impossible – to raise, perhaps because the financing climate has changed, or the business has hit unforeseen hurdles that make it less desirable? This thought should make entrepreneurs uncomfortable. Declining extra investment when it was offered, then finding it was needed after all but is now not available, is the nightmare scenario that eventually nudges management teams in the direction of accepting more cash than originally planned and coming to terms with the additional dilution. As many an entrepreneur will attest 'Better to have a smaller slice of a big pie than a big slice of a burnt pie'.

Entrepreneurs should think very carefully before saying no to extra money when offered.

WHAT DO WE MEAN BY BUILDING VALUE?

Throughout this chapter we have referred to 'value' and 'building value' within a start-up. Indeed, that is the title of the book, but what does 'building value' really mean? Is value measurable as revenue or profit, or is it something less tangible? There are many examples of businesses with billion-dollar valuations that never made a profit, and in some cases don't even have a product on the market (see Figure 2.8). The biotechnology industry is a case in point, where companies build value by developing promising new drugs or progressing clinical trials. These companies may have enormous valuations, and the valuation should reflect the inherent value in the future potential of the drug, assuming it works…

Valuations are dealt with in Chapter 6, but this gets to the heart of how companies build value and hence high valuations. The value within a company and the valuation of the company ought to match but they are not always the same – and mismatches occur when overexuberant markets (private or public) place high valuations on ventures that have potentially valuable technologies but haven't yet delivered. Again, going back to the example of biotechnology, 'value' is created by developing and owning intellectual property related to new and important science, perhaps something that opens the way to new therapies for serious diseases. This does not necessarily need to be a new drug product; it

What Do We Mean by Building Value?

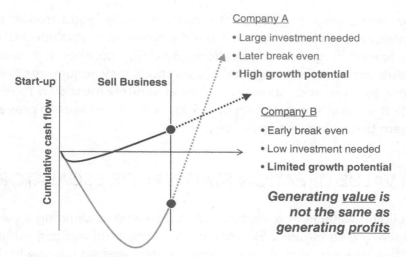

Figure 2.8 Value is not the same as profit.
The example shows two very different businesses crossing the Valley of Death. Company A represents the typical cash-flow profile of a science or technology-based new venture of the sort backed by VCs. The Valley of Death is as wide as it is deep as the business develops its complex product, but the business plan suggests the upside is potentially unlimited, with cash going through the roof once sales begin. Company B is different. It has the sort of cash-flow profile that a consultancy business might display, with a relatively small Valley of Death (hiring an office, paying salaries) prior to revenues increasing gradually as the consultancy gains more clients. If we sold both companies on the same day – represented by the vertical line – which one is worth more? The loss-making Company A, which appears to be on the up but may yet enter a new Valley of Death, or the steadily growing and profitable Company B? Remember, everything to the right of the date of sale is the future and therefore unknown. Despite the uncertainty, most will choose Company A, unable to resist the temptation of unlimited upside. Hence the conclusion that generating value is not the same as generating profit. This is the reason why science-based and technology-based new ventures are often valued at billions of dollars before they are profitable, or in some cases before they have generated revenue.

could be an enabling technology or science that paves the way to a new approach or opens a new route to discovering an exciting class of drugs, sometimes known as a platform technology. Owning important intellectual property (patents) in the biotechnology field is a sure route to building a valuable company, as global pharmaceutical companies are often prepared to pay large sums to own a promising new area even before that area is mature.

In other industry sectors, building value may relate to creating a powerful brand name, or growing substantial user numbers, owning data or having geographic reach. Whatever 'value' is, it can be very different in different industries but a good maxim for entrepreneurs in any sector is *build a company that is needed by or feared by global corporations*. By doing so, they will create value and those same global corporations may acquire the business as it provides something they absolutely must own to enable the growth of their own business, or in some cases to prevent them becoming a serious competitor.

A VALUE CREATION STAIRWAY OR ESCALATOR?

Building value in new ventures can be viewed as climbing a value stairway (see Figure 2.9). Beginning on the bottom floor, a team with some intellectual property or an idea sees no change in the inherent value of its business until it achieves a tangible milestone, such as proof of principle that its nascent technology works. At that point its value is inherently greater, as it is more likely to work. The value within the business then remains largely the same until the next tangible milestone, such as demonstration of a first functioning prototype of the product and so on. Building value is a stepwise process until the business reaches a point where it has reliable, repeatable revenues and building value occurs on a

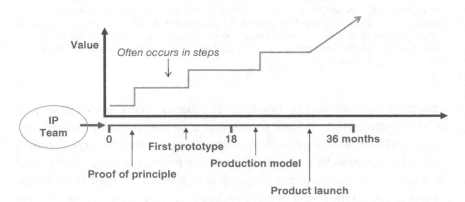

Figure 2.9   The stairway to value.
The process of value creation in start-ups is sometimes represented as a stairway, with value created in a series of distinct steps. Value is not created in a smooth curve until reliable, repeatable revenues occur and these can be measured using rational measures. In the pre-revenue phase, tangible milestones such as a proof of principle or a first prototype create immediate leaps in value, which then remains flat until the next milestone is achieved.

smooth predictable curve, perhaps changing from the stairway to ride the next part of the journey on a valuation escalator where progress is smoother.

Example Case Study

Developing a Milestone-based Approach

The following practical case study provides an opportunity to put the milestone-based approach into practice. Readers should work through the Nanomachines case study before looking at the model answer and comments available at the beginning of Case Study Solutions.

Nanomachines: Creating Value through Milestones

The principle of 'milestone-based financing' is almost universally applied in the world of entrepreneurial finance. Venture capital firms are very careful to ensure that the high-risk investments they make are mitigated by staging their commitments to companies. At the same time, entrepreneurs sometimes find it useful to raise finance in a series of rounds.

The chart below represents the cash flow and technical/commercial milestones for a fictional start-up 'Nanomachines'. This is typical of the kind of opportunity that VCs invest in and shows a negative cash flow for several years followed by the launch of a product and subsequent positive cash flow.

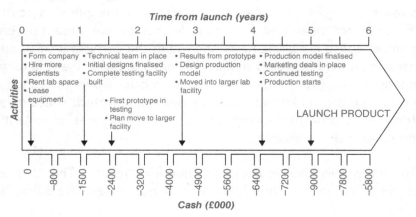

The Task

Assume the role of an entrepreneurial team pitching to a VC and consider how possible financing rounds might be constructed based on the principles of milestone-based financing used by VCs. Remember, as with most business cases, there are few 'right' or 'wrong' answers and this is especially true in entrepreneurial cases. Consider points such as:

- Where are the value inflexion points?
- How much investment do you raise to build the company in stages?
- What are the advantages for the team to raise investment in stages?
- What are the disadvantages?

SUMMARY OF CHAPTER 2

This chapter has focused on equity finance as a core investment tool for start-ups and growing ventures to raise the finance needed to build the business. Although venture debt is an exception for more developed ventures aiming to extend their cash runway, selling shares is how most start-ups finance the journey to the Promised Land.

Central to the entrepreneurial finance journey is the concept of milestone-based financing, in other words raising sufficient finance to reach a tangible, value-adding milestone (value inflexion point). This does not mean raising enough finance to hire a team or rent facilities, these are basic functions within the competence of any manager. It means raising sufficient finance to prove that the technology works, prove that the business model works or launch a product on the market with revenue being generated. These milestones should be measurable and definite and most importantly should de-risk the investment.

The title of this book is *Building Value* for a reason. This chapter has highlighted that building value is not always the same as generating revenue or profit, and can come in many forms, whether it is developing intellectual property, clinical trials results, data or numbers of clients. All of these are, of course, proxies for (or early indicators of) eventual commercial success in the form of revenues or profits, but many companies become valuable assets well before they generate revenue or become profitable. The phrase 'build a company that is needed by or feared by global corporations' is a good mantra for entrepreneurial teams to adhere to. If they do, they are more likely achieve a high-value exit…

Which brings us to the final point: the exit. The venture capital business model demands an exit within a 10-year time frame and founders of companies raising venture capital need to understand and work towards that goal. The milestones along the way, denoting financing rounds at increasingly higher share prices, allow VCs and founders to mark their progress as 'the market' values their potential higher and higher. On paper, founders can become multi-millionaires as the value of their share of the business climbs, but for reasons explored in later chapters, that value cannot be turned into cash until the exit, when all shareholders have the opportunity to harvest value.

Think in milestones and dream of exits; nobody makes real money until the exit…

REFERENCES

Hargreaves, R. (2021). *Business Angel Investing: Everything You Need to Know About Investing in Unquoted Companies.* Harriman House.

Shane, S.A. (2008). *Fool's Gold: The Truth Behind Angel Investing in America.* Oxford: University Press.

Chapter 3

A History Lesson

BEGINNINGS

It is a popular assumption that the venture capital industry really took off in Silicon Valley in the 1970s, and common culture associates the rapid growth of venture capital with the birth of the silicon chip industry. But the roots of entrepreneurial finance are much deeper than this, and history provides some interesting lessons about the interactions between entrepreneurs and the investors who back them. A careful analysis even reveals that some of the concepts and principles underpinning modern venture capital such as elements of preferred shares and liquidation preferences existed in a primitive form 5,000 years ago.

Landes et al. (2010), in their excellent book *The Invention of Enterprise*, explain how, in ancient Mesopotamia around 3000 BC, the Sumerians developed a system of backing merchants selling and distributing the produce of large estates associated with palaces and temples. Palaces would advance these merchants a defined number of commodities to sell in distant lands, with payment expected on their return from lengthy voyages – sometimes lasting 5 years or more, or perhaps at harvest time when dealing with domestic crops. They were even provided with salaries or rations and a means of transporting goods. If they met the agreed return target, they were free to keep the surplus they generated, or bear the losses they incurred. They operated at a risk and therefore were entrepreneurs, with the palace and temple administrators providing the capital with which they conducted their trade. Arguably this may represent some of the first recorded instances of entrepreneurial finance in action.

Interestingly, this happened around the same time as one of the key innovations in human history: the development of the wheel. Scholars believe that the Mesopotamians first invented the wheel for use in pottery making but then expanded upon this concept to place an axle through the centre and attach it to a cart. This would have represented a step change in the efficiency of transportation for both people and goods, and enabled a more effective long-distance trading relationship with other cultures. This innovation, just as innovations in transportation today, accelerated and expanded the notion of trade. It is difficult to provide evidence that the development of the wheel and the first evidence of entrepreneurial finance are connected but it is tempting to speculate that it bears similarities to the acceleration in growth of the venture capital industry in 1970s Silicon Valley.

The notion of sharing profits based upon a journey with both a beginning and an end will be revisited throughout this book in discussions of the venture capital business model and its dependence on carried interest as the basis for performance-related pay. A start-up is like a journey, it has a clearly defined beginning and when it depends upon venture capital investment it must also have a clearly defined end, which we call an exit. As we shall see in later chapters, there are similarities between the structure of ancient trading deals and the relationships between modern entrepreneurial teams, VCs and the investors (Limited Partners, LPs) who invest in their funds. The structuring of fixed-life modern venture capital funds may be compared in some ways to the 5-year trading voyages of the Mesopotamians, with a rewards structure based on a fixed management fee (like the rations provided to the Mesopotamian merchants) and a risk-based share of the profits.

What ancient civilisations also understood, perhaps better than modern-day investors, was the need to occasionally write off or forgive debts after disastrous harvests or shipwrecks that yielded no return on their risky investment. As Michael Hudson writes in Landes et al. (2010), in the case of poor harvests, debts were forgiven to avoid a widespread impact on society – there was little sense in ruining the men who might later be called upon to defend the kingdom. The Mesopotamian rulers understood that ruining its pool of labour would lead to disaster across their wider society.

Some aspects of this are observed in the formal relationship between LPs and the VCs they back, in which the losses of a fund are borne by the LPs. The VCs managing the fund share in the profits but are insulated against the majority of the losses if the fund fails. This may seem like an asymmetric relationship that tempts risk-taking by VCs but that is the point, their job is to invest in risky start-ups. Sometimes they fail. Usually, the winners in a venture capital fund's portfolio far outweigh the failures, but in the event of a fund-wide failure then the debts are effectively written off. This is not 'forgiveness' in the Mesopotamian sense, it is a simple reflection of the risk apportionment that VCs and LPs sign up to.

VENTURE CAPITAL THROUGH HISTORY

Beyond the early beginnings of enterprise first recorded in Mesopotamia, economic growth has for centuries been supported by enterprising investors who have identified the potential for capital gains and have, in turn, facilitated many of the changes that have steered the course of history. From Queen Isabella of Castile's funding for Christopher Columbus's voyage into uncharted waters in 1492 to J.P. Morgan's investments in Thomas Edison's promising inventions in the late 19th century, to modern Sand Hill Road venture capital firms pushing the limits of technology and progress skywards in Silicon Valley, instances abound of relationships between risk-tolerant investors and visionary entrepreneurs who have long disrupted the status quo and left far-reaching imprints on all that has followed since. Today's venture capital industry derives from this long-standing human dynamic – between those with a vision and those with the means to realise it – and has, through a gradual proof of concept, carved its own existence out of this natural chain as a conduit designed to maximise the chances for collective success, under a 'high-risk, high-reward' investment model. It has grown hand-in-hand with Western free-market capitalism since the post-war days of 1946 to become a major agent of global economic progress – a verdict validated by the remarkable fact that among today's US public companies founded since 1975, venture capital-backed companies account for half in number and three-quarters in value (Gornall and Strebulaev 2021). But how and why is this the case?

World War II and the Push for Innovation

Amidst the total warfare that raged across the globe until 1945, each belligerent nation underwent domestic upheaval on an unprecedented scale to mobilise its collective resources in the desperate effort for victory. The United States, already a global economic power at the outbreak of war, oversaw a massive centralisation of military, civilian, scientific and industrial force following the bombing of Pearl Harbour and its resulting entry into the conflict in late 1941. President Roosevelt's newly organised War Production Board brought together civilian industries and redirected them for wartime production. Businessmen became civil servants, and leading professors were assembled as military-minded technocrats. An exponential increase in munitions production followed over the next few years (leading Joseph Stalin to ultimately declare that 'the war was won by American production'). There was a corresponding storm of technological innovation. Jet engines, radar, synthetic rubber, penicillin, electronic computers: just a few examples of the extraordinary scientific breakthroughs facilitated by this convergence of nationwide effort. Arguably the most globally consequential innovation of all resulted from a meeting of minds atop the mesas of New Mexico's Pajarito Plateau, led by J. Robert Oppenheimer: the world's first nuclear fission bomb ended the war and inaugurated a new 'Atomic Age'. Thus, the stage was set for the soaring tensions of the Cold War, as technological innovation turned into a matter of national security for the principal powers, the United States and the USSR. Within this global race for progress, the jolts of innovation sparked during the war would usher in

vast new horizons of commercial opportunity for investors, entrepreneurs and those shrewd enough to bridge the gap.

ARDC

One professor-turned-military technocrat was Georges F. Doriot,
regarded today as the 'father of venture capital' (Gompers 1994).
Born in France in 1899, he emigrated to America in the 1920s to
study at Harvard Business School, staying on afterwards to teach.
He was soon recognised for his inspiring qualities, and, as one
former student put it: 'his strong affinity toward technology and
the notion that what you [have] today isn't going to be around 20
years from now'.[1] Having become a naturalised American in 1940,
he was appointed as Head of Research and Development in the
office of the Quartermaster General during the war. At the inter-
section of scientific innovation, industrial production and military
demand, he personally assessed the potential of new products
and facilitated their routes to the frontlines, earning the rank of
Brigadier-General and the Distinguished Service Medal for his
achievements.

Upon returning from service, his acute awareness of new, untapped
technologies and their potential commercial applications
prompted him to found American Research and Development
Corporation (ARDC) in 1946, alongside MIT President Karl
Compton, Boston Federal Reserve Bank President Ralph Flanders
and Massachusetts Investors Trust Chairman Merrill Griswold
(Rosegrant and Lampe 1992). At a time when investments in innovative start-ups were reserved strictly for wealthy families who
could afford the risk, ARDC raised its capital from publicly issued
bonds instead – a bold new concept, especially amid a lack of
public investment ethos in the long wake of the 1930s Depression.
Its mission to aid 'the development of new or existing businesses
into companies of stature and importance' pioneered a progres-
sive business model that focused not just on supplying risk capital
for promising young companies, but also on *building value* by providing industry knowledge, hands-on management experience
and networking connections, the so-called *money plus* that will be
discussed again and again throughout this book. This paradigm,

and the nascent venture capital industry for which it would in time become the standard, were truly vindicated when a 1957 ARDC investment became venture capital's first 'home run' story.[2]

DEC: Venture Capital's First Home Run

Engineers Ken Olsen and Harlan Anderson had been recruited to MIT's Lincoln Laboratory during the war, with the task of using emergent computer technology to develop a flight simulator for the Air Force. Their efforts spawned several innovations under 'Project Whirlwind' that would ultimately form the basis for air defence systems. A few years later, in 1947, the Nobel Prize–winning invention of the point-contact transistor by Bardeen, Brattain and Shockley would soon prompt them to begin working towards building a new version of their Whirlwind computer, with transistors instead of vacuum tubes. When, in 1956, they noticed a peculiar student fascination with one of their consequent models, the primitive yet interactive computer TX-0, they sought to capitalise on this unexplored market with their own commercial enterprise, which they named 'Digital Computer Company'. A tour of the local equity firms of Massachusetts soon revealed a distinct lack of investor interest in the uncertain, fledgling market for computers.[3]

Doriot, however, sensed the potential of their idea for a computer that could turn clunky mainframes into something more accessible and affordable. To allay investor trepidation, he insisted Olsen and Anderson rebrand to 'Digital Equipment Company', and with his $70,000 investment for 70% equity, the stage was thus set for their fortunes to be forever changed. A string of mildly successful digital modules preceded DEC's creation of the Programmed Data Processor (PDP) mini-computer series, which culminated with the PDP-8 in 1965 – the first commercially successful computer in history, with over 50,000 units sold at $18,500 a unit.[4] A blockbuster 1966 IPO returned a 'home run' $35 million for ARDC.[5] Olsen and Anderson had proven the commercial appetite for computers, and Doriot had proven beyond all doubt that venture capital could change the world. Their mutual success symbolised, too, a blossoming kinship between high-tech business and the venture capital industry that was destined in time to forge a new world of opportunity on the US western frontier, in California's Santa Clara Valley.

The Turn of the Century and the Closed World of Private Equity

It may be no coincidence, however, that the venture capital industry first arose on the East Coast in Boston, Massachusetts. Indeed, graduates and professors of nearby institutions like Harvard, MIT and Boston University had been making the city a beacon of entrepreneurship and innovation for decades by the time that ARDC was founded. When, for example, Scotland's Alexander Graham Bell arrived in 1872 to work as a professor at Boston University, he was immediately 'swept up' by the buzzing atmosphere among local inventors and scientists. His subsequent success story there was indebted to Boston's embrace for change and, in fact, bears certain hallmarks of a future model of venture capital. In 1874, two local Boston acquaintances, attorney Gardiner Greene Hubbard and leather merchant Thomas Sanders, agreed to commit their personal finances to support Bell's experiments in developing the world's first telephone. Having risked bankruptcy for years, these two financiers would prove crucial in steering the fledgling Bell Telephone Company's management and distribution, overseeing its later ascent as telecommunications giant AT&T (Rosegrant and Lampe 1992). Indeed, its R&D department, known as Bell Laboratories, would later foster some of the most pivotal inventions of the 20th century, including the transistor – a technological cornerstone that paved the way for the meteoric rise of Silicon Valley and the onset of the so-called Information Age.

This rather extraordinary example of 'friends, family and fools' angel investing success belies the fact that, during the late 19th century, investment in innovative, potentially lucrative tech enterprise was the preserve of only the wealthiest elites: those who had forged their own financial empires amid the dizzying progress of the Industrial Revolution.[6] The Vanderbilts, Whitneys, Carnegies and Phipps, the Morgans, Rockefellers, Mellons and Warburgs all actively mobilised their considerable fortunes to support propitious industries of the day, like steel, electricity, railways, oil and textiles. By also setting aside portions of their family assets for high-risk investments, as Henry Phipps Jr did following the sale of Carnegie Steel Company in 1901, these wealthy families began to establish alternative routes to success for well-connected entrepreneurs, laying the groundwork for later modes of start-up investment.

American Royalty: Adapt or Die

When, amid the depths of the Great Depression, strict banking investment restrictions were imposed under the Glass–Steagall Act, these unorganised and fragmented family firms began to be formalised, as professional managers were hired to ensure continued growth. Out of these practices sprang some of today's most venerable venture capital and private equity firms – from Phipps's Bessemer Venture Partners to Rockefellers' Venrock and E.M. Warburg & Co. (later Warburg Pincus). Front runner among these family-funded professional organisations was, however, J.H. Whitney & Co., which emerged alongside ARDC in 1946 with a similar plan in mind: to commercialise new wartime technologies. Its founders, who are today credited with coining the term 'venture capital' by the elision of the word 'adventure', were Jock Whitney– the beneficiary of a family fortune built on railways, cotton gin and fleets – and Benno Schmidt – a talented Texas lawyer who had helped oversee economic relations with America's wartime allies. They soon struck a winning formula, playing a pivotal role in the start-up successes of fertiliser plant Spencer Chemical Company, later sold to Gulf Oil,[7] and of powdered orange juice company Florida Foods Corporation – now known under the household name 'Minute Maid' – later sold to Coca-Cola. Thus, from two separate strands blossomed the foundations of modern venture capital. One was academia, as symbolised by the talismanic visionary Doriot, who would in his later years go on to found the internationally renowned business school INSEAD. The other was an American elite that had risen to the fore through industrial innovation and sought to maintain their position through much the same.

Venture Capital: From Experiment to Industry

DEC's success in the late 1950s coincided with the rise of another minicomputer company on the opposing coast that would forever change the landscape of American enterprise and accelerate the growth of venture capital as a viable means of start-up success. Fairchild Semiconductor's founding in 1957 can be credited to two factors: audacious venture capital backing and mutiny. The so-called 'Traitorous Eight' scientists who defected from their authoritarian boss William Shockley and his California company Shockley Semiconductor had been enticed by pioneer VC Arthur Rock, who had persuaded businessman Sherman Fairchild into carving out a semiconductor division from one of his many companies. Working for New York corporate finance firm Hayden, Stone & Co., Rock worked out a deal that secured 20% equity of the infant Fairchild Semiconductor, which inevitably rocketed to pre-eminence over the following years as a trailblazer in the field of transistors and integrated circuits. Its employees would go on to found the so-called 'Fairchildren' that catalysed the growth of Silicon Valley, with both high-tech companies like Intel and AMD and elite venture capital firms like Kleiner Perkins and Davis and Rock – the Bay Area's first venture capital firm, in 1961.

The growth of an industry as inherently risky as venture capital was held on a short leash for its formative decades during the post-war era. It was in 1979, at a time of seismic change in Western economic policy, when drastic measures were being sought by leaders to combat the 'stagflation' that had dogged the 1970s, that the leash was lengthened – and venture capital took flight. A reinterpretation of the wording of the 1974 Employee Retirement Income Security Act now meant that pension funds, which had to handle their money with the care of a (helpfully ambiguous) 'prudent man', were allowed to allocate 10% of their capital towards venture capital investment.[8] Struggling high-tech start-ups like Microsoft and Apple saw an unprecedented influx of investment, and a chain reaction of innovation followed at dizzying speed.

Naturally, this fireball of newly unregulated capitalist growth hit a few road-bumps and proved to be as unstable as it was enticing. Older firms like Whitney's and Warburg's transitioned away from the frontier world of Silicon Valley start-ups to the more reliable corporate finance, whilst newer, bolder venture capital firms like Sequoia, Caulfield & Byers and Kleiner & Perkins forged ahead on the now-established Sand Hill Road – venture capital's very own Wall Street – driven by the hunt for the next home-run investment.

A new world of individualism was afoot, and aspirations had never been higher. In Oliver Stone's 1987 movie *Wall Street*, Gordon Gecko's declaration that 'greed is good' epitomised the sudden excesses that the finance industry soared towards, just as Moore's Law rationalised the incredible rate of achievement in transistor technology that laid the groundwork for the 1990s.

Choppy Seas: The Dotcom Boom

The development and rapid growth of internet companies emerging in the mid to late 1990s felt to those of us in the industry like a new Industrial Revolution. In fact, those are the very words we used to describe it. It was a period of limitless opportunity, as entrepreneurs realised how the internet could open new markets for their existing businesses and how entirely new businesses could be developed from an ability to aggregate buyers and suppliers and remove inefficiencies from supply chains.

The first wave of 'dotcoms' (as they were quickly named) focused on retail, the so-called business-to-consumer (B2C) segment. VCs looked for goods and services that could be marketed and sold via this new electronic medium and focused on items that were high value and easy and cheap to ship. It may now be forgotten by many, but Amazon started as an online bookstore enabling customers to browse an online catalogue of books that were then shipped directly from a warehouse located somewhere that real estate was cheap. By getting rid of the expensive shop front in prime real estate areas of cities, the price advantage offered to customers was hard to beat. In the heady days of the late 1990s this business model was applied to everything from pharmacy products to Christmas trees on both sides of the Atlantic. The term 'bricks and mortar' became a byword for old-fashioned business models that were outdated and uneconomic and were soon to be extinct. Who needed an expensive bricks and mortar shop when a virtual shop was available on every computer terminal connected to the internet?

As the investment market for B2C dotcoms became saturated, its attractiveness began to fade and was followed by what was perceived as a far more sophisticated, high-value investment opportunity – that of business-to-business (B2B) opportunities. A common phrase used by VCs towards the end of the 1990s was something like 'we don't do B2C anymore, only B2B'. It was perceived that B2B offered scalability in lucrative, high-value markets and did not require the huge marketing budgets of B2C companies. The general idea behind B2B companies was that the internet provided a perfect marketplace for goods and services traded between companies – areas that had previously been occupied by agents, intermediaries and distributors whose business models depended on taking a cut of the transaction. The disintermediation of these go-betweens led to online marketplaces in everything from laboratory supplies to parts for industrial machinery and farm equipment. There was seemingly nothing that the internet could not transform, and a string of high-profile venture rounds and IPOs followed, but then revenues slowed (or in some cases failed to appear entirely) and investors realised that valuing a dotcom at hundreds of millions of dollars when it had the revenues of a local grocery store did not make sense. What followed was a sharp reversal in stock prices and investor sentiment, beginning with the B2C companies and then spreading to the B2B sector. It was to become known as the dotcom crash.

In 2000, the supply of venture capital finance was turned off. Businesses that had found it easy to raise a couple of million on an idea and a business plan in 8 days now found it impossible. Overexuberant VCs found themselves burdened with large portfolios of dotcom businesses with no hope of reaching the Promised Land without the input of almost endless marketing budgets, which depended on new financing rounds that never appeared. There was a raft of attempted mergers between loss-making companies, followed inevitably by bankruptcies. VCs learned the hard way that merging two loss-making companies did not suddenly produce a success. Companies failed and so did entire venture capital funds. The 'nuclear winter' for VCs that followed 2000 was alleviated slightly by a biotechnology boom. The sequencing of the human genome was nearing completion towards 2003 and the positive investor sentiment this created led the financing world to believe it was on the cusp of a new revolution. Some commentators said the 20th century had been the century of physics, and the 21st century would be the century of biology. Several biotechnology companies rode this wave of sentiment to raise large sums of finance and deliver great exits for the VCs that backed them.

Twenty-five years after the dotcom crash, we can see that the entrepreneurs and VCs of the late 1990s were not wrong. They were just too early. At the time of writing this book, online businesses dominate both retail and business services. We are all familiar with what has become of some of those early movers. Amazon is no longer an online bookstore and its dominance across sectors is beyond anything most VCs imagined in 1999. Traditional retailers around the world have either gone under, downsized or adapted, and high streets in many countries have struggled to reinvent themselves under the burden of the 'bricks and mortar' that VCs talked about long ago.

What the dotcom crash of 2000 illustrated nicely was that the venture capital industry – when faced with a perceived business revolution – overinvests, creates a bubble and then overcorrects when reality bites. The creation of investment bubbles is nothing new and has occurred for hundreds of years; there are numerous instances of this behaviour throughout the history of the venture capital industry (a phenomenon referred to as herding[9]), but the dotcom crash was particularly borne of a mentality within the venture capital industry that missing opportunities is unforgivable and that land grabs will always occur in the face of new technology. The conclusion for entrepreneurs is that they exist in a sea of uncertainty, where investor sentiment is on a knife edge and they had better hope – when they raise money in a strong market – that they raise enough to see out the downturn which will inevitably come.

The Financial Crisis of 2009

The financial crisis of 2009 was an altogether different experience for the venture capital industry compared to the dotcom crash almost a decade earlier. In the immediate aftermath of the collapse of Lehman Brothers and the global credit crunch, the venture capital industry took a cautious view and focused on supporting its existing portfolio companies rather than making new investments.

VCs worried about the obvious impact on their ability to exit investments, since investment banks which normally conducted IPOs on stock markets and mergers and acquisitions between venture-backed businesses were paralysed. But day to day, smaller technology-focused companies seemed to be impacted minimally, and the venture capital business carried on… for a time. The serious impact emerged when venture capital firms set about raising new funds in the immediate aftermath of the crisis: the large financial institutions which normally invested in venture capital had simply turned the taps off upstream. During this period it was incredibly difficult for VCs to raise new funds from the investors who sat upstream from them in the global financial chain, and consequently entrepreneurial ventures found it increasingly difficult to raise money. Times were bad.

In response to the bad times, central banks around the world reduced interest rates close to zero to encourage faltering economies and this had the expected, but perhaps still surprising result. Money hates a vacuum, and investors constantly seek the best returns, so with global interest rates at record lows, investors sought these returns by buying riskier and riskier assets. One of these risky assets was the venture capital industry, and money finally began to flow into funds. As interest rates remained low for years, a trickle of investment into venture capital funds turned into a deluge, and as the decade wore on, ever larger venture capital funds were raised. As funds became larger, they deployed capital faster and set about identifying more entrepreneurial start-ups to invest in. The demand for venture capital, however, did not climb at the same pace as the size of the funds, and so a huge supply of venture capital began chasing fewer high-quality deals. The unsurprising result was, yet again, that start-ups of lower quality raised too much money, valuations climbed and a bubble emerged.

The COVID-19 Pandemic of 2020

When COVID-19 began to spread globally in early 2020, an email circulated within the venture capital community. Memories of the dotcom crash loomed large for those of us who had been around to see it and a leading West Coast VC, sensing the impending crisis, sent a circular to its portfolio companies warning of the likely financial impact. Portfolio companies were instructed to preserve cash, cancel new hires, pause new projects and get ready for the long haul. Other VCs wrote similar communiques to their own portfolio companies and an air of caution spread quickly. We all anticipated a crash and in the spirit of *money plus*, we would not allow our portfolio companies to fall into the dotcom bear trap of 20 years previously. How wrong we turned out to be, at least for the duration of the pandemic. Further quantitative easing (low interest rates) from central banks, various national COVID-19 loan schemes, government funds and furlough payments pumped more cash into an already exuberant market for risky investments. The outcome was predictable.

This cash-driven frenzy was accelerated by the stellar perfor-mances of new technology companies enabling remote working, and the 'new normal' that we would all adapt to. Life sciences companies were back in the spotlight, providing remarkable new vaccines, treatments and diagnostics. This continued apace until 2023, when interest rates began to rise to combat inflation around the globe and the venture capital market cooled dramatically. The money supply dried up and trading for many companies became more challenging as a cost-of-living crisis hit. The supply and demand equation for venture capital altered dramatically, making it (again) very difficult for entrepreneurial companies to raise capi-tal that only a few months earlier would have been easy. Some within the venture capital industry had never seen such a down-turn. After all, it had been a decade of impressive growth on the NASDAQ and raising and investing funds had appeared relatively straightforward. Those in the industry for less than a decade bemoaned the terrible financing climate, but it was really just a return to reality. Good companies will always raise money. The terms of investment might be harder (and we will explore later in this book exactly how they may change) and it will take longer to raise capital, but isn't that just a return to how it was before? Look back at Henry Ford's journey and remember the lessons of asset parsimony.

Entrepreneurs and VCs are afloat on a sea of unpredictable sen-timent. Plan accordingly.

SUMMARY OF CHAPTER 3

This chapter does not attempt to write a comprehensive history of the venture capital industry, in fact it doesn't even scratch the surface. Business history is a fascinating subject and many learned scholars have written extensively in this area – charting in detail the key events of the development of the global venture capital sector. What this chapter has attempted to do, however, is to draw parallels between ancient business models in which enterprising investors backed visionary entrepreneurs and the behaviour and structures of the modern venture capital industry. History demonstrates that waves of technical innovation have often been accompanied by similar surges in financial innovation, sometimes supporting great leaps forward and at other times ending in financial catastrophe. At the very least, thinking about historical events sheds light on how closely linked entrepreneurship and high-risk investment have always been, and will continue to be…

The significant events against which the venture capital industry has evolved include war, global financial crises, pandemics and occasionally misplaced beliefs in how the future will evolve. The history of the venture capital industry is a turbulent one, as entrepreneurs and investors strive to predict and understand new business opportunities based on very few facts and imperfect information. The notion of herding – in which the venture capital industry overinvests and then overcorrects in the 'next big thing' – occurs time and time again. Many have said that it is difficult to see the bubble when you are inside it, and the ominous phrase 'but it's different this time…' to describe a developing bubble should ring in the ears of entrepreneurs and VCs. It is *never* 'different this time…', and exuberance in a particular investment sector is always repaid with a substantial fall at some point – we just need to learn to anticipate the fall and know it is coming at some point. Often, when a sector is overhyped, it is written about extensively in the media and by the time we are reading about it daily with a nagging feeling that we are missing out, it is already too late to invest. Hype and herding are elements of the entrepreneurial finance ecosystem that are hard to shake off, but being aware that they exist is the best tool entrepreneurs and investors alike can have in their armoury to avoid being caught out when the fall comes.

The next chapter will examine in detail the business model and structures underpinning venture capital funds and will attempt to enlighten potential entrepreneurs about the economics of the investment they are seeking to raise. Understanding business models is the only way to understand how VCs evaluate and invest in new ventures. By understanding the business model, a great deal of conflict can be avoided when it comes to negotiating the right deal. There are certain concepts embedded within the structure of venture capital funds that dictate the terms that VCs will seek, and it is difficult for them to navigate round such principles. Knowing where and how to push effectively is the best route for entrepreneurs to get a good deal.

NOTES

1. The talented Georges Doriot, *The Harvard Gazette*, 24 February 2015.
2. Jones, D.W. https://homepage.cs.uiowa.edu/~jones/pdp8/faqs/
3. The archives of the *New York Times* 1966.
4. The archives of the *New York Times* 1963.
5. Jones, D.W. https://homepage.cs.uiowa.edu/~jones/pdp8/faqs/
6. Ibid.
7. The archives of the *New York Times* 1966.
8. Jones, D.W. https://homepage.cs.uiowa.edu/~jones/pdp8/faqs/
9. Ibid.

REFERENCES

Gompers, P.A. (1994). The rise and fall of venture capital. *Business and Economic History* 23 (2): 1–26.

Gornall, W. and Strebulaev, I.A. (2021). The economic impact of venture capital: Evidence from public companies. SSRN 2681841.

Landes, D.S., Mokyr, J. and Baumol, W.J. (2010). *The Invention of Enterprise: Entrepreneurship from Ancient Mesopotamia to Modern Times*. Princeton University Press.

Rosegrant, S. and Lampe, D. (1992). *Route 128: Lessons from Boston's High-Tech Community*. Basic Books.

Chapter 4

Business Models

CAPITAL GAIN

Venture capital exists to accelerate the development of high-risk start-ups and shepherd them across the Valleys of Death to the Promised Land of profitability and continued self-sustained growth. In the long run, venture capital-backed companies cannot defy the fundamental laws of economics and business; they must become profitable, but the venture capital model does not necessarily require companies to achieve profitability within the tenure of their share ownership – they simply have to deliver an *exit*. As we have seen in earlier chapters, delivering an exit depends on generating value – whether it be through intellectual property, revenue growth or customer numbers and data. Exits may arrive well before a company becomes profitable and the mantra 'Be needed by or feared by global companies' often drives the strategy of young companies with a view to generating the highest value exit for investors and entrepreneurs alike.

The exit is an absolute requirement for VCs to realise the goal that sits at the centre of their business model: *capital gain*. Despite the seemingly sophisticated nature of the venture capital industry, its business model is one of the simplest and oldest that exists: buy low and sell high (perhaps more accurately described as 'buy very low, sell very high' to reflect the high risk of failure within the portfolio — the winners must be *extreme* winners to pay for the substantial losses generated by failing companies within the portfolio (see Figure 4.1). This is the mindset that drives VC behaviour and hence decision-making at every level: how will this investment generate capital gain via an exit and when?

VCs do not invest in companies with the goal of sharing in the profits of the business for the long term. Their goal is to buy shares, help build value and generate a capital gain by selling their shares in the cleanest and simplest exit that can be engineered, usually via acquisition by another company or an IPO on a liquid stock market. Exits are discussed in more detail in Chapter 9, but for now it is sufficient to recognise that this is a central pillar of the venture capital business model and is at the front (and back) of any VC's mind during the decision-making process of investing.

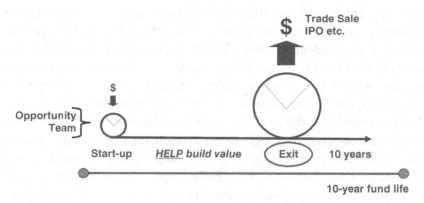

Figure 4.1   The role of VCs in building value.
At the centre of the venture capital industry sits an adaptation of one of the oldest business models on earth, that is to buy low and sell high... or in this case buy very low and sell very high, because we are dealing with substantial risk and that is reflected by buying shares at a low price. Helping the team to build value is an essential element of all true venture capital investments, to deliver an exit within a 10-year time frame consistent with the lifetime of most venture capital funds.

The essence of the venture capital business model is remarkably simple for VCs: back a start-up and help it along the journey to deliver an exit and hence generate a capital gain. The problem lies in executing the business model, and it turns out that this is not as simple as it sounds. Launching a start-up and building it into a successful company is fraught with challenges and crises along the way. Ask any entrepreneur and they will give numerous examples of the unexpected challenges they face on this journey, as illustrated in Figure 1.2 which showed the multiple Valleys of Death that growing ventures cross.

AGENCY

There are many differences between VCs and business angels, but perhaps the most notable difference is their source of investment funds. Business angels are investing their own money, but VCs are fund managers investing other people's money. VCs raise money from other investors, pool it into a fund and build a portfolio of investments in early-stage ventures. Their specialist role in the financial food chain is to act as *agents* for the ultimate investors in start-ups – the investors who put money into their funds with the desire to back high-risk start-ups but not necessarily the specialist skills (or the time) to do so. This is the gap that VCs fill.

VCs are specialised intermediaries in the financial food chain.

VCs generally market themselves as specialists in identifying and evaluating the best possible investment opportunities within their chosen target sectors. Some specialise in life sciences, others in tech or energy. Within their specialised sector, they build an investment strategy, akin to the business plans that entrepreneurs develop, and they pitch it to potential investors. Their strategy will often self-impose certain geographic restrictions (e.g. life sciences start-ups in Europe) or with a preference for certain stages of the investment cycle (e.g. Series A or Series C), although most VCs will have a mix (or agreed portions) of the fund they are permitted to deploy in certain geographies or at different stages.

INFORMATION ASYMMETRY

The role of VCs as agents is to manage the information asymmetry that exists between entrepreneurs and their ultimate investors, the pension funds, banks and other investors who sit far upstream from them. What exactly does this mean? Entrepreneurs will always know more about their businesses than the investors who back them. Although it may not seem that way in a world where VCs and other investors go to great lengths to understand the businesses they back, ultimately the entrepreneurial team behind the business is one or two steps ahead – they always know that little bit more. That is information asymmetry: the imbalance between the information possessed by the entrepreneurial team and the information possessed by the investors who back them. VCs manage this information asymmetry – they develop skills and tools to smooth out this imbalance and enable rational investment decisions based on the best information available. Their ongoing role in monitoring the performance of investments is enhanced by their appointment to the board of directors of the companies they back and provides a main gateway for managing information asymmetry for their investors. The role of a VC on the board is not to spy on investments and report back to investors, but to be an 'investor director' does provide privileged access to information and allows them to make further decisions about how and whether to invest more capital in the company as it progresses.

FUND STRUCTURES

Just like any other investor relationship, the link between the managers of venture capital funds and their investors is governed by a form of shareholders agreement. This agreement is structured in most cases as a Limited Partnership Agreement (LPA). The detailed legal mechanisms through which LPAs operate is beyond the scope of this book and depends on the legal jurisdiction within which they operate, but LPAs are usually fixed-term, tax-transparent partnerships binding the investors to the fund managers for a 10-year period (see Figure 4.2).

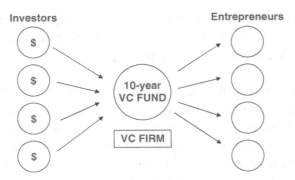

Figure 4.2 The role of VCs as intermediaries.
The venture capital industry uses an adaptation of one of the oldest business models on earth, buy low and sell high, but they are doing so on behalf of investors who put money into their funds. VCs usually structure their business as a partnership, and the venture capital firm raises a fund to invest in start-ups from investors such as pension funds, banks, major corporations and sometimes government organisations. To do this, the VCs develop a business plan focused on investing in particular sectors and they go out to pitch their fund strategy to investors (LPs) who deploy a fraction of their total funds into the venture capital sector.

The classic 10-year LPA is the dominant form of agreement between VCs and the investors who back them (the Limited Partners, LPs), committing the investors to put up the money for investment when required by the VC. At the same time, the VC is committed to investing the cash within their chosen sector and making investment returns for the LPs within the 10-year life of the fund. The cycle of raising a venture capital fund, identifying, investing and exiting from a portfolio of high potential investments within its 10-year lifespan is routinely referred to as the *venture capital cycle*. The 10-year time constraint placed on venture capital funds is an important and challenging hurdle, as occasionally great ideas do not receive venture capital investment because they are unlikely to deliver an exit within the term of the LPA.

The 10-year LPA is further split into two 5-year periods, the first being termed the *investment period*, in which VCs focus on identifying and investing in new companies. The second 5-year period is termed the *management period*, during which VCs are only permitted to reinvest in companies they already backed during the investment period, and they must focus on growing those businesses towards an exit. This is why the venture capital industry is sometimes criticised as having a short-term bias – the nature of their funds means they must operate to this rhythm and there are times when, unfortunately, generating exits becomes a driving force in the VC's decision-making process.

Taking this a step further, a number of industry observers refer to VCs as engaging in 'grandstanding': they push portfolio companies towards an exit event too soon, before the moment of maximum value has arrived, because they need an exit to assist their own chances of raising a new fund, or just to give some good news to their investors. This goes against the idea that investor-directors on the board of a company must act in the interests of all shareholders and is a very clear example of a potential conflict of interest, which must be managed accordingly. The artificial constraint of the 10-year LPA on the natural process of innovation has been talked about in the world of entrepreneurial finance for years and, although there are alternative funding structures available, the LPA has survived. This may be due to its advantages in measuring and distributing the rewards of a venture with a defined endpoint, not unlike its historical roots in the trading adventures of the merchants who went before.

It is important to note that when a venture capital firm raises a fund via an LPA, the entire fund does *not* sit within a bank account controlled by the VC. When the LPs sign an LPA, they are committing to sending cash to the VC to make their investments when the firm formally requests the cash via a 'drawdown notice'. There is no optionality here; if the investment is within the scope of the fund and the VC follows the policies and procedures laid out in the LPA, then the LPs must comply with the drawdown. The penalties for failing to comply are severe, and any LP who fails to send the cash will likely lose its entire investment placed in the fund to date.

This drawdown arrangement suits both LPs and VCs. On the one hand, it serves to manage and monitor a VC's investment behaviour – ensuring that every time the fund makes an investment, the VC communicates to the LPs what the investment is and summarises the investment thesis for backing a particular start-up. The LPs do not have a say in the investment decision, they cannot block it or make changes unilaterally, nor can they refuse to participate (assuming the investment is within the scope of the LPA). Usually, however, there is an advisory board comprised of the most significant LPs in a fund who will meet on a regular basis to monitor its progress and approve changes to the investment strategy if needed.

The drawdown approach is useful for VCs too. It means they do not have the responsibility of managing bank accounts containing huge amounts of cash (perhaps impacting their regulatory status), but it also means that one of their performance measures – the internal rate of return (IRR) – is maximised as the 'clock only starts ticking' for the IRR calculation from the moment cash is drawn down into the fund for making a particular investment and not before. Although IRR is important, the ultimate measurement of performance for venture capital funds is the cash-on-cash return (i.e. cash returned to the LPs compared to cash invested by the LPs). This is a remarkably simple measure, but is equally remarkable for being difficult to achieve within the life of the LPA and the remuneration of VCs is tied very closely to making returns to the LPs.

CARRIED INTEREST AND LOAN REPAYMENT POINTS

Venture capital firms have two sources of revenue from their fund management activities, both of which are paid from the total funds they raise. First, there is an annual management fee paid by the LPs for managing the fund. This covers all running expenses for managing the fund, from salaries to office rent and travel to board meetings. Second, and more importantly, there is a share of the profits generated from successful exits, termed 'carried interest' (see Figure 4.3).

Annual management fees for almost all venture capital funds are equivalent to 2% of the total committed capital of the fund, usually paid quarterly by the LPs according to their share of the fund. In some cases, the annual management fee is higher during the 5-year investment period (e.g. 2.5%) and lower during the 5-year management period (e.g. 1.5%) as it is assumed most of the 'heavy

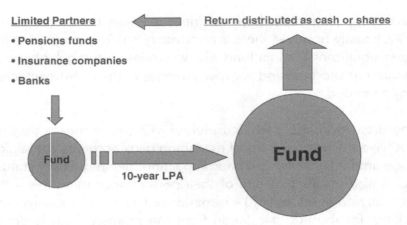

Figure 4.3 The flow of funds.
VCs raise their funds from investors such as pension funds. The investments are pooled into a venture capital fund usually structured as an LPA, and the investors are termed Limited Partners (LPs) reflecting the fact that they are largely passive partners in the fund with the VC acting as the 'General Partner' with responsibility for managing the fund. The investments into the fund are made in the form of loan commitments, which the VC 'calls' from the LPs over a 10-year period to make investments. The 'fund' is not really a fund at all, in that it does not sit in the VC's bank account – it is only an obligation of the LPs to send money to the VC according to their allocated portion of the commitment whenever the VC requires it to make an investment. Once the VC has made the initial investments they want to make within the 5-year investment period, they will then seek to maximise the returns to the LPs by delivering the best possible exits during the management period, or even before the end of the investment period if opportunities arise. Once the entire fund has been returned, including management fees, the venture capital firm is rewarded with 20% of the profits, the so-called 'carried interest'.

lifting' work has been done by the end of the investment period when new investments are identified, evaluated and negotiated. After that, the main activities are restricted to monitoring, adding value via money plus, reinvesting in further rounds and delivering an exit. Although management period activities appear simpler, most VCs will agree that they are often the hardest part of the fund management process, and delivering exits can take up a significant proportion of any VC's time.

> *Putting money into companies is relatively easy compared to getting it back out…*

Carried interest is the term used by the venture capital industry to describe the profit share that flows from the fund to the venture capital firm once the entire fund has been repaid from the proceeds of exits. The point at which the fund is repaid completely is termed a loan repayment point (because the money committed to the venture capital fund by the LPs is a form of loan) and it must be repaid in full before the VC's share of the profits (the carried interest) begins to flow. This includes repayment of all the 2% annual management fee amounts paid by the LPs. Everything must be repaid (salaries, costs, etc.) before the loan repayment point is reached and the fund is regarded as fully repaid. Sometimes there is a minimum expected annual return (termed a hurdle rate) which the VCs also need to repay to the LPs before they receive carried interest, and this may be as high as 8% per annum, creating a substantial hurdle for early-stage venture capital funds backing risky start-ups.

> *Reaching a loan repayment point is a major milestone and kick-starts carried interest.*

To illustrate how carried interest works, it is useful to consider an example. Assume a venture capital firm raises a $100 million fund structured as a 10-year LPA. Over the course of 10 years, the fund pays to the venture capital firm (via a legal construct known as the General Partner) a 2% annual management fee. This means that a total of $20 million in fees is paid to the VC over the 10-year period. This leaves $80 million of capital in the fund for investment into target companies. Carried interest is only paid to the VC (via another legal construct called the Founder Partner) when the entire $100 million is paid back (the so-called loan repayment point). The total amount invested, and the entire management fee, must be repaid before carried interest is triggered, so $80 million of investment must generate at least $100 million of returns to reach the loan repayment point. This example does not consider the impact of any additional hurdle rates, which would further increase the loan repayment point and, of course, push it further away over time.

The example above illustrates that carried interest is usually paid out based on the returns of the entire fund; in other words, after reaching a loan repayment point when the entire fund (including management fees and hurdles) is repaid. The carried interest is usually shared out among the partners in the venture capital firm according to their employment contracts. Senior partners (sometimes called General Partners) are equity partners in the venture capital firm itself and usually retain the lion's share of the carried interest, with junior partners and associates receiving proportionately less. When venture capital firms manage multiple funds, some partners (termed fund partners) will have carried interest attached only to the funds they were hired to manage. Therefore, just as in most organisations, there is a hierarchy within venture capital firms via which carried interest is apportioned, and this may change as the firm raises successive funds over time. This hierarchy plays an important role in the investment decision-making process and is discussed later in this book.

Regardless of hierarchy, carried interest within a fund is not usually allocated to partners based on whose investments within that fund *succeeded* or *failed*, it is pooled and shared out across the partnership as described above. This is intended to ensure that the entire venture capital team works for the good of the fund as a whole, rather than their own individual interests. It is easy to imagine that if this were not the case, individual partners would promote their own deals and maximise their own individual rewards. The allocation of carried interest based on performance of the entire fund avoids such individualist behaviour and gets everyone in the firm pulling in the same direction. Naturally, if a pattern develops where one or two partners make poor investments but share in the carried interest pool, they may find themselves having a conversation with the senior partners about their performance, their share of the carried interest and ultimately their position in the team. As in any business, there is internal competition for status, pay and promotion, and fund carry is intended to minimise this behaviour and align all partners in the venture capital firm towards a simple, common goal: maximise returns for the LPs within a 10-year time frame.

The allocation of carried interest based on overall fund performance is termed 'fund carry', and is the dominant form of reward in the venture capital industry. An alternative is 'deal carry', where carried interest is paid out for individual deals – perhaps even before a loan repayment point is reached. This can sometimes be observed when VCs have been able to negotiate with LPs to accelerate the point at which they begin receiving carried interest, but problems arise if the fund subsequently fails to reach a loan repayment point. In these cases, mechanisms exist for clawing back carried interest paid out on earlier successful exits, but it becomes messy and in the long run is best avoided.

The remuneration model for VCs described in the previous paragraphs is commonly referred to as the '2 and 20 model', describing the 2% management fee and the 20% carried interest. In some rare cases, venture capital firms that have consistently managed high-performing funds can negotiate larger fees, in particular greater carried interest. The question is, what do the LPs who invest in venture capital funds expect for the fees they pay; in particular, the 2% per annum simply for managing the fund, which appears unconnected to the performance of the fund?

MONEY PLUS

There is an easy answer to the question above. LPs expect VCs to *proactively* manage the fund. They expect the managers of the funds they invest in to do more than simply choose investments and wait for the exit. True VCs' investments are not passive. They do not simply negotiate the biggest equity share possible in return for an investment followed by a period of observing and waiting, there is active engagement on the journey to the exit. This is important and is expected by the LPs who invest in venture capital funds – they want active management for the substantial fees they pay to the VC.

Money plus and active engagement from a VC should also be expected by the entrepreneurial teams behind start-ups. As explained in Chapter 2, selling equity is expensive, and founders surrender economic upside and control in return for the investment they need to build the business. But they should expect much more than just the money. The VC usually takes up a seat on their board of directors, and this should be a proactive relationship. It should not be a relationship where the VC shows up at board meetings every few months and drinks the coffee, makes a few notes and leaves promptly in a fast car. The most important word in the phrase is 'help'. A VC's role is not only to choose potential winners when they make an investment, but to help guide the entrepreneurial teams they back along the way to a successful outcome – it is a hands-on relationship with the aim of nudging performance upwards.

Some VCs have a more hands-on style than others. VCs who position themselves as 'lead investors' focus on originating opportunities, taking the lead on evaluating and negotiating the investment and then recruiting other VCs to join a syndicate to invest on the same terms. Syndicate building and the reasons for it are discussed in a later chapter, but it is common practice in the field of entrepreneurial finance when investment rounds are too big for a single investor. Investors who take less of a lead role – often those managing larger funds with a focus on later-stage investments – are referred to as 'followers'. There is a slightly derogatory air about this descriptor, and very few VCs will go into a meeting with an entrepreneurial team and describe themselves as followers, but some are naturally more inclined to do this. Some VCs will have a mixed model, where they play a lead role in some deals and act as a follower in others; sometimes this relates to who found the deal first, sometimes it relates to skill sets within the firm and sometimes the geographic location of the start-up. VCs usually prefer to be the lead investor for something close to home both in terms of location and sector specialism.

Which model offers the greatest return per unit of effort put in by VCs is the subject of much debate within the industry and research by academics. It is notoriously difficult to compare the success of individual venture capital funds to each other as, being limited partnerships, they have few requirements to publish their performance. VCs focused on later-stage investments say that early-stage investing, backing completely new start-ups which invariably require them to play the lead role, is a huge amount of work that is not reflected in the returns for their funds. VCs focused on backing, or in some cases creating, brand new start-ups will claim that the only way to make the best returns is to play the lead role and get into companies very early at a low price. The venture capital ecosystem contains both groups who major in one area or another and focus on one investment philosophy or another. There is, it seems, room for both approaches but entrepreneurial teams would be well advised to do their research and target VCs who best fit their needs.

HOW VCs DEPLOY THEIR FUNDS

VCs see their world as a series of financing rounds within a portfolio of companies. They build their portfolio of companies based on the investment strategy they pitched to potential LPs in their fund, and they seek to execute that investment strategy by discovering, or in some cases creating, the best set of opportunities they can find, choosing the best ones and negotiating a favourable set of investment terms. The milestone-based financing strategy discussed throughout Chapter 2 is central to the VCs' ability to build and manage their portfolio of investments in stages (see Figure 4.4).

Just as entrepreneurs focus on raising capital to cross the Valleys of Death in stages to minimise dilution of their equity ownership, VCs focus on using milestone-based financing to mitigate the risks of backing a portfolio of start-ups, each of which could fail at any time. By committing to investments over a series of investment rounds, in stages, they use the performance of start-ups to gauge the level of risk they are taking by putting further investments into any one individual company.

Having made an investment in a start-up company, each time that company raises a further round of finance, the VC will have the right, but not the obligation, to invest part of the investment round to maintain their stake in the company. This is called investing *pro rata* (from the Latin 'in proportion'). This is a crucially important concept for managing a venture capital fund, as it means every time there is a new investment round in an existing portfolio company the VC has already backed, they must make a fresh investment decision about whether to reinvest (and how much) depending on the progress the company has made against its business plan and compared to the other portfolio companies the VC has backed.

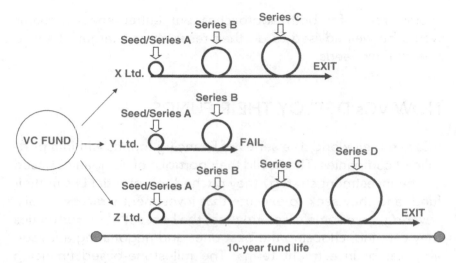

Figure 4.4   Building a milestone-based portfolio.

The venture capital industry has an adaptation of one of the oldest business models on earth – buy low and sell high. In Chapter 2, Figure 2.6 shows how entrepreneurs should build a milestone-based financing strategy, recruiting VCs over a series of investment rounds of increasing size and valuation to minimise their equity dilution. VCs mirror this approach by viewing their first investment as only the first of a series of investments they will be expected to make into portfolio of companies until exits can be generated. In the example above there are three portfolio companies that undergo a series of investment rounds in which the VC may invest to maintain their stake in each of them. Company X and Company Z deliver successful exits after three or four rounds of investment, but Company Y fails. The milestone-based financing shown in Figure 2.6 and the milestone-based approach shown above are two sides of the same coin; for the entrepreneur, it minimises dilution and for the VC, it mitigates risk. It is a process of increasing commitment to each other on the journey towards an exit.

The important point is that investing *pro rata* is a right, not an obligation, and the VC could decide not to reinvest at all if a company is doing badly. Failing to invest *pro rata* will cause dilution of the VC's stake in the business but if the company is struggling or failing to deliver on its promises, this is a decision the VC should make.

THE DYNAMIC ALLOCATION OF CAPITAL

Human nature means it is tempting for VCs to save struggling companies in which they have invested. Nobody wants a failure within the portfolio against their name, but the shared nature of carried interest should ensure that individual VCs within the firm, acting in the interests of the fund's overall performance, should make the decision to cease further investments into a company that may never cross the Valleys of Death. Sunk costs are just that, and VCs should focus on the potential winners that could deliver 10× returns rather than propping up companies that may only just return the original investment. This sounds like common sense but in the heat of a rapidly changing investment environment with the pressures to make investment decisions, the clarity required to make such brave decisions may be hard to find.

The decisions to invest and reinvest in companies within the portfolio rarely rest with an individual. Such decisions within a venture capital fund are made by reaching a consensus within the firm, comparing all available investment opportunities. The senior partners will have the biggest say, often forming an investment committee to ensure good governance and that the investment complies with the scope of the fund. In the case of existing companies within the portfolio seeking further investment, the decision will depend on progress against the business plan on which the original investment was made, allowing for pivots in strategy and the obvious challenges that all companies face.

When an investment is made in a new company for the first time, not only is there a decision to invest in the current round, there is also a budgeting decision to 'reserve' approximate funds for supporting future financing rounds as the company continues its milestone-based financing strategy through Series B, Series C, and so on. This is only an internal budget reserved by the VC, it is not a legally binding or firm commitment made to a portfolio company. In the shareholders' agreement signed by a venture capital fund when it invests in a company there is always a right, but not an obligation, to maintain its equity stake in the business by investing its pro-rata share. That budget will change constantly as the portfolio progresses, and funds that were previously reserved for a portfolio company may be decreased or removed altogether if it appears that a company is failing. In some cases, reserved funds for a company may even increase if the VC believes this company is going to be a big winner. This is called dynamic capital allocation and is represented in Figure 4.5.

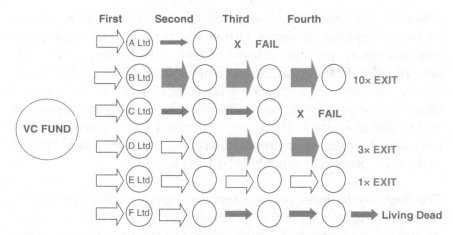

Figure 4.5 Dynamic allocation of capital across a portfolio.
When a venture capital fund makes first-round investments in a set of companies (in this case represented by Companies A to F), the VCs will budget for a series of further investment rounds in those companies. The 'neutral position' is that VCs assume they will invest pro rata (in proportion) to maintain their stake in the business, but this will change depending on individual company performance. In the second round of investments, Companies D, E and F receive their pro-rata investment (represented by a white arrow) but Companies A and C are judged to be poor performers and receive substantially less (represented by a small darker arrow). Company B is judged to be an outperformer and the VC will seek to invest a higher amount (represented by a thicker grey arrow). In the third round of investments, a similar pattern emerges, with some companies outperforming expectations and others underperforming. Company A receives no investment from the fund at all and goes on to fail. In the fourth round, Companies B and D emerge as the consistently high-performing businesses that will drive the performance of the fund. There are two failures in the portfolio in which the fund will lose some or all of its investment. There is one company, Company F, which is described as the 'living dead'. This is a term used in the venture capital industry to describe companies that neither succeed nor fail but instead lead to another problem – a company that does not provide an exit. The key message from this example is that in order to maximise returns from the fund, VCs should direct extra investment to the likely winners in the portfolio rather than attempting to prop up the likely losers. A 10× return on an investment in which the VC invested more capital will return far more than preventing an investment loss of 1×…

RAISING SUCCESSIVE VENTURE CAPITAL FUNDS

VCs do not simply raise a fund, invest in it and retire from the industry 10 years later at the termination of the LPA. When VCs remain in business for a long period of time, they set about raising a series of funds, one after the other; they do not wait for 10 years to raise the next fund as shown in Figure 4.6. The reason for this lies in the fact that only during the investment period, the first 5 years of the fund's life, are they permitted to seek and invest in new opportunities.

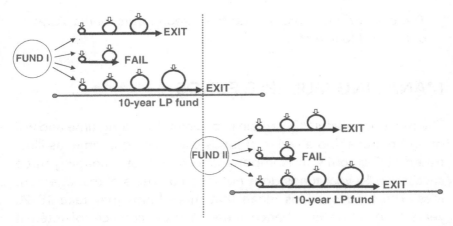

Figure 4.6 Raising the next fund.
Venture capital firms raise their second fund (Fund II) when they have generated sufficient track record to enable them to do so but before the management fee from Fund I comes to an end. Prospective LPs will examine the venture capital firm's financial performance by looking at the valuations of their Fund I portfolio companies, but primarily the exits generated. The balancing act VCs must play is raising their second fund at the moment when they have sufficient track record but before the management fee for Fund I ends. The goal is to have a continuous (and sometimes overlapping) management fee from Fund I and Fund II to continue to grow the firm. The most successful venture capital firms have managed multiple successive funds such that as one investment period ends, another begins.

The second 5 years of the fund's life, the management period, is when they are supposed to be supporting, reinvesting and exiting from the portfolio they have built during the investment period.

To achieve continuity of their business and to ensure a constant ability to be in the market for new investments, VCs must raise a subsequent fund ready to invest just as the investment period of the previous fund comes to an end. Ideally, VCs must be ready to start investing a new fund after 5 years. This depends, however, on them establishing sufficient track record in the first fund for LPs to have sufficient confidence to reinvest.

So, when is the right time for a VC to raise a new fund? The answer lies in the fine line between establishing sufficient track record through exits and revaluations in the portfolio from Fund I and prior to the management fee ceasing or declining due to exits. Importantly, the VC must also be seen to be in the market for making new investments. If they are not, the entrepreneurial community quickly loses interest in them.

There is nothing more useless to entrepreneurs than a VC without a fund to invest...

MANAGING MULTIPLE FUNDS

The most successful VCs remain in business for a long time and will often be managing a series of funds overlapping in time, as illustrated in Figure 4.7. It is important to note that managing three successive 10-year funds does not mean 30 years of management fees. The fund overlaps mean that three funds may take 18–20 years to manage and hence there may be conflicts of interest between successive funds as their activities overlap. Separate funds cannot make investments into each other's portfolio companies, as one set of LPs cannot be seen to bail out the misfortunes of another (or indeed benefit from their good fortune). On a more subtle level, how should an individual venture capital fund manager split their time between managing the investments of Fund I,

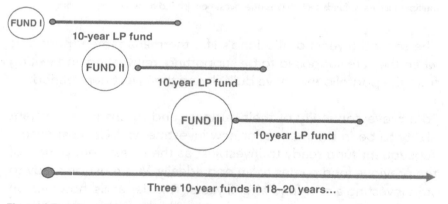

Figure 4.7 Managing overlapping funds.
Successful VCs manage a series of funds, each overlapping with the previous one; as one fund enters the management period after 5 years, a subsequent fund is launched to provide fresh capital to invest in new businesses. Because money flows through a fund only once and cannot be 'recycled' to reinvest in new deals, it is important for VCs to raise new funds in a timely manner to ensure continuity of their investment activities, and importantly continuity of management fees. Although many funds managed by a VC will contain many of the same LPs, funds cannot 'cross invest' in portfolio companies from a previous fund – to avoid conflicts of interest. For example, using capital from Fund II to bail out a struggling company in Fund I would be against the interests of LPs in Fund II. In general, investments in a single portfolio company must all come from within the same fund. As VCs become more successful and raise successively larger funds, this contributes to the equity gap discussed earlier.

whilst making new investment for Fund II and thinking about fundraising for Fund III? This issue of time allocation is a serious point, as the venture capital fund manager could potentially be receiving payment for a full-time management role by two separate sets of LPs in two separate funds. There are ways in which this is managed to ensure that VCs do not get rich simply by raking in management fees from large funds, but it is an issue that needs managing.

Funds may overlap temporally but may vary in scope. In Figure 4.7, Fund I and Fund II may have different investment scopes and strategies and even a different geographic focus. It is important for entrepreneurs to know from which fund a VC is intending to invest in their business. Is their investment the last one from Fund I or the first one from Fund II, meaning a difference of 5 years in terms of exit horizon...?

THE VENTURE FUND LOOP

There is more to venture capital than picking the winners. When can a VC truly call themselves a VC? Probably when they have raised a fund, successfully invested in it, made returns to the LPs and raised a subsequent fund.

VCs have several simultaneous activities they must undertake when managing multiple successive funds. They must invest in new companies whilst exiting ones from the previous fund. They must manage the inevitable crises that emerge in the existing portfolio whilst retaining a creative and open mindset towards the future investments they plan to make as they identify the next wave of groundbreaking technology. They must manage investor relations with existing LPs whilst pitching to LPs (who may or may not be the same) for the new fund and ultimately, they must return profits to trigger carried interest (see Figure 4.8).

The above is not intended to generate sympathy for VCs from the entrepreneurial community. Instead, it is intended to paint a picture of the pressures these investors feel as they manage a multitude of different tasks. The message for entrepreneurial teams

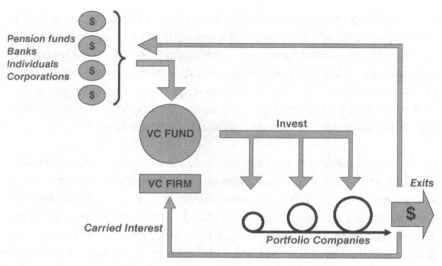

Figure 4.8   The venture fund loop.
The venture fund loop is completed when a loan repayment point has been reached and all the capital committed by LPs has been returned with carried interest fully paid. Arguably, a VC is not a 'true' VC until their first fund has been fully returned to LPs and a second fund raised. Venture capital is, therefore, much more than choosing good investments. It is raising a fund, investing and managing a portfolio, raising a second fund and making further investments. How VCs manage their time between making new investments, whilst acting as a director on the boards of existing portfolio companies and thinking about raising the next fund is a hot topic of discussion within the industry, and something which all experienced VCs must manage.

raising finance is to know what to look for, what questions to ask and to make the VCs' lives easy and hence more likely to say yes to an investment in their start-up. Understanding the VCs' business model, fund structure and position within the venture capital cycle is crucial in understanding their decision-making process.

Modern pirates: venture capital of another sort?

In an MBA class in San Francisco, Al Crawford recounted his career in the navy as a helicopter pilot. He had substantial experience patrolling the Gulf of Aden protecting commercial shipping from raids by modern-day maritime pirates. When I talked about the business model of VCs, Al immediately recognised the business model as almost identical to that operated by the pirates he had encountered. What he told me was along the following lines:

In the local area, normally near a town, there is usually a 'Pirate King'. The locals will approach the Pirate King with an offer to go out and conduct piracy on his behalf. The Pirate King will probably receive a few offers from different men with different amounts of piracy experience and he will select the men that he wants from the pitches he receives. He will then 'invest' by supplying them with a vessel, a crew and a supply of piracy equipment such as weapons, ladders and satellite phones. He then sends them off to sea, possibly mitigating his risk by making them do some human trafficking, and taking money from people for the transportation, to offset his costs. The Pirate Captain selected by the Pirate King will be expected to pursue any reasonable piracy target or opportunity.

If the Pirate Captain is successful in capturing a vessel, he will be rewarded by the Pirate King with a portion of proceeds that he may share with his crew. Depending on whether there is a ransom paid, the payout may be immediate and come directly from the Pirate King, or the Pirate Captain might be allowed to delay his exit and wait for the details and scale of the ransom to become clear and potentially get a larger amount.

The similarities with the relationship between LPs, VCs and entrepreneurs are multifaceted. The Pirate King may be viewed as a powerful LP funding the Pirate Captain (a VC) to build a portfolio of risky ventures (captured vessels), any one of which could deliver a blockbuster exit with the payment of a ransom or two. The vessels, arms and funding provided to the Pirate Captain are akin to the management fee paid to VCs to operate their investment business day to day, but the real payoff is the carried interest (share of the profits) when a ransom is paid. It is not an exact metaphor, but it goes back to the ancient business models of Babylonian merchants and 19th-century whaling agents, with the management fees and carried interest bearing a striking resemblance to the modern pirates and VCs alike. It appears to be an ancient business model that gets to the heart of the risky venture.

CORPORATE VENTURE CAPITAL

Although the 10-year LPA is the dominant fund structure within the venture capital industry there are alternatives, including some VCs or government-backed agencies that operate an 'evergreen' approach, raising funds on an annual basis or receiving an annual budget from their parent organisation.

Corporate venture capital is a subsector of venture capital that has periodically grown and then receded according to the economic cycle. Many large international corporations have developed the ability to make direct investments in start-ups. In the 1990s, such investors were sometimes regarded by the venture capital industry as being naive, having lengthy and unpredictable decision-making processes, and worst of all attaching special conditions to their investments that compromised the financial exit. They were not desirable investment partners from the perspective of the VCs who dominated the entrepreneurial finance ecosystem. But then corporates got smarter, they started to hire VCs from the mainstream industry and structure their investments in such a way as not to compromise their ability to co-invest and co-exist with purely financial venture capital funds. Corporates often engage in venture capital investments as part of an open innovation strategy; either to learn about new areas adjacent to their core business, or to expand into new areas without necessarily changing their core strategy or committing assets from their core business.

There are numerous examples of successful corporate venture funds, and some have been in business for a very long time – like Intel Capital and Johnson & Johnson Development Corporation. Others, such as Google Ventures, are more recent entrants, and the credibility they bring to a start-up is consistent with the money plus concept. Not only do they bring validation from a major incumbent in the industry, but they may also bring technical resources, knowledge and routes to market, but this comes at a price. Entrepreneurial teams who accept venture capital investment from a corporate venture capital fund must ensure they are not prevented from doing business with the competitors of their corporate backer. They must also ensure they do not agree to conditions which constrain their exit route in any way. Harvesting

Corporate Venture Capital   **81**

maximum value at exit is the golden mantra for entrepreneurs, and any deal with a corporate VC that prevents this – such as rights of first refusal to buy the company – is to be avoided at all costs.

Having an investment from a corporate VC knowledgeable in the industry often provides validation of a start-up's technology or business model and can be a valuable tool to attract other investors, but the risk lies in the perception that the corporate investor may have attached special conditions to their investment or favourable terms that will limit the exit routes. There is a balance between the validation provided and the risk of negative investor perceptions. It is often said that the ideal number of corporate venture funds backing a growing venture is zero or two. An investment from one corporate VC suggests special terms might be in place, but an investment from two corporate VCs will clearly signal that there are unlikely to be special terms in place for both – they can't both have rights to buy the company…

Corporate venture capital exists in several forms. The simplest, most informal structure is one in which corporates make occasional investments *ad hoc* into individual enterprises which they believe to be relevant to their core strategy. Sometimes these investments sit alongside a commercial relationship with the venture, such as a licensing deal or a co-marketing agreement for a new product, and sometimes an equity investment is part of the deal. Decision-making for such investments is often complicated and can go as far as the very top of the organisation, with CEO and CFO approval being required. This is often forthcoming for the initial corporate investment but may be problematic if the start-up comes back for *pro-rata* contributions to further investment rounds, by which point a commercial deal may have ended. Sometimes this manifests itself in issues as simple as requiring shareholder approval for future investment rounds; even if the corporate is not investing, it may be an achingly slow process to gain the required signatures from the appropriate signatories who need to be identified within a corporate management structure.

Ultimately, the reasons why an equity investment may be part of a commercial deal such as this are many and varied, but such investments may create conflicts of interest and challenges in the future that need to be managed carefully. Sometimes start-ups need to ask the question whether equity investments as part of a commercial deal are worth the challenges that often emerge in the future...

More formal corporate venture capital arrangements exist when corporates form a ring-fenced pool of capital to be invested in start-ups and external ventures at various stages of growth. These pools of capital can exist either as an annual budget for investments, or a separate fund structure such as a classic LPA – in which the corporate is the sole LP with a management team who act outside of the corporate parent. The latter arrangement mimics the mainstream venture capital industry closely and therefore enables the corporate VC to invest alongside VCs with minimal conflicts of interest. The corporate LP fund structure has found favour with many corporates eager to align their interests with the mainstream venture capital industry, making co-investments easier and decisions quicker. Under this model, venture capital fund managers can make investment decisions rapidly and ensure their decisions are consistent with the principles of venture capital investing, rather than the latest strategic direction adopted by the corporate parent. It also enables corporates to recruit and reward experienced venture capital managers with a reward model they are familiar with – management fees and carried interest over a 10-year cycle.

How corporates measure success for their corporate venture investments depends on their goals for making investments in the first place. The two axes of measurement are usually financial returns or strategic gain. The reasons a corporate venture investment is made, or a corporate venture fund is set up, may be predominantly financial returns or predominantly strategic advantage (e.g. insight into a new area of technology), or a blend of the two. Measuring financial returns is easy via capital gain and the IRR, but measuring a strategic gain is harder and many corporates have struggled with this. How an equity investment impacts a set of strategic goals within the parent organisation depends on the goals, and subtle changes in corporate culture that improve innovation are almost impossible to quantify. More importantly, the decision to invest in a start-up or growing venture is more easily understood when a financial return is the main reason for the investment; but justifying an investment in a start-up with 'strategic reasons' can be vague and ill-defined. The usefulness of an equity stake in a start-up can disappear overnight if corporate strategy pivots away, leaving an orphan investment in an area that is no longer of interest. Making individual investments based on financial potential within a corporate venture fund with a well-defined scope is often the only way to get close to resolving these issues for corporate venture fund managers. It is the least problematic approach but by no means perfect.

It is clear to see that for entrepreneurs seeking to raise finance, engaging with a corporate venture fund has some advantages in providing market credibility and other resources but there are problems too, ranging from decision-making within the corporate to conflicts of interest and problematic exits. Entrepreneurs are best advised to check the goals, structure and decision-making process before deciding that an investment from a corporate venture fund is a good idea.

The ideal number of corporate venture capital investors in a company is zero or two. Make sure no investor, be they corporate or otherwise, has special rights that compromise an exit...

SUMMARY OF CHAPTER 4

For those seeking to enter the venture capital industry, this chapter has provided an introductory guide to the inner workings of venture capital funds. For those seeking to raise finance from VCs, this chapter provides something more important: an insight into the venture capital business model that underpins and colours every decision they make. Understanding the venture capital business model means that entrepreneurs seeking to raise capital can anticipate the questions that may arise and how they might best fit their business plan to deliver what VCs are looking for.

The chapter began by explaining that the venture capital business model is an adaptation of one of the earliest business models known to humans — buy low and sell high (and aim for a capital gain). VCs are financial intermediaries, fund managers who act on behalf of investors in their funds to seek out and invest in the best selection of entrepreneurial ventures they can find. They are agents for their investors, with a remit to manage the enormous information asymmetry that exists between complicated entrepreneurial ventures and the ultimate investors who provide the financial resources to grow – the LPs in venture capital funds.

Although alternative structures exist, such as those found within corporate venture funds, the '2 and 20' model underpinning most LPAs is by far the dominant form within the mainstream venture capital industry and tends to provide the backdrop for most venture capital investments. Understanding the pressures on venture capital fund managers and where they are within the venture fund loop is not intended to garner sympathy for VCs, it is intended to illuminate the pressure points that entrepreneurs can address in making a VC's investment decision easier. Highlighting the potential for an exit and the timelines to doing so are one example of solving the multitude of problems a VC will anticipate in making investments.

Understanding the venture capital business model is key to understanding investment decisions.

Chapter 5

A Day in the Life

In the previous chapter we examined the predominant business model and fund structure utilised in the venture capital industry, the so-called '2 and 20' model in which venture capital funds are structured as limited partnerships (via LPAs), and how VCs play the role of financial intermediaries managing the information asymmetry between the investors in their funds and the entrepreneurs they back.

Anyone entering the venture capital industry for the first time might imagine that the job is simply picking new investments. The previous chapter illustrated that being a VC is much more than that, but imagine you are a newly recruited associate arriving at your desk for your first day of work at a venture capital firm. Most firms hire new associates to find investment opportunities, known in the venture capital industry as 'deal flow'. How would you go about finding new opportunities before your competitors working for other funds? How would you source proprietary deal flow leading to great returns? After all, only by finding proprietary deal flow early can venture capital funds produce better returns than their competitors...

86   A Day in the Life

The question may be answered readily by considering a further question: How did you get the job in the first place? Venture capital firms do not hire new associates or partners to sit at their desks and wait for deals; they hire new associates and partners who already bring new deal flow with them. Students often ask the question: What is the best way to secure a job in the venture capital industry?', and the answer is quite simply to generate deal flow before you show up at the interview. There are many bright graduates and MBAs in the world, and many experienced managers with successful track records in investment banking, consulting and working with start-ups, but what sets apart successful candidates gaining a job in the venture capital industry is being in possession of potential investment opportunities.

Attending networking events and conferences, being active in industry discussion forums and building powerful networks within the entrepreneurial community are all essential ingredients to building strong proprietary deal flow. Anyone interested in working in venture capital should start this process before they even get to the job interview. Sourcing deal flow in venture capital is all about networks and the stronger the network, the better the chances of a great investment.

Similarly, for new entrepreneurs seeking to raise finance, building warm contacts with participants in the entrepreneurial community – such as the CEOs of growing ventures – is the best way to gain access to VCs via 'warm contacts'. Operating via warm contacts who know VCs and are trusted by them is an infinitely more efficient means of generating investment interest than 'cold calling' VCs. VCs rely on 'qualified leads', opportunities that are recommended to them by people they trust. For entrepreneurs and VCs alike, active networking within the entrepreneurial community is an essential short-cut to generating the best deal flow and the best opportunity to raise investment for a new start-up. It is all about people...

This notion relates to a concept usually referred to as 'social capital'. It is well established that entrepreneurs who have previously built a successful company and who have raised venture capital from investors before will go straight to their network and raise more capital and raise it quicker. First-time entrepreneurs, on the other hand, are often bewildered and may take an almost random approach to identifying potential investors. Meanwhile, those with some business experience will follow a more structured approach, perhaps like the process an investment bank would follow – they identify lists of investors and target them in a rational, stepwise process to maximise their chances of raising money. The entrepreneurs who raise the most and raise it the fastest, however, are those who have done it before; they have the greatest social capital. Likewise for VCs, those who have built the greatest social capital in the entrepreneurial community find the best deals quicker and more efficiently.

> *Proprietary deal flow is the life blood of venture capital funds. It is a people business...*

OPPORTUNITY

At this point it is worth spending some time considering what we mean by 'opportunity'. There is an entire field of academic study directed at defining what an opportunity 'is', but in essence an entrepreneurial opportunity is simply a *fit* between an underutilised asset and an unfulfilled need. This reduces the concept to a very simple phenomenon: an empty warehouse (an underutilised asset) may easily fulfil a customer need for storing inventory. This is, by definition, an entrepreneurial opportunity, but it is generally not the type of opportunity backed by the venture capital industry. VCs seek opportunities that are protectable, scalable and often technologically sophisticated. The essence of 'opportunity' as perceived within the venture capital industry is that the business model should be *scalable*, and preferably scalable without limit. VCs seek to invest in opportunities within large, global markets with unlimited upside. They are not interested in small businesses based on niche opportunities, or in which scalability is constrained for any reason. For example, a consultancy business that is growing steadily is generally not something VCs will back as every time new clients are won, new consultants must be hired to deliver the services; the business model is not very scalable. A new piece of software, however, can be sold in unlimited quantities without incurring a similar increase in costs.

VCs back scalable opportunities...

SUPPLY AND DEMAND

Chapter 4 highlighted that the supply of venture capital and the demand for venture capital by entrepreneurial start-ups must be in balance to ensure that the venture capital markets operate efficiently. When the supply of venture capital is in excess compared to the demand from start-ups and growing ventures, we tend to see the development of investment bubbles. Valuations increase as VCs pay higher prices to invest in a scarce number of high-potential opportunities, the quality of available investment opportunities gradually declines and the return on investment declines. Hence, investment bubbles eventually deflate or burst suddenly.

The same is true of opportunities. At times of great technological change, such as the years following the development of the World Wide Web, there were a plethora of new dotcom opportunities with endless new business models attached. Entrepreneurs were extremely active in innovating or discovering how new opportunities could impact human lives, but as time wore on it became more difficult to identify opportunities with the unlimited upside sought by the venture capital business model. Within a few short years it seemed as if all the most valuable opportunities had been taken by those who were quickest to move, and the entrepreneurs that followed struggled to identify and develop opportunities that could offer the same potential returns. Again, the venture capital industry witnessed, and played an active role in, the inflation and bursting of a technology bubble.

The preceding paragraphs highlight the risky nature of investing in new waves of technological development. Business generally dislikes risk, managers like predictability and large corporates like to know what they're dealing with. Entrepreneurs and VCs, however, have the opposite view of risky markets. They embrace risk and thrive on it because it is there that they find the greatest opportunities. At times of great change and in imperfect markets, where information is poor, the greatest opportunities are often found. This is why the venture capital industry specialises in deeply technological areas underpinned by science and engineering and areas in which a sophisticated level of knowledge leads to only the smartest entrepreneurial teams being able to capture opportunities. VCs focus on areas such as technology, life sciences, healthcare, energy and so on, as these areas are constantly undergoing great change. Nobody ever seems to have the solution to the energy crisis or the healthcare needs of large populations, but it is within challenges such as this that entrepreneurs find large markets to tap into with the innovations they develop. The Valleys of Death encountered by entrepreneurial teams attempting to conquer these opportunities are large and numerous, and the venture capital industry attempts to provide the finance required to cross them.

Uncertainty, chaos and imperfect markets lead to the greatest opportunities.

For VCs, the trick to managing risk in these circumstances is that they are highly specialised and only invest in areas where they have deep knowledge. This is an aspect of venture capital that many first-time entrepreneurs do not understand. VCs are not endowed with a special gift to see the future, they do not have a crystal ball in which to gaze and predict with any level of certainty what will happen 1 year, 2 years, 5 years or certainly 10 years from now, but they manage the risks they face by specialising. They restrict themselves to investments within the field of expertise they possess and when they raise a new fund, they do so within a very limited scope. The business plan they pitch to potential LPs is based on investing within a specific technological field, with specific business models, geographic locations and stages of growth. By doing so, they manage the risk encountered in these unpredictable markets and provide themselves with a significant advantage in identifying, evaluating and investing in new opportunities.

When a venture capital firm raises a new fund, it agrees with the LPs an investment scope and investment strategy. Within this scope they will develop a plan for building a portfolio of investments in subsectors they believe to be the future. For example, within a $100 million life sciences fund to be invested in the United States, VCs might define four or five strategic areas within which they want to build their portfolio, they will seek to identify the leading innovators and entrepreneurs within those areas and then populate their subsectors within the portfolio as they go forward. In other words, they are proactive. They seek out opportunities to fill their portfolio according to a predetermined strategy; they do not simply wait for random opportunities to come to them. The key is that VCs are *proactive* rather than reactive when it comes to finding deals to invest in (see Figure 5.1).

> VCs find the deals they want to do. They don't wait for them to arrive...

The question posed at the beginning of this chapter was, therefore, a little unfair. New VCs do not arrive at their desks on day one with a blank sheet of paper and a quest to find deal flow without limits. The firm they join will have raised a new fund with a defined investment scope, a defined investment strategy and a timeline for

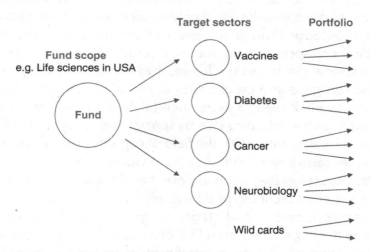

Figure 5.1 Proactive design of the portfolio.
Venture capitalists pitch their funds to LPs with a defined scope and a strategy to build a portfolio in target sectors they believe will yield strong returns and which match their own track record and skills as in the example above. VCs don't wait for ad-hoc deals to come to them, they go out with a purpose to execute their portfolio strategy but with room for manoeuvre – they leave gaps for 'wild cards' they had not perceived as target sectors. VCs need to be strategic yet open minded to new and unusual opportunities that might turn out to be their biggest winners.

building a portfolio containing several high-priority subsectors. Their hunting grounds, therefore, are constrained, and their task is to go and identify the leading innovators and entrepreneurs within specified subsectors. This immediately feels like an easier task, and any new VC will have expertise within the field they have been hired into: they will know people, they will have a network and they will probably have arrived on day one already equipped with potential opportunities to pursue. New recruits are hired to find deals and they will spend a period mapping out an innovation landscape to identify where they can find those with the greatest potential to develop new companies. Don't wait to land the job before starting that process...

IS A BUSINESS PLAN WORTH IT?

There is a difference between a business plan and an investor pitch. Business plans exist primarily for the entrepreneurial team to evaluate their market, determine their strategy and devise a plan to execute. It is a document that serves to align the management team and orient them towards common goals; to make sure everyone is on the same page with regard to where the business is going. A clear strategy is essential for any business, and maximising the chances of success for a highly risky start-up depends on a business plan that contains a good analysis of the market, the competition, the business model, pricing strategies, barriers to entry and financial forecasts showing a range of scenarios for how the business may grow. Crucial among these financial forecasts is a cash-flow analysis that serves as the starting point for the discussion of how much capital the business should raise. In earlier chapters we talked about crossing the Valleys of Death and how difficult it is to predict the capital required to do so. However, building a *pro-forma* cash-flow model that shows a range of scenarios is the best framework for deciding how much, when and in what stages a start-up should raise finance.

In the old days, a business plan for a start-up would tend to be a weighty document containing a series of chapters much like this book, beginning with an introduction, an overview of the business setting out the problem, the solution and examining different aspects of the business. It was a formal document but was immediately out of date as soon as it was printed, as the environment changed and new information came to light. Entrepreneurial teams now tend to develop their business plans via a presentation (slide deck), which contains largely the same information but is far more amenable to change, and more readily adaptable in the rapidly shifting sands of the entrepreneurial world.

Compared to a business plan, whether written as a formal document or developed as a flexible slide deck, an investor pitch is an altogether different document with a different goal in mind. The investor pitch is intended for an external audience: it is a sales document communicating the grand vision of the start-up and with the express intention of raising capital to finance the entrepreneurial journey. It is not a detailed business plan with a consideration of the pros and cons of the business opportunity; it is a sales document based on the business plan aimed squarely at raising money from investors. More importantly, it is not a *single* document. It turns out that entrepreneurs do not need a single pitch, they need a series of pitches each designed for a specific audience and a specific context. In fact, it could be argued that an entrepreneur's life consists of a series of pitches, each one designed to enable the raising of capital to move the business further along towards its grand vision.

LIFE IS A SERIES OF PITCHES

Entrepreneurs often seek guidance on how best to pitch to investors, and the first lesson is to realise that there is no single pitch, but a series of them each with a specific goal.

The first pitch entrepreneurs need to develop is a one-line pitch, a sentence capturing the vision in a very simple statement to be understood by anyone passing, perhaps in a glancing conversation with a non-expert. This does not mean developing a corporate-style mission statement, full of buzz words and jargon, but a description that anyone can understand intuitively and see the opportunity in the blink of an eye. This type of pitch is useful in all sorts of scenarios, from networking events to social encounters, where chance can play a role in connecting entrepreneurs (eventually) to potential investors. Being at an event or even a party with like-minded people might just lead to such a connection. These days, entrepreneurial teams often focus on connecting via social media platforms, which of course is useful but only goes so far. Social media connections do not necessarily translate easily into the human connection that comes from face-to-face interactions, and having a snappy one-line description of a business idea goes a long way to developing that.

The next evolutionary layer beyond the one-line pitch is a 30-second 'elevator pitch'. This phrase is well known in the entrepreneurial community and in the business world in general, but the idea is to develop a pitch to a potential investor trapped with you in an imaginary elevator ride, which provides about 20 seconds to successfully deliver it. It is more than a one-liner but less than a full-blown presentation. The idea is to create intrigue and a desire to learn more about your idea, with the goal of being invited to a meeting to pitch the full story.

The full story, in other words the *real* pitch, is usually accompanied by a slide deck compact enough to send electronically to investors as a 'teaser' document. It should be capable of being read and understood without any accompanying verbal pitch/voice-over, and should be self-explanatory in making clear the vision for the business and the reason to invest now. The purpose of a teaser pitch such as this is to secure a face-to-face meeting, either in person or via a remote meeting platform. The teaser pitch should be no more than 10 slides in length and when used in a meeting scenario should aim to be 'talked through' in about 15 minutes, perhaps supplemented by a series of backup slides that might extend the pitch to around 20 minutes.

An investor pitch such as this is not usually given as a formal 'speech'. VCs do not sit and listen patiently whilst entrepreneurial teams deliver a scripted, rehearsed pitch only to save their cutting questions for the end. They will ask questions all the way through the presentation and will divert the pitch into areas crucial for their investment decision, which may throw the team off balance and off course. This approach by VCs is partly driven by a desire to make the meeting efficient – they simply want to obtain the information required to make a decision – but it also serves a purpose in evaluating how a team behaves and responds. If a management team does not cope well with being thrown a few awkward questions in a pitch, it is unlikely to do very well in a fast-moving business environment. If a management team responds impatiently or displays a level of irritation at being asked questions, or perhaps refutes those questions too abruptly, this indicates to VCs that it may turn out to be a difficult working relationship going forward.

The best pitches are those of about 20 minutes in length, which are guided by a series of slides, but which are not overly scripted and are given confidently and informally. There are plenty of online guides from experts on entrepreneurial pitches focused on the slide contents and the messages to be delivered. This book will not deal with the best structure for a slide deck, but the way in which that presentation is delivered is just as important. Investor pitches sometimes vary in structure between different industries in which cultural norms are different, but being confident, relaxed and informal is a universal advantage for entrepreneurs. It makes investors aware that the team knows what it is talking about and reassures them regarding the future working relationship. Reading from a script, responding abruptly to questions and giving the impression of someone who does not listen are huge red flags for VCs.

> *Entrepreneurs should anticipate a conversation, not rehearse a speech.*

NETWORKS, CONNECTIONS AND REPUTATION

VCs are very active when it comes to using their networks to identify proprietary deal flow. This means using 'warm' contacts within their networks to identify 'qualified leads' – opportunities from people they trust and who understand their business model and the ingredients of a good venture capital deal. Roughly translated, warm contacts often mean the senior management teams of companies they've previously backed or within their existing portfolio who have 'passed the test': they understand the venture capital business model and have achieved some kind of quality threshold by raising money from the investment community.

Somewhat surprisingly, the array of warm contacts who may supply qualified leads to a VC also means other VCs investing within their sector. This might sound strange: previous chapters have indicated how competitive the venture capital industry can be; VCs compete to raise their new funds from a defined set of LPs who may be considering rival venture capital funds. If successful, they are then competing for the same deal flow opportunities in which to invest those funds, so why would VCs talk to each other about proprietary deal flow. The answer lies in *syndication*. VCs often identify and evaluate deals that are too big for them to invest in alone, and they will seek out other VCs to co-invest with them to mitigate their risks by investing only *part* of the financial capital required to fill the round. But this is not the only reason VCs syndicate deals. They syndicate deals to gain access to other skills, complementary networks and knowledge to improve their investment decision. Sometimes a second opinion – another VC's view – may help them avoid a potentially disastrous investment or may lead to a better decision, with an improved investment structure or valuation. It may also lead to greater *money plus* after the investment. By sharing an investment opportunity, VCs may be able to increase the performance of the venture by recruiting additional VCs with complementary skills, knowledge and networks, and be willing to give up some of the upside in return.

There is one further reason why VCs talk to their potential rivals. Not only do they mitigate the financial risks of an investment by recruiting additional financial firepower and skills, they also hope that if they share a potential investment with another VC, the favour will be returned by other VCs sharing a deal in return. In this way, the venture capital industry is, at the same time, competitive and collaborative. VCs sometimes like to hunt in packs by co-investing with other VCs they get along with, who they like and respect for the quality of their decision-making, the views they bring and the added value they can deliver to a portfolio company through money plus.

There is some danger in this approach, as VCs who work together may often adopt overly similar views of the market, leading to uniformity of investment decision-making within the industry. This may contribute to the creation of speculative bubbles, as VCs follow each other into deals they all agree look good at the time. In risky sectors with uncertain futures there is a perception of safety in numbers, and venture capital funds may be more comfortable if they believe other funds will sink or swim together with them. Overall, however, second opinions really matter when the future is uncertain and new technologies are unproven. Tapping into the expertise of an erstwhile rival can minimise risks for both investors.

The risk for entrepreneurs in all of this, of course, is that collaboration between VCs could lead to collusion in negotiating the deal. The next chapter will discuss how the best valuation for start-ups raising investment can only be achieved when entrepreneurs create competitive tension around their opportunities. Seeking rival bids and rival term sheets from multiple VCs is the only surefire way to ensure they are raising investment on the best terms. This process ends up being short-circuited if rival VCs are, in fact, talking to each other and this needs to be carefully managed by entrepreneurial teams.

Potential collusion between VCs however is rare, and is something they are very careful to avoid. A VC's reputation means everything to them. A VC with a negative reputation within the entrepreneurial community is going to find it very hard to access the best investment opportunities. Entrepreneurial teams do not want to communicate their innovations to VCs with a poor reputation, and VCs know this. They work hard to maintain a strong reputation in the market because they know that having a strong reputation will not only allow them to access the best deals, it will also help them to invest at *lower* share prices. It is well documented that entrepreneurial teams will accept investments from highly reputable VCs at lower share prices than they otherwise would. Some studies have attempted to quantify this, but it varies between sectors and depends on what we mean by 'reputation'; suffice to say, VCs preserving their reputation means getting access to the best deals, investing at lower prices and therefore generating greater returns. Doing anything which damages that reputation will undoubtedly impact the returns for their fund in the long run, and hence their chances of raising the next one. Therefore, VCs need to be very careful about making sure they are perceived well within the wider entrepreneurial community.

This care includes preserving their reputation with entrepreneurial teams they *reject*. Ask any VC the percentage of opportunities they reject, and they will give you a figure somewhere between 95% and 98%. In other words, VCs spend the vast majority of their time declining opportunities and saying 'no' to the entrepreneurial teams who pitch to them. This leaves a lot of disappointed entrepreneurs, therefore saying no in the right way is really important for VCs. Entrepreneurs reading this, who may have been rejected by VCs, will likely be sceptical at this point. Sometimes VCs and other investors simply don't respond, or they give very few reasons for declining an investment opportunity. However, it turns out this is not in their best interests. Saying no to entrepreneurial teams and giving rational, well-thought-through reasons for doing so results in those teams going away with a good impression (or at least a less negative impression) of the VCs who said no. It might mean they come back in 6 months or even a year having fixed the problems the VCs highlighted; it might mean they go away and tell other entrepreneurial teams that even though they were rejected, they got some good feedback, and this VC is certainly worth talking to. By saying no but providing rational, well-thought-through reasons for doing so, VCs leave the door just slightly ajar but open enough for entrepreneurial teams to return with a better plan or direct other entrepreneurial teams towards that open door. Rejected teams may even become the 'warm leads' described earlier, and become a source of qualified leads. The goal for VCs is to cast the net wide enough within the entrepreneurial community to generate the best possible deal flow in the most efficient manner. By creating as positive an experience as possible with the entrepreneurs they reject, the door is always left slightly open…

Maximising deal flow in the most efficient manner by having a clear, proactive strategy for identifying opportunities, casting a wide net for qualified leads – including via entrepreneurial teams they reject – is only the first step in the venture capital deal flow process prior to the next stage of the process: screening and evaluation.

THE SELECTION PROCESS

Having identified the best possible sources of deal flow available to them, most VCs follow an almost uniform selection process, organised in a series of stages leading to progressively greater engagement with a start-up. This deal-flow process is akin to the process that many large corporations use when managing projects through to successful endpoints. The venture capital deal-flow process is, however, skewed towards rejecting deals early, efficiently and *cheaply*. The volume of opportunities that are fed into the venture capital deal-flow process means that VCs cannot spend the time required to evaluate all deals in detail. They must *triage* deals according to initial screening criteria. Screening involves identifying whether the opportunity fits the scope of the fund, is at the right stage, is raising an amount of capital consistent with the fund size and fits within some aspect of the proactive investment strategy for building the fund's portfolio.

This often involves an initial meeting with the entrepreneurial team; a first pitch attended by one or two members of the investment team. This initial pitch is the point at which around 90% of opportunities are rejected. The mindset and philosophy of VCs operating a deal-flow process is that if opportunities are likely to be rejected, they should be rejected as early as possible. This is intended to minimise the opportunity cost of spending too much time on unlikely deals that cause them to miss another high-potential opportunity. The risk in this approach is, of course, that by doing so they fail to see a hidden gem – if only they had spent the time to look. Every VC has their so-called 'Beatles moment', the moment when they said no to something that went on to become a global success, just as some in 1960s Liverpool predicted those four young men would amount to nothing in the music business. But this is the price the VC sometimes must pay for operating an efficient deal-flow process in which they are evaluating a lot of opportunities.

The good news for entrepreneurial teams who are invited back for a second meeting is that they are, by definition, likely to be in the top 10% of ventures the VC is looking at. They know their chances of progressing and raising capital are, therefore, greatly enhanced when they are invited back. Phase two of the deal-flow process involves a much more detailed evaluation of the opportunity. This preliminary due-diligence phase will involve the VC crawling over every aspect of the start-up. Nowadays, most start-ups create an

The Selection Process   99

online data room where they deposit their investor pitch, the business plan, the financial projections and all the supporting data they can muster to enable VCs to evaluate the business as efficiently as possible. It is in everyone's interest for the VC to make a rapid decision – whether that decision is positive or negative. Time is precious for both entrepreneurial teams and the investors who back them, and reaching a decision efficiently (even if that decision is 'no' or 'not yet') is helpful in general.

Access to online data rooms and sharing of detailed proprietary information with a potential investor should only be done after they have signed a confidentiality agreement (also known as a non-disclosure agreement, NDA). The right time to sign a confidentiality agreement is when a VC requests access to the data room and the confidential information it contains, and not before this point. It would be unwise for an entrepreneurial team to require an NDA before the first pitch, or even before the second pitch. VCs see so many opportunities that putting hurdles in the way provides an easy reason for them to say no. They just don't have the time. It is a misperception among entrepreneurs that VCs will steal their ideas – that is not the business they are in: raising a series of venture capital funds and investing in the best entrepreneurial ventures they can find. Signing an LPA is a serious legal obligation to their LPs, and they are not about to forsake it by stealing an entrepreneur's idea and running off to do it themselves. It would not be a good business decision for them when they are already managing an investment fund for which they receive a management fee and the potential for carried interest.

What is of course possible, and even likely, is that VCs are constantly being educated by the start-ups that pitch to them. VCs are in a privileged position, gaining access to a wide number of entrepreneurial minds at the forefront of their industries. All the information that VCs gather when they evaluate opportunities will naturally form part of their decision-making process as they go forward. This is unavoidable and is a risk that entrepreneurial teams must be prepared to take to raise capital: to some extent, they are all educating the investors they talk to. This is different, however, to sharing *confidential* information they do not wish to be leaked out beyond the VC they are talking to. This is when signing an NDA becomes useful. Sharing confidential information with a VC who may invest is one thing, but that information leaking out into a wider network is quite another. By signing an NDA, VCs agree not to share that information with any other party – including companies they have invested in or may invest in at some future date. Signing NDAs when a VC enters the data room is good practice, ensuring that confidential information is not leaked to third parties, including competitors who may be operating in the same, or adjacent, markets.

HOW TO PICK A WINNER

There is no crystal ball to provide a reliable shortcut in evaluating high-risk, early-stage ventures operating in uncertain markets. An important point outlined in this chapter so far is that investment decision-making is a *process*, not a single moment. VCs evaluate opportunities using a process that is organised and rational and usually involves many pitches and meetings between the entrepreneurial team and the VC. It takes time. In fact, multiple meetings over an extended period are an important part of the venture capital due-diligence process. VCs will often challenge management teams with a new piece of information, or a new question, and will send them away to develop a solution prior to the next meeting. How the entrepreneurial team responds to this is an important element of the VC's due-diligence process. If the team goes away and devises a well-thought-through response and returns with sensible suggestions and new insights, this is a positive indication of how they will behave following the investment. If, on the other hand, the team is defensive and does not appear receptive to new ideas and challenges, this will be regarded negatively by most VCs. Teams who are wedded to their way of doing things are going to have a hard time engaging with the venture capital community.

> *Entrepreneurial teams who are open to ideas usually raise more investment.*

Asking any VC what they look for when evaluating an investment opportunity will lead to a range of responses. But there are common themes that rise to the surface across a range of industries and between different investors. This book cannot hope to provide the ultimate 'answer', but it does aim to provide guidelines and a framework within which most VCs will operate. The following represent the most common evaluation criteria most VCs mention when asked; the order and *emphasis* may change, but broadly speaking VCs evaluate opportunities along the following lines.

A *Potentially* Huge Market

VCs invest in start-ups with unlimited upside potential. This means focusing on start-ups with the potential to transform and disrupt global markets. The word 'huge' is intentionally vague, but it indicates that the markets start-ups must operate in are certainly not local, regional or even national. They must be international in nature and preferably global. This is not to say that businesses should launch with a plan for global domination. In fact, launching a start-up in multiple international markets would not be credible, but it *is* credible for start-ups to start small and *aim* big. Beginning the business by securing a solid position in the home market is sensible, but to command the attention of leading VCs the ambition must be to conquer international markets.

It is important to note the emphasis on the word *potentially*. Sometimes start-ups create new markets that previously did not exist or did not exist in any substantial way. Sometimes potential customers may not even comprehend the needs they might have until an innovation opens possibilities previously undreamt of. The invention of the telephone is an obvious example. Many potential customers would not have imagined the need to communicate instantly with someone until the telephone opened the possibility to do so. The smartphone market and beyond is testament to how far that potential market has developed…

A Top-Rate Team

It is difficult to build a top-rate team in a brand-new start-up, and very few start-ups come with anything like a complete team of top-rate experienced entrepreneurs and professionals. What VCs look for is the beginnings of a top-rate team: founders who they believe they can build around and who are receptive to the concept of bringing in high-quality management to help them build the venture.

What makes a top-rate team is hard to define. How VCs evaluate a potential team is even harder. There are many studies showing how teams with diverse ranges of skills and experience outperform others, but most VCs will agree that a mixture of industry expertise within the target industry sector and venture-building expertise is the ideal mix. Sometimes entrepreneurial teams with little experience in the market they aim to address are blessed with a naive energy: they believe they can do anything. This is useful, as being optimistic is often the only way to survive the multiple crises that lie ahead. However, bringing in team members who understand the industry the start-up is targeting adds a dose of reality to enable the entrepreneurial team to avoid catastrophe.

Some VCs go to the lengths of carrying out psychometric testing to establish how the skills and experiences within the team fit. Most, however, will rely on their experience and observations in numerous meetings to get a good idea of how a team will perform. How the team responds to the challenges posed by VCs, both in and between their meetings, provides great insight into how successfully they will build their business going forward.

A Pathway to Create Protected Value

Chapter 2 discussed the concept of 'building value'. It highlighted that value is not necessarily the same as generating revenue or profits. In the life sciences industry, for example, building value can involve generating scientific data, intellectual property in the form of patents, or clinical trials data. In the tech industry, building value might mean developing proprietary algorithms or generating large amounts of data to provide a competitive advantage. These are protectable assets, which create barriers to entry for competitors who cannot easily replicate them or find a way to engineer around them, and therefore they are essential for locking in the value created in the business.

Sometimes VCs appear to back start-ups whose ideas can be easily replicated, but in these cases the pathway to creating protected value may rely more on executing faster and better than other competitors. Growing fast rapidly depends on investing large amounts of capital, and some entrepreneurial teams have been adept at gathering very large financial backers behind them to outcompete other players through weight of capital. Sometimes the best technical solution doesn't win the race, it is the management teams who were able to execute faster with more resources behind them who end up delivering the winning solution. An ability to raise capital may not seem like a pathway to creating value, but if a company can lock in a market before others, and create a strong dominant brand in that market, then it has built value which it can protect via its brand and an established supply chain within that market.

A Scalable Business Model

If there is one word that summarises what VCs look for in a business, it is *scalability*. The key ingredient for all venture capital-backed businesses is that they must be scalable without adding a unit of cost every time a unit of revenue is generated. Chapter 2 illustrated the Valleys of Death for two very different businesses, the first a steadily growing consultancy business and the second a technology-based business that required high levels of R&D funding prior to the launch of its product. Even though the technology-based business requires substantial investment, once it starts to sell its product or service, the sky is the limit and its business model does not depend on adding resources in a similar ratio. The consultancy business, on the other hand, will require new consultants to be hired according to a certain ratio when new clients are secured. This is not a scalable business and is very unlikely to secure venture capital investment.

VCs seek unlimited upside through scalable businesses.

A Pathway to Exit

VCs do not look for a fully defined set of exit routes when they invest in a company, but they do look for recognition within the entrepreneurial team that an exit will occur, and it will occur within an expected time frame. It is not possible to define an exit route precisely, and building a business designed to be acquired by a specific global corporate is usually not a good idea: nobody knows the strategy of that corporate 5 years from now and how it may change going forward (perhaps not even its own senior leadership team). The fundamental principle is to build a company that will be successful, self-sustaining and ultimately profitable, whilst also being open to an acquisition or other form of exit. Creating multiple exit routes and therefore flexibility is usually the most important factor VCs consider when they evaluate a business. Almost the first question that crosses the mind of any VC when an entrepreneurial team walks through the door is: How will I sell my stake in this business 5–10 years from now? This is certainly running through the minds of every VC listening to an investor pitch for the first time and entrepreneurial teams would be wise to remember it, but not to dwell on it.

DECISION DYNAMICS WITHIN A VC FIRM

It would be wrong to assume there is a single decision-maker in most venture capital firms or a single moment when decisions are made. Venture capital firms are usually constructed as partnerships and the management structure is relatively flat. Investment decisions are made via consensus among the partners, supported by associates and analysts. It is rare that a single all-powerful partner sitting at the top of the firm will call the shots.

Most of the time, when an entrepreneurial team engages with a venture capital firm, their first meeting (part of the screening process) will usually be with junior partners or associates. In turn, these junior partners will usually be working with a more experienced colleague and will quickly bring them into the discussion if they believe what they have seen looks like a promising venture. This small deal team will conduct follow-on meetings with the entrepreneurial team, challenging them, guiding them and moulding the opportunity into something they believe they can share with the broader partnership. That initial team will become 'deal champions' for the new venture and, once comfortable, they will recommend this investment to their partners seeking the go ahead to spend further time and resources on conducting due diligence. This second phase of due diligence will require additional resources and team members to help evaluate the opportunity. Over a series of meetings, sometimes taking several months, there will be a cycle of discussions between the deal team and the entrepreneurial team as they work together through the process.

SIGNING A TERM SHEET

If all goes well the deal team will, at a certain point, be ready to present this opportunity to an investment committee, which usually comprises a group of the more senior partners operating the fund. The decision point reached at this meeting will be whether to negotiate a term sheet with the entrepreneurial team. Term sheets are the documents through which VCs make investment proposals to start-ups and are discussed in Chapter 7.

The negotiation of a term sheet not only serves to establish whether there are terms of investment the deal team and entrepreneurial team can agree on, it also serves to illustrate how the entrepreneurial team will behave in a real business scenario. How they react to an initial term sheet (usually one that they disagree with) is an important part of the due-diligence process for the VC. If an entrepreneurial team simply signed the term sheet and accepted all the terms, this would be a worrying sign. VCs expect the entrepreneurial teams they back to be astute businesspeople and tough negotiators, and they like to see evidence of that during their own deal negotiations. Negotiating in a logical, rational and calm manner is a strong signal that the entrepreneurial team understands the journey that lies ahead and can navigate the many challenges they will face. In conclusion, it is good for entrepreneurs to negotiate hard, and it improves their chances of reaching a good deal.

Once a term sheet is agreed, the venture capital deal team will take this back to the investment committee and seek final approval to sign the term sheet on behalf of the fund. This is an important moment because, as described in Chapter 7, this commits the VC and the entrepreneurial team to work together towards a final, legally binding agreement following which investment will flow into the company.

COMMON REASONS FOR REJECTION

Why VCs reject investment opportunities is of course related to start-ups scoring badly against the key headlines listed above, but this is not the complete story. There are other factors often hidden from view that contribute substantially to why VCs reach a decision 'to pass' on what appears to be an otherwise interesting opportunity.

Often this may relate to a form of 'institutional memory' – a bad experience with a related company in an adjacent field. This may relate to similarities in technology, the market, geography or more often the business model. Any one of these, or a combination of all four, could lead to a decision that having backed a similar opportunity in the past there is nothing to suggest that trying it again would lead to a better outcome. VCs will often recount how wisdom takes over from analysis as their careers progress; they build enough experience along the way of what works and what doesn't work to be led by gut feeling. The corollary of this wisdom is that sometimes they pass on an opportunity that rational analysis would suggest is a good one, but experiences of the past colour their judgement and create a risk bias leading to a poor decision. The risk for VCs, of course, is that they fail to remain open to new ideas and new management teams just because they had a bad experience in the past of something that on the face of it appeared similar.

> We've seen this movie before, and we don't like the ending. We don't want to see it again…

An intermediate response that lies somewhere between yes and no is 'yes, but…'. In other words, a conditional offer to invest, one that is predicated on satisfying some preconditions. Such preconditions may relate to establishing proof of concept with the technology or showing traction in the market by securing initial customers and generating early revenues. Sometimes, 'yes, but…' might mean making changes to the management team by hiring new senior leaders or in some cases parting company with one of the start-up's founders. This can lead to a great deal of stress within the entrepreneurial team if it's clear that raising money depends on a co-founder leaving the business. Any decision about whether to accept such a condition is a delicate one and must be dealt with carefully – what if the team agrees to it but the investment deal falls through anyway? Now they may have let go a valuable team member, perhaps destabilising the entire business, and they have still failed to raise the finance they need. More common, and usually less controversial, is the requirement to change aspects of the business plan, refine the business model and the financial projections, and these changes are much easier to address.

HOW VCs COMPETE FOR DEALS

It would be easy to assume from everything in this chapter so far that VCs exist in a plentiful sea of opportunities and that all they need to do is find the right ones. In other words, there is an unspoken assumption that entrepreneurial opportunities and start-ups usually outnumber the VCs investing in any one sector, resulting in enough to go around for everyone. This implies that VCs are the scarce resource and will always hold the power in any negotiation. But this is not true. Out of every 100 entrepreneurial opportunities, VCs are likely to reject the same 98; they look at the same parameters, they evaluate markets in a similar way, and they assess the capabilities of teams using similar approaches. It is likely, therefore, that a very small subset of opportunities will form the target for VCs operating within that market. The competitive dynamic therefore flips around from one in which start-ups are competing for scarce venture capital to one in which venture capital is competing for a scarce number of highly desirable or 'hot deals'.

How should a VC compete to win the right to invest in a hot deal? The obvious answer is to pay more – to pay a higher share price for the investment it is making and therefore diluting the founders and other existing shareholders less. Clearly this would be desirable for the entrepreneurial team, but it is not the answer for VCs aiming to make the best returns. Any fool can pay more; the trick for VCs is to win deals without paying a higher share price than the competition. This is where the allure of money plus comes into play. VCs will promote their additional value to the entrepreneurial team; they will highlight their reputation, credibility, track record, network, experience and financial resources to put themselves in a strong position to win the right to invest without paying a higher share price. Indeed, as we saw earlier, VCs with a strong reputation not only win deals – they win the right to invest at lower valuations or share prices, and this is fundamentally important to maximising the returns of the fund.

Any fool can pay more. Money plus is how VCs win deals.

EVALUATION GOES BOTH WAYS

It is essential for entrepreneurial teams to recognise that the power to make a deal is not all in the hands of the VCs. Evaluation goes both ways, and in the case of hot deals it is often the entrepreneurial teams who choose which investment offer or term sheet to accept. This choice should be based on the money plus investors can provide and should not merely be a function of price. The right investor for a start-up can be the difference between success and failure, and factors such as reputation, network, experience and other non-financial resources will often play a part. How this translates into success is difficult to measure, but the personal chemistry established between the VC's deal team and the entrepreneurial team should be a key ingredient of the decision of which investor is the right one.

Entrepreneurial teams go about this in a variety of ways, but speaking directly to CEOs and entrepreneurs previously backed by a VC will illuminate how they really are. VCs should be open about providing access to the CEOs within that portfolio; indeed, they often work to promote the portfolio as a 'family' – organising away days or strategic retreats for the senior leadership teams of the companies they have backed. This is aimed at promoting innovation and an exchange of ideas with the goal of maximising the performance of their portfolios. Therefore, asking for an introduction before the deal is even completed should not be a problem.

The sorts of questions an entrepreneurial team should ask of those CEOs range from the help they could obtain in routes to market but should focus primarily on personal chemistry and the role they are likely to play as a director on the board of their start-up. Being proactive and adding value at board meetings is an essential component of money plus, and establishing that VCs will show up regularly and contribute – rather than holding a seat on the board in name only – is crucial.

SUMMARY OF CHAPTER 5

This chapter has sought to provide an insight into the day-to-day operations within a venture capital firm and began by considering how a newly employed VC would go about identifying potential new deals. Top-rate, proprietary deal flow is the lifeblood of any venture capital fund: without finding the best deals, VCs cannot hope to deliver the best returns. Understanding how VCs use their networks, underpinned by qualified leads, is essential to understanding how they perceive the entrepreneurial ecosystem around them. They even rely on the 98% of entrepreneurs they reject to act as quasi-ambassadors for their fund, putting out the word that even though they were rejected, at least they received good feedback. Perhaps they will return with a revised or upgraded business plan at some point in the future.

This chapter has also discussed how VCs evaluate and compete for the highest-quality entrepreneurial opportunities. Investment decision-making does not lie with a single individual or rest at a single moment, it is a process of reaching consensus within a partnership and one that can take several months. Building consensus within the partnership lies in the hands of the deal champions who will shepherd an opportunity through the venture capital process. This small team, perhaps a partner and an associate within the firm, will take responsibility not only for evaluating the investment but also for moulding it into something that they believe the partnership will back, managing this process and helping entrepreneurial teams understand how decisions are made within the fund structure.

The next chapter will examine one of the most important questions entrepreneurial teams ask: How much equity to sell to raise the finance required to build the business? This might be like asking how long a piece of string is, and indeed it is more art than science. There are, however, frameworks within which to understand early-stage valuations and the approaches VCs and entrepreneurial teams may take in an attempt to reach an agreement using rational argument with minimal conflict.

Chapter 6

Valuation

HOW MUCH EQUITY DO ENTREPRENEURS HAVE TO SELL?

How much equity entrepreneurial teams must sell to raise the capital required to build their start-up is the million-dollar question, quite literally. The question always remains the same, but the answer changes, and it changes frequently according to the financial climate at the time.

Chapter 1 talked about the supply of, and demand for, venture capital finance and Figure 1.4 showed how the NASDAQ index has risen and fallen with alarming regularity over time, it being a reasonable proxy for the state of the venture capital industry. When supply and demand for venture capital are in balance the global innovation engine roars ahead, but when they are not, we see investment bubbles inflate and burst as investor exuberance evaporates and confidence falls. As supply and demand for venture capital change, the price of equity in start-ups rises and falls. Too much venture capital chasing deals and the price of start-up equity rises; too little supply of venture capital and the price of

111

start-up equity falls as entrepreneurial teams scramble to find money to sustain their ambitions. In other words, the valuation of start-ups and growing ventures is market-based rather than being dictated by measurable, predictable corporate finance metrics used for larger, more established corporations.

Valuation of start-ups is what investors are prepared to pay...

THE EXAMPLE OF UBER

Many authors and commentators have written about Uber as a high-profile tech start-up turned global corporation. Uber has become so ubiquitous it has changed from a brand name to a *verb*: we have all '*Uber'd*' somewhere. Uber has become synonymous with how humans transport themselves over short distances from A to B and now incorporates other services such as food delivery. But the financing history of Uber is relatively short and serves to illustrate some key points about the valuation of start-ups and growing ventures.

Uber raised an early seed round of just over $1,500,000 from several high-profile tech business angels. This investment round appears to have valued the business at just under $4,000,000. Over subsequent years the company raised nearly $25 billion in over 20 private financing rounds, many of which included high-profile VCs. The company's last private financing round was $600,000,000 in 2018, valuing the company at around $69 billion. This valued Uber at more than the market capitalisation of General Motors at the time; the question is: How can this be so? How can a relatively young tech company, far from profitability at the time, be valued higher than a well-established global automobile manufacturer?

There are many other examples of high-growth companies with a visionary idea achieving multi-billion-dollar valuations before they turn a profit, or in some cases before they generate revenue, and it is this point that gets to the heart of the issue of how start-ups are valued.

WHAT IS AN IDEA WORTH?

Entrepreneurs always believe their ideas are worth something and usually that 'something' is more than anyone else believes they are worth, especially potential investors. The reality is that ideas are of limited value unless something is done about them. Execution, or the ability to execute an idea, is an essential part of the inherent value of any idea. A market opportunity is only a business opportunity if an entrepreneur displays some possibility of making it happen.

Ideas therefore are relatively worthless from a venture capital perspective until there is sufficient evidence they can become the basis for a real business. This viewpoint places a great deal of value on so-called 'traction', a demonstration by the entrepreneurial team that their business opportunity has some momentum either via proof that the technology works, or better still proof that the business model works via generating revenue from paying customers. Evidence that the idea works and that consumers will pay for it are fundamental in ascribing a valuation to an early-stage idea.

How much an idea is worth, even with some evidence that it works, is difficult to establish – and the question of how much equity an entrepreneurial team must raise to make their idea real is similarly challenging. The remainder of this chapter will demonstrate that in the early stages of growth, this is very much *art* rather than science.

VALUE VERSUS VALUATION

Chapter 2 discussed in detail the simple notion of building value, making the point that building value is not necessarily the same as generating a profit, or even generating revenue. It relates to how start-ups can generate substantial value in other ways, sometimes related to intellectual property, market penetration, data or branding. Figure 2.8 illustrated this concept by comparing the cash-flow profiles of two companies crossing the Valleys of Death, one of which was a steadily growing, revenue-generating company and the other a typical technology or science-based start-up that seemed to offer great potential for future growth but was not there yet. The question of which company is more valuable on a particular date makes the point quite neatly. Most observers will conclude that the loss-making (but potentially high-upside) company is worth more; they would pay more for it, or invest at a higher share price because of the future growth potential. But that growth potential is far from certain and could wither away at any time or be delayed significantly as the company enters new, unexpected Valleys of Death.

Therefore, *value* is a somewhat nebulous concept and varies from industry to industry and across time as technologies and economies evolve. *Valuation*, on the other hand, should be a more precise concept. The valuation of a start-up, arithmetically, is simply its share price multiplied by the total number of shares in issue at the time. The problem is calculating that share price with any level of accuracy when the risks within an early-stage venture are so high. The share price and therefore the total *valuation* of the company ought to reflect the inherent *value* that has been built (or will be built) within the growing venture. Because of the uncertainties in building new ventures and the risks associated with technology failures, management performance or market growth, making the valuation match the inherent value is remarkably difficult. The ups and downs of the NASDAQ are illustrative of the challenges that even expert observers experience in accurately placing a valuation on early-stage companies.

> *Valuation is simply the share price multiplied by the number of shares in the company. The problem is agreeing it…*

DIVIDING THE START-UP EQUITY PIE

Dividing the equity for a brand-new start-up is about dividing the equity pie fairly (see Figure 6.1). This might seem a strange thing to say, given that earlier chapters made clear that to maximise their returns VCs seek to own the largest share of equity that they can negotiate, and conversely entrepreneurs seek to minimise their dilution by selling as little equity as possible. This puts them at opposite ends of the negotiating table and suggests there must be a winner and a loser in any such discussion. In reality, this is not necessarily the case.

Dividing the Start-Up Equity Pie

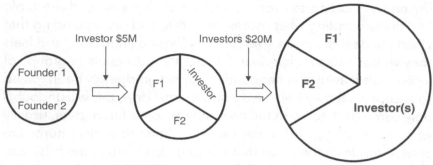

Motivation and *Alignment* of Interests

Figure 6.1 Dividing the pie.
In the example above, two founders have started a company in which they each own 50% of the equity. They raise $5 million in a first-round investment in which they sell around one-third of the equity in the company to an investor. In a subsequent round they raise a further $20 million from investors, likely to include their existing investor and additional new investors required to support such a large round. The ownership stakes of the two founders are consequently diluted but the prize is bigger. The goal in reaching an agreement for the equity split in the early stages is driven more by human factors such as motivation and alignment towards a common goal rather than purely financial metrics. That goal is delivering a high-value company and eventually a high-performing exit.

VCs understand that a demotivated management team is never going to deliver the best outcome, and it is not in their interests to squeeze the entrepreneurial team to the point where they are not motivated to deliver. The key point in any of these discussions is that motivation to deliver an *exit* is fundamental, as without an exit nobody makes real money. There are rarely winners if there is no exit, and this depends on the entire team – including entrepreneurs and investors – pointing in the same direction. Agreeing the price of an investment in a start-up is not a simple transaction with a finite end; it is the beginning of what is likely to be a lengthy partnership through the ups and downs of growing a venture.

> *Equity in start-ups is about motivation towards a common goal… delivering the exit.*

Negotiation of equity in start-ups is therefore as much about human behaviour as it is about financial engineering or the analysis of complex spreadsheets. It is about understanding how individuals are motivated and how best to knit the team together towards the goal of building value and, over time, delivering the exit for investors. Building companies is a people business and deciding how to share out the equity at the beginning must be driven by 'reading the room', looking at those around the table and understanding what makes them tick, and understanding that when the deal is agreed, everybody is aligned, motivated and feels they've been dealt a fair deal. If there are individuals or groups of individuals leaving the negotiation having grudgingly been forced to accept what they believe is a suboptimal deal, this will undoubtedly come back to harm the company at some future date, usually at a crucial stage of the exit process. When financial returns are crystallised from the value that has been built within the business, scores are often settled between aggrieved groups of shareholders who have nursed a grudge from the outset.

Fault lines in the equity agreed at the outset often reveal themselves when an exit is close; groups of shareholders – including the entrepreneurial team – can finally calculate how all that hard work may translate into cash, and this clarifies their thinking as to whether they will accept a particular exit price or not. A good exit price for one shareholder may not be a good exit price for another, and this sometimes depends on the equity split that was agreed very early in the company's life. Why then would anyone have agreed to an equity split that they felt at the outset wasn't fair? The answer is sometimes that desperation to raise money will always make entrepreneurs compromise if they have no alternative, but this does not mean squeezing the team is a 'win' for the VC. The win only comes when a financially successful exit is delivered, and returns are distributed. It is often said that a smaller share of a bigger pie is more important than a bigger share of a small pie, or even a pie that disappears altogether if the company fails. Being generous with one another around the initial negotiating table, strange as it may sound, can offer benefits that are very hard to quantify with a financial spreadsheet. Understanding each other's business models clarifies the perspective of both entrepreneurs and investors in the negotiation that lies at the core of the VC– entrepreneur relationship, a relationship that must endure inevitable crises, multiple Valleys of Death and existential challenges that could kill the company. Having an equity deal that works for all will help weather the storm.

It is important to remember that even equity splits agreed at the outset are not necessarily baked in forever. Sometimes adjustments are made at an exit if one group of shareholders believes the deal is insufficient for them to sign the required documentation, and this group is often the management team who are expected to deliver the deal. If the management team believes it is not sufficiently rewarding for them, then the exit will likely not happen. It is almost impossible to force the sale of a company with an unwilling management team who are not motivated to get the deal over the line, and whether actively or passively obstructive, their actions may ultimately kill an exit opportunity for the investors. VCs know this and are often prepared to create what is known as a *management carve out* to ensure the team is motivated to complete the transaction if their equity has been diluted substantially. The management carve out is a reallocation of the proceeds from an exit transaction, either by distributing new equity in the form of options or by allocating cash from the transaction to create an exit bonus. The details often depend on how the proceeds of an exit are taxed, and a carve out may be structured as a mix of cash and equity. However it is structured, the goal remains the same and equity agreements may need to be rewritten or adjusted around the time of the exit to get the deal over the line. This benefits the VCs and other investors, who are usually prepared to surrender a small portion of their returns to generate a return in the first place; they would rather have a slightly lower return rather than no return at all…

The golden rule of equity: 'felt fairness' is the only solution…

VALUATION TERMINOLOGY: PRE- AND POST-MONEY VALUATION

An important lesson in how VCs and entrepreneurial teams negotiate valuation is simply understanding the language they use to do so. They will usually not talk about the percentage equity they will own; instead, they usually refer to something called the 'pre-money' valuation and 'post-money' valuation. Pre-money and post-money valuations are not valuation methodologies, they are simply the names given to the valuation of a company before and after an investment and represent the language used commonly during these negotiations.

This is best illustrated by considering a simple example. If an investor, ABC Ventures, invests $2 million in a company in return for 50% of the equity, what is the company worth (a) immediately before the investment and (b) immediately after the investment? It would be easy to conclude that before the investment, the company might be worth zero or close to zero, because as discussed earlier – an idea alone is worth very little. However, the pre-money and post-money valuations are simply numerical values placed on the potential of the business via an investor agreeing to invest at a certain price. By agreeing to invest $2 million for 50% of the equity in the business, ABC Ventures is (by definition) stating that 100% of the company is worth $4 million immediately after the investment has landed in the company's bank account. The post-money valuation is, therefore, the valuation of the entire business immediately after a new financing event occurs. If 100% of the equity in the business is worth $4 million and $2 million of that value is in new 'unused' cash, then the valuation of 100% of the business immediately before the cash went into the company's bank account must necessarily have been $2 million. This is the pre-money valuation and is a notional valuation placed on the business via the act of an investor agreeing to invest. It approximates to but is not necessarily the same as the enterprise value of a business. Enterprise value considers debt and preferred stock, which pre-money valuation typically does not, but they are closely related cousins in the lexicon of valuation terms.

THE GAME OF OFFER AND ACCEPTANCE

The example of pre-money and post-money valuation above considers a single investment round, with ABC Ventures backing a company and buying 50% of the equity. But what about subsequent rounds? What happens to valuation then?

As discussed previously, most new ventures will raise a series of investment rounds, ideally of increasing size and share price as the business grows through a series of value-adding milestones and crosses multiple Valleys of Death. The share price for those investment rounds is always set by the new, incoming investors and not by the existing investors. New, incoming investors will price the

The Game of Offer and Acceptance   **119**

round objectively from an external perspective based on their analysis of the business potential. They carry out their due diligence and arrive at a conclusion, from which they will offer to invest at a certain price – the new pre-money valuation of the business. It is the role of existing investors to accept that price by co-investing alongside them on the same terms and conditions. When the new round is complete, the new post-money valuation is established. New, incoming investors usually set the price in every round, but existing investors are expected to support that round by investing their *pro-rata* share of the round or an alternative pre-agreed proportion of the round acceptable to the new investors (see Figure 6.2).

When a new share price is established via the act of new incoming investors pricing an investment round, all existing shares in the business are repriced at the new share price. Existing investors, founders and other shareholders can therefore mark their investment holdings up to the new share price and this is how VCs represent the valuations of their investments in their own accounts

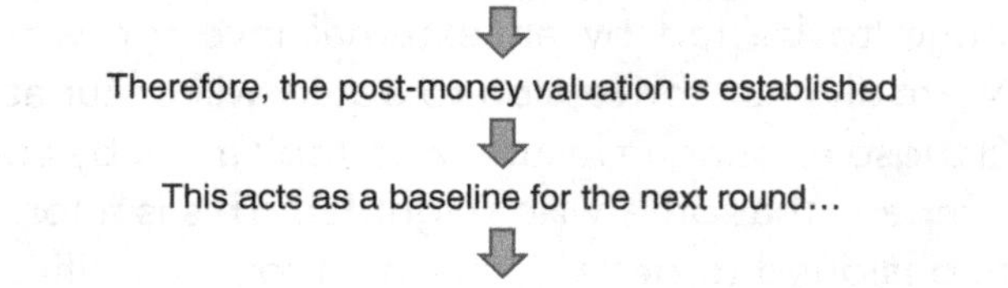

New incoming investors 'price' the deal by offering to invest at a proposed share price (the pre-money valuation)

⬇

The Board negotiates prior to seeking shareholder approval to accept the offer

⬇

Investment flows into the company

⬇

Therefore, the post-money valuation is established

⬇

This acts as a baseline for the next round…

⬇

Figure 6.2   The game of offer and acceptance.
The game of offer and acceptance is a delicate dance performed by potential investors in the business and those who already hold shares. It is for the new investors to price the deal by offering to invest at a proposed share price, usually described as the pre-money valuation. The board of directors of the company raising money will usually negotiate the terms of such an investment but ultimately it is for the existing shareholders to approve the offer. It is important that existing shareholders both approve the offer and 'put their money where their mouths are' by co-investing on the same terms. Once the round is complete, the new post-money valuation is in place – being the sum of the pre-money valuation plus the money raised. The post-money valuation of this round will provide a baseline for the pre-money valuation of the next financing round to be negotiated with yet more new incoming investors.

prior to any exits being delivered. The share price established at a new investment round determines the valuation of all existing shareholdings. Share prices rarely change in between financing rounds, perhaps only when there is a serious impairment to the business due to commercial events or market changes. The share price set by incoming investors in a new financing round is regarded as the 'fair market price' for all shares in the business and for this reason, existing investors rarely if ever set the price of investment rounds due to conflicts of interest resulting from the shares they already own. It would be an easy temptation to set new share prices high to mark up the value of their existing shareholdings.

Sometimes, of course, there are investment rounds organised solely by the existing investors in a company. For example, if there are no external investors willing to back the growing venture, perhaps because it has struggled or even because the financing climate is very difficult, then existing investors must make the decision to go it alone. They must back their portfolio company without external help and therefore it is difficult to set a new valuation. This may be handled in several ways, but the most common solution is to invest in the form of a *convertible loan*.

A convertible loan (or loan note) is, as the name suggests, a loan made by the existing shareholders to their business that will convert into equity on the same terms and conditions as the next equity round to be led by an external investor, whenever that occurs. Normally that conversion to equity will occur at a discount to reward those existing investors who took a risk by continuing to back a company that otherwise might fail. This is a form of bridge financing, designed to get a company through a difficult financial patch when it cannot raise external investment and when the normal process of offer and acceptance will not work. The terms of convertible loans will be discussed in a later chapter, where the conditions will depend on the urgency of the situation and the risk that existing shareholders are taking.

Understanding pre-money and post-money valuations is simply a matter of understanding the language used to discuss valuation. It does not move us any closer to establishing what the right price of the deal is, simply how we talk about it. So, how is the right price established for a venture capital deal?

VALUATION METHODOLOGIES

Science only works when you can measure something, and with start-ups and early-stage ventures, measuring anything at all can prove to be impossible. Investors are sometimes dealing with unproven technology, an unproven management team and vague market potential. Measurements become inaccurate and unreliable and therefore a considerable degree of judgement is required; this is where valuation becomes *art* not science in the early stages. Only when investors can measure something reliable, such as revenues, growth or profitability, does valuation take on a more scientific and rational approach. Figure 6.3 shows how valuation methodologies change with stage of development, a schematic often reproduced by investment analysts to show how, as businesses evolve, it becomes easier to place a rational valuation on them when there is something to measure.

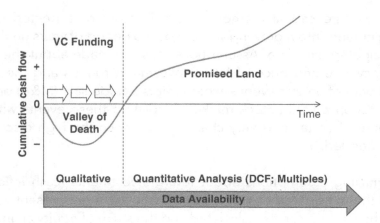

Figure 6.3 When art becomes science.
For start-ups and early-stage ventures in the Valleys of Death, opportunities to measure reliable financial information are limited. Reliable, repeatable revenues are at that stage a futuristic dream, and valuation depends on largely qualitative information – it is little more than a guessing game influenced by timing, reputation and market conditions. Only when businesses climb out of the Valleys of Death, producing reliable financial performance data, can valuations be estimated using more traditional corporate finance techniques. No wonder the venture capital industry sometimes gets it wrong…

Valuation

Nevertheless, there are some approaches that can help to place a range of valuations on early-stage businesses, helping investors and entrepreneurs to align around a common perception of the valuation of a business. First among these is the venture capital method, written about extensively by several authors, most notably Paul Gompers and Josh Lerner in their seminal text *The Venture Capital Cycle* (Gompers and Lerner 1999).

THE VENTURE CAPITAL METHOD

The venture capital method is an adaptation of the net present value/discounted cash-flow methodology used in many corporate finance scenarios based on future cash flows, revenues and profits. The method works well for more established businesses with more reliable future cash flows but is more challenging for early-stage ventures with a great deal of uncertainty and risk. The problem is that the discount rate applied for high-risk start-ups and early-stage ventures will need to be so high as to make the calculation less reliable, and therefore less useful for investors who know their markets.

The venture capital method uses a forecast of expected cash investments into a growing venture over a period of years until the anticipated exit date. Assumptions must be made about the frequency, size and price of future investment rounds and the size and date of an exit event – whether it is a trade sale (M&A) or via an IPO on a liquid stock market. Predicting these events with a degree of certainty is very challenging, hence the high discount rate needed.

By making assumptions about future investments (cash inflows) and the anticipated exit date (cash outflows), a net present value for the start-up can be calculated and the share of equity an investor must own to generate a return can be deduced – thus informing the decision to invest or not.

It is more likely that VCs will use this approach to 'check' the pre-money valuation they are offering based on their knowledge of market conditions, but it is unlikely to be the primary source of their views of valuation. VCs will employ the venture capital method when auditing their portfolios, or indeed demonstrating to potential LPs that the valuations at which they have made investments based on market knowledge are consistent with the rational framework provided by the venture capital method.

VALUATION IS A MARKET-DRIVEN NEGOTIATION

Valuations in early-stage ventures are driven by the market, and the market is comprised of investors who are prepared to buy shares in risky early-stage ventures. This market is a mix of VCs, business angels, corporate investors, family offices and others. Valuation is what investors are prepared to pay to own a stake in a venture that may ultimately fail or may deliver fantastic returns.

Entrepreneurial teams can only locate the market valuation of their company by talking to sufficient potential investors to establish how the market views the business. By talking to enough investors with a deep knowledge of the market, a pattern will begin to emerge, and a range of valuations will gradually enter the conversations with investors.

For investors, frameworks like the venture capital method may form a useful benchmark, but often they are driven by competition from other VCs, and in the scramble to win the right to invest in a hot start-up, frameworks often go out of the window. Ultimately, competition is key…

For entrepreneurial teams seeking to maximise the valuation of the growing venture, generating competitive tension to invest in the business is the most reliable way to raise the price. VCs hate to lose deals and although they never seek to pay a higher price, sometimes they must do so. Entrepreneurial teams who are adept at generating competitive tension will retain a greater proportion of the equity in their business by negotiating higher share prices in investment rounds.

Rational measures are a benchmark, but market conditions drive the valuation discussion.

FINANCING HISTORY

Completely new start-ups raising their first investment round will have very little in the way of a financing 'history'. Perhaps they have raised a friends and family round or small seed round from angels, sometimes in the form of a convertible loan. But for growing ventures that have raised previous rounds of investment, their historical record plays an important role and potential investors will ask questions about this as they begin to form a view about what price they are prepared to pay to back the venture. The financing history can be broken down into three components.

1. *Valuation of the last round.* The post-money valuation of a previous financing round serves as a baseline for the pre-money valuation of the next. If the company has made substantial progress since the last financing round, and the financing climate has remained constant, then the company should command a premium for the pre-money valuation of the new round. Although entrepreneurs should never reveal their expectations for the pre-money valuation (as discussed later in this chapter), the post-money valuation of the previous round is a fact; it will be self-evident from the company's capitalisation table and can be shared with potential new investors.

2. *Historic cash.* The total amount of capital raised historically by an early-stage company provides another (usually lower) baseline for new investors considering an investment. If the post-money valuation of the previous round is regarded as the first step up the valuation stairway, the historic cash raised might be regarded as the basement. There is little chance the existing shareholders will accept a pre-money valuation lower than the cash they have put into the company so far – unless they are desperate.

3. *Participation by existing investors.* The extent to which the existing investors in an early-stage company can follow their

investment and participate in the new round is a major determinant of the valuation. If existing investors are unable to participate *pro rata* – or perhaps not at all – this either signals a lack of confidence in the company or an inability to invest as a result of having no cash reserves to do so. In either case, new incoming investors will seize upon this opportunity to invest at a bargain price. Having investors who cannot back the company further is one of the most damaging scenarios for a company in terms of defending its valuation. For this reason, it is essential for entrepreneurial teams to establish at the outset that any investor they raise capital from can back them through a series of future financing rounds. Existing investors must always play their part in a new round by investing *pro rata* (or close to it) to preserve the valuation.

TIMING

Getting the timing right is perhaps one of the most important factors in determining the valuation at which investors are prepared to back a start-up or growing venture. Entrepreneurial teams leaving it too late to begin the fundraising process, resulting in a negotiation of valuation very close to the point where the business runs out of cash, can have a disastrous outcome, as they may need to accept a low valuation just to keep the business afloat. The time horizon or 'cash runway' until the business runs out of cash should be foremost in the minds of management teams when they think about raising their next round of capital.

Based on the maxim discussed earlier – that the best time to raise money is when you don't need it – beginning the fundraising process when the cash 'runway' is lengthy is the best approach. The same business raising capital when it has 6 months, 6 weeks, or only 6 days of cash left in the bank will command a very different valuation, even though during those 6 months the business may well have hit important milestones. A company that is backed into a corner by a lack of cash will not be able to negotiate a good valuation; the management team and the board may need to accept investment at almost any price to survive and avoid insolvency. The practical result is that management teams must begin the fund-raising process early, well before they ever get to the stage of really needing the money...

The time to raise money is when it isn't needed; start early to avoid disaster...

REPUTATION

When it comes to competing to invest in the best entrepreneurial opportunities, VCs do not want to rely upon simply investing at a higher valuation than their competitors. As the saying goes, *any fool can pay more*, and if they win deals only when they pay more than others, then they will never deliver a better performance than rival VCs. One of the factors that enables VCs to invest in the best deals without necessarily paying a higher valuation, is reputation: their reputation to deliver money plus and the cachet of being associated with their fund. The credibility attained by start-ups when they raise capital from a highly reputable VC is worth something, and entrepreneurial teams are prepared to pay for it. Entrepreneurs will sacrifice equity for credibility by accepting investment at a lower valuation when the VC brings a powerful reputation. VCs know, therefore, that their reputation is paramount, and it translates into lower valuations when they invest.

The same is true, in reverse, for serial entrepreneurs – their reputation enables them to push the price up in a negotiation with VCs. Well-known entrepreneurial teams, or teams with highly reputable directors on their board, will command higher valuations compared to first-time entrepreneurs with an equivalent idea. Rightly or wrongly, VCs will invest at higher valuations when the entrepreneurs they back have a strong track record of previous success. As any investment documentation will warn, past performance is no guarantee of future performance, yet in the rarefied atmosphere of investing in start-ups it counts for something, and that something is reflected in the higher valuations paid by VCs.

SOMETIMES MORE IS… MORE

There is a curious effect on the valuation when entrepreneurial teams seek to raise more capital. Sometimes simply the act of raising more can increase the perceived valuation of the business, even when inherently it is the same. A business that has a pre-money valuation of $10 million when raising, for example, $5 million might – in the eyes of investors – have a higher pre-money valuation if it were raising $10 million. The effect of this is that businesses can sometimes raise more capital by selling precisely the same amount of equity as they would have for a smaller round. It is hard to explain why this is the case, but instances like this exist. Perhaps it indicates to investors an entrepreneurial team with greater ambition, greater confidence and a more aggressive approach to building the venture. It alters investors' perception of the risk in the venture and provokes a looser approach to pre-money valuation. It also highlights the challenges of placing rational valuations on early-stage ventures; beauty is often in the eye of the beholder and sometimes more is simply that, more…

Raising bigger rounds raises the perceived valuation…

NOT ALL SHARES ARE CREATED EQUAL…

This chapter has focused so far on the simple matter of dividing equity along the lines of a straight percentage, in theory a straightforward ratio of ownership and rights reflected by a number. But it is more complex than that, as the numerical 'valuation' can be misleading. The complication arises because VCs often do not buy ordinary shares when they invest; they buy special types of shares referred to as preferred shares or preference shares, which command not only special voting rights but also a variety of special economic returns. Chief among these is the so-called convertible, redeemable, preferred ordinary share, commonly referred to simply as the preferred share or double-dipping preferred share.

This aspect of the venture capital investment process is often little understood by first-time entrepreneurial teams, but it has a substantial impact on their shareholding and importantly on their portion of any payout at exit. Understanding this, and understanding the alternatives, is crucial for arriving at a suitable compromise with investors during a valuation negotiation – where to push to achieve the best outcome depends on the entrepreneurial team's expectations for the exit, both in terms of timing and magnitude, and for the VC it can be an important indicator of where the team's true levels of confidence lie.

The concept of the double-dipping preferred share is simple. Having made an investment, the investor receives their money back plus interest, like a loan, and then in addition receives their share of the equity. In other words, the investor receives their initial investment plus a fixed interest rate or cumulative dividend depending on how long the investment has resided within the company before any other distribution or payout to shareholders. The preferred shares behave like a straightforward loan with interest but with an added twist: preferred shares go on to behave just like ordinary shares and they receive an appropriate proportion of the equity as well. Double-dipping preferred shares therefore behave both like a loan and pure equity, benefiting from a repayment of the principal plus interest and participation in the upside delivered via their equity shareholding. It appears as if they have the best of both worlds: the security of a loan with interest and the potential high returns that come with an equity investment in an early-stage, high-risk venture.

The immediate response from entrepreneurs reading this text will be that this is grossly unfair. Why should VCs or other investors receive a double dip into the proceeds of any exit? Earlier, this chapter made the important point that alignment of interests and motivation towards a common goal (delivering a successful exit) is key to establishing a fair split of the equity, but the concept of preferred shares seems to go directly against this principle. So, what argument could a VC make to justify them holding preferred shares and not ordinary shares like the entrepreneurial team? The answer lies in *information asymmetry*. VCs will argue that the founders and management team know far more about their own business than the VC can ever hope to, despite all the due diligence they carry out. It is as simple as that. VCs will argue that preferred shares compensate for this information asymmetry by providing downside protection against the risks of everything going wrong, resulting in them losing their entire investment. In such risky ventures, mitigating the risks brought about by information asymmetry is achieved, at least in part, by the VCs holding preferred shares.

Preferred shares compensate investors for the effects of information asymmetry.

PREFERRED SHARES, PREFERENCE SHARES AND CASCADES

Preferred shares combine the features of a loan with the features of an equity investment. In other words, the 'upside' potential of owning shares in a start-up with some degree of 'protection and certainty' via a loan with interest. Of course, this is not entirely true, as making a loan to an early-stage, high-risk venture is only worthwhile when there is money to repay the loan. If the business fails completely there is unlikely to be any repayment, but what about poor performance or partial successes rather than complete failures? Start-ups in general do not generate sufficient cash to pay dividends, interest or repayment of loans. They can only do so at an exit which is sufficient to deal with the debt, so if a start-up fails completely, preferred shares are of limited use, but if a start-up just performs poorly, or with modest success, the preferred shares may receive some repayment. If the start-up performs a little better, the preferred shares may get repaid in full, with interest, before anything that is left over is distributed to the equity shareholders according to their percentage shareholding. This is more easily illustrated by considering a simple numerical example.

In the earlier example used in this chapter to illustrate the notion of pre-money and post-money valuation, an investor – ABC Ventures – bought 50% of the equity in a start-up for $2 million. The example did not consider the qualitative nature of these shares, simply the numerical split of equity. It assumed 50% ownership of equity meant a 50% share of the proceeds of an exit based on a simple numerical ratio, but what happens at an exit if we assume the investor buys its 50% equity all in *double-dipping preferred shares* as opposed to ordinary shares? How is ABC Ventures rewarded at an exit after 5 years and how are the founders impacted by ABC's ownership of double-dipping preferred shares?

Below we consider a series of exit valuations assuming double-dipping preferred shares with an 8% annual interest rate that accumulates on the balance sheet of the start-up until it can be paid out at exit (note that an 8% interest rate on $2 million after 5 years equates to a total of approximately $1 million in cumulative interest). In the following examples, the pre-money and post-money valuation has been further modified by the introduction of a 10% option pool; it is normal for VCs to require that companies create an option pool of at least 10% for the reward and retention of existing and new management talent. Usually, although the requirement for an option pool specifies 10% of the post-money shareholding, it is generally paid for by the shareholders before the investment takes place and therefore is subtracted from the pre-money valuation. In this case, therefore, the true pre-money valuation for the founders is not $2,000,000 but $1,600,000, giving them an equity ownership of 40% of the equity after the investment, with the option pool consisting of 10% and the investors holding 50% just as they did in the earlier example before the option pool was considered. As will be discussed in a later chapter, 'who pays for the option pool' is always up for negotiation, but for the following examples assume the founders pay for it.

The shareholdings are therefore represented as follows:

ABC Ventures:	50% equity all in double-dipping preferred shares
Founders:	40% equity all in ordinary shares
Option pool:	10% options over ordinary shares

Given this split of the shareholdings, what is the impact of preferred shares in a range of exit valuation scenarios?

Scenario 1. The company performs badly after the investment and is sold for $4 million after 5 years, the same as the post-money valuation following the ABC Ventures investment. It has, therefore, not generated any additional value and the investors may be glad

Preferred Shares, Preference Shares and Cascades **131**

to be rid of it since it is probably taking up the VC's management time in attending board meetings without the prospect of a good return.

<u>The answer is as follows:</u>

- ABC loan: $2,000,000 principal + $1,000,000 cumulative interest
- Total preference: <u>$3,000,000</u>
- 100% equity remaining: <u>$1,000,000</u>
- ABC 50% share: $500,000
- Founders 40% share: $400,000
- Option pool 10% share: $100,000

- Total return for ABC: <u>$3,500,000</u>

ABC Ventures receives 87.5% of the proceeds, despite only having 50% equity ownership. Contrast this with the $2,000,000 ABC Ventures would have received if it had bought 50% of the equity in ordinary shares. It seems like a terrible deal for the founders and option holders. However, from the perspective of ABC Ventures, it will argue that it made the investment based on a business plan that promised great success – the information asymmetry inherent in the transaction led them to a poor investment decision and they have been compensated accordingly.

It may seem that a $3,500,000 investment return on a $2,000,000 investment is pretty good, but this is not how a VC will see it. Chapter 4 discussed the venture capital cycle and how funds flow only one time through the cycle. A $2,000,000 drawdown from the LPs into the fund has been transformed into a $3,500,000 return, which must then go straight back to the LPs. It cannot be reused or recycled for further investment and will be regarded as a poor investment, and certainly not the return the LPs were expecting from a venture capital fund to which they pay a 2% management fee and 20% carried interest. ABC Ventures will regard a $3,500,000 return on a $2,000,000 investment as a modest return to its LPs, but

132   Valuation

at least they have managed to recoup some form of return from a venture into which they placed that money and their faith. Too many of these types of investments and ABC Ventures will not be in business very long, and they will not be raising their next fund on very good terms, if at all.

Due to the competitive pressure for venture capital funds to perform well, staying ahead of the competition is an important goal and recouping some form of return from poor to modest-performing investments may mean the difference between raising the next fund and not. Ordinary shares simply would not provide any worthwhile return in this scenario. In the example above, the founders receive a $400,000 return from their equity ownership and the option pool receives $100,000 return. Taken together, this might be seen as a reasonable return for the management team of a venture that, in the end, did not deliver on its grand plan. The debate as to whether this is fair or not could rage on for the rest of this chapter, but let us examine further scenarios before reaching any conclusion about fairness.

Scenario 2. The company performs a little better and is sold for $10 million after 5 years, over double the post-money valuation following the ABC Ventures investment. It has generated some additional value compared to the investment price and will be regarded as a modestly performing investment. How do the double-dipping preferred shares play out at the time of this exit?

<u>The answer is as follows:</u>

- ABC loan: $2,000,000 principal + $1,000,000 cumulative interest
- Total preference: <u>$3,000,000</u>
- 100% equity remaining: <u>$7,000,000</u>
- ABC 50% share: $3,500,000
- Founders 40% share: $2,800,000
- Option pool 10% share: $700,000
- Total return for ABC: <u>$6,500,000</u>

Preferred Shares, Preference Shares and Cascades **133**

In this scenario, ABC Ventures receives 65% of the proceeds for its 50% ownership. This is still substantially more than if ABC Ventures had invested $2,000,000 for ordinary shares but it is not as extreme as the previous scenario. For the founders and the option pool it seems that things are heading in the right direction...

Scenario 3. The company performs a little better and is sold for $20 million after 5 years, five times the post-money valuation following the ABC Ventures investment. It has generated a good return and will be regarded as a decent performer within the portfolio. How do the double-dipping preferred shares play out at the time of this exit?

<u>The answer is as follows:</u>

- ABC loan: $2,000,000 principal + $1,000,000 cumulative interest
- Total preference: <u>$3,000,000</u>
- 100% equity remaining: <u>$17,000,000</u>
- ABC 50% share: $8,500,000
- Founders 40% share: $6,800,000
- Option pool 10% share: $1,700,000

- Total return for ABC <u>$11,500,000</u>

In this case, ABC Ventures receives 57.5% of the proceeds for 50% ownership and from the perspective of the founders and option holders this begins to feel a little better and approaches what the returns would have been if the ABC Ventures investment was made in pure ordinary shares.

Scenario 4. The company performs very well and is sold for $200 million after 5 years, 50 times the post-money valuation following the ABC Ventures investment. It has generated an excellent return and it is likely to be regarded as one of the best performers within the portfolio. How do the double-dipping preferred shares play out at the time of this exit?

134   Valuation

<u>The answer is as follows:</u>

- ABC loan: $2,000,000 principal + $1,000,000 cumulative interest
- Total preference: <u>$3,000,000</u>
- 100% equity remaining: <u>$197,000,000</u>
- ABC 50% share: $98,500,000
- Founders 40% share: $78,800,000
- Option pool 10% share: $19,700,000

- Total return for ABC: <u>$101,500,000</u>

In this final scenario, ABC Ventures receives 50.75% of the proceeds for 50% ownership and this is almost identical to the return it would have received if it had made the investment purely in ordinary shares. From the perspective of the founders, there are unlikely to be too many complaints or accusations of an unfair deal; they have been rewarded handsomely, with almost $80 million hitting the founders' bank accounts.

The conclusion from the four scenarios above is clear: as the exit price climbs, the impact of the double-dipping preferred shares begins to disappear until eventually their effect is almost com-pletely invisible compared to ordinary shares. Double-dipping preferred shares therefore penalise management teams and founders in scenarios such as poor to modest exits. As the exit price climbs, the impact of preferred shares falls away. Preferred shares could therefore be seen as a tool to incentivise manage-ment teams to deliver high-performing exits and to make sure they are not content simply to deliver a modest return in which they would receive a substantial equity payout.

ABC Ventures' argument that preferred shares compensate it for information asymmetry holds true in these scenarios; when the company performs as per the business plan there is little harm done by the preferred shares. If the business underperforms, then

Preferred Shares, Preference Shares and Cascades **135**

the preferred shares compensate ABC Ventures for the information asymmetry it will argue it was subjected to. It could be said that if founders and management teams of start-ups are confident in their abilities to deliver a high-performing exit, they should be less concerned about preferred shares and simply focus on delivering that exit. The preferred shares are there because the venture capital fund managers who invest in them are themselves under pressure from their LPs to deliver high returns and this is just one tool at their disposal to help them do that.

There is one further scenario to consider: what if a company is sold for less than the post-money valuation of the investment made by ABC Ventures? What if the company is sold for only $3,000,000, just enough to pay the preferred shareholders their investment plus interest?

<u>The answer is as follows:</u>

- ABC loan: $2,000,000 principal + $1,000,000 cumulative interest
- Total preference: <u>$3,000,000</u>
- 100% equity remaining: <u>$0</u>
- ABC 50% share: $0
- Founders 40% share: $0
- Option pool 10% share: $0
- Total return for ABC: <u>$3,000,000</u>

In this scenario, the founders and the management team receive absolutely nothing for their efforts, and this presents a special case. It would not be rational for anyone to work for free and in a scenario where the investors are pushing the founders and management team to deliver an exit like this, they are simply unlikely to stay. These scenarios do exist when companies have performed very poorly for whatever reason and a low-priced sale to an acquirer is preferable to the company becoming insolvent. Insolvency can

136 Valuation

be a painful process for the directors of any business, including investor directors appointed by a venture capital fund. The opportunity cost and personal liability involved in fulfilling the role of a director, discussed in a later chapter, are best avoided by executing some form of exit, even at a loss.

But if the nature of the preferred shares means that those who are expected to do all the work to deliver an exit, and get it over the line, are likely to receive no reward, then something must be done to keep the founders and management team in place and motivated to deliver even a poor exit. The other shareholders must be prepared to re-examine the original equity deal and share out the proceeds of such an exit with the founders and management team. This is often referred to as a *management carve out*, a special deal agreed near the time of an exit to guarantee that the management will stay, remain motivated and importantly strive to deliver the best deal they can under the circumstances. Management carve outs will be discussed in greater detail in Chapter 9.

ALTERNATIVES IN THE MARKET...

There is an alternative form of preferred share, one that contains some of the features of a loan and therefore offers the investor downside protection but does not penalise other shareholders to the same extent as the double-dipping preferred share. This is called the non-participating preferred or preference share. It is important at this point to clarify some terminology: preferred share and preference share are often used interchangeably to mean the same thing. For ease and simplicity, this book uses the term *preferred* share to refer to *double-dipping preferred shares* and uses the term *preference* share to refer to their less toxic *non-participating* cousins.

> *Preferred share:* The participating 'double-dipping' preferred share in which investors receive their initial investment and cumulative interest **and** their equity share.
> *Preference share:* The non-participating preferred share in which investors receive their initial investment and cumulative interest **or** the equity share.

Alternatives in the Market... **137**

Note the difference highlighted in **bold italics** in the descriptions above. Preferred shares allow investors to claim back the loan **and** equity but preference shares force investors to choose between claiming back their loan **or** their equity, **not both**.

Compared to the previous example, if ABC Ventures invested its $2,000,000 as *non-participating preference shares*, the returns profile at exit would look a little different under the same scenarios. In each scenario, ABC Ventures must choose whether to receive a return based on its loan plus interest or whether it wishes to convert its preference shares to ordinary shares and receive the corresponding share of its equity. It cannot do both.

Scenario 1. The company performs poorly after the investment and is sold for $4 million after 5 years, the same as the post-money valuation following the ABC Ventures investment. How do the non-participating preference shares play out at the time of exit?

If ABC Ventures chose to participate via ordinary shares, it would receive a return based on its 50% equity share of the exit price (i.e. $2,000,000). But if ABC Ventures chose to receive a return based on its $2,000,000 loan and the $1,000,000 interest received, it gets $3,000,000. Clearly this is the better choice for ABC Ventures.

Having chosen to receive the $3,000,000 preference return, ABC Ventures' 50% equity ownership is then effectively 'cancelled' and it is no longer regarded as a shareholder for the purposes of the calculation. The $1,000,000 equity is split between the remaining ordinary shareholders accordingly – their shareholdings in this case being effectively doubled by the cancellation of ABC Ventures' shares.

Summary:

- ABC loan: $2,000,000 principal + $1,000,000 cumulative interest
- Total preference: $3,000,000
- 100% equity remaining: $1,000,000

138   Valuation

- ABC share: –
- Founders 80% share: $800,000
- Option pool 20% share: $200,000
- Total return for ABC: $3,000,000

In this scenario, ABC Ventures receives 75% of the proceeds for its 50% ownership. Compare this to the 87.5% share of proceeds if it had invested in double-dipping preferred shares and the 50% it would have received if it had invested in (or chosen) ordinary shares. The non-participating preference share sits between these two extremes.

Scenario 2. The company is sold for $10 million after 5 years. How do the non-participating preference shares play out at the time of this exit?

This time, if ABC Ventures chooses to convert its preference shares to ordinary shares it will receive its 50% equity share of the sale price, which in this case provides a $5,000,000 return. This is greater than the $3,000,000 it would receive by electing to receive its $2,000,000 loan and $1,000,000 interest. Consequently, the founders receive their 40% share of the exit price ($4,000,000) and the option holders their 10% share ($1,000,000).

Summary:

- ABC Ventures 50% share: $5,000,000
- Founders 40% share: $4,000,000
- Option pool 10% share: $1,000,000
- Total return for ABC: $5,000,000

ABC Ventures receives a payout entirely based on its ownership of ordinary shares. It has chosen to convert and consequently receives a 50% payout based on 50% equity ownership.

In all further scenarios discussed in the previous example, ABC Ventures will choose to convert to ordinary shares as this pays out more than simply receiving its loan plus interest. In other words, there is a 'crossover point' where conversion always makes sense. This crossover point is when conversion to ordinary shares provides one cent more return to ABC Ventures than simply receiving back $3,000,000. The crossover point in this example is when the company is sold for more than $6 million (see Figures 6.4 and 6.5).

UNPLEASANT COUSINS...

Just as the preference share provides a more lenient, less toxic variety of share than the double-dipping preferred share, there is also a less lenient, more toxic alternative in the market that VCs will sometimes deploy. These are double-dipping preferred shares with a multiple liquidation preference. This means the VCs receive a multiple of their loan plus interest and then participate in their appropriate equity share. For example, a 2× liquidation preference in the above examples would provide ABC Ventures with $4,000,0000 return on its loan plus $1,000,000 of interest before it participates in its appropriate equity share. The impact of this is obvious to see and there is no need to work through the same examples, it is worse in every scenario for the entrepreneurial team.

But it does not stop there, in some circumstances 3× liquidation preferences provide investors with a 3× multiple and so on. These sorts of terms are most frequently observed when venture capital is in short supply, the financial climate is poor and new ventures are desperate to raise money under almost any circumstances. Investors will claim that the greater risk due to a poor financial climate means that they need additional downside protection in a risky investment; they may even claim that there is greater information asymmetry when companies are desperate to raise money and capital is scarce. Perhaps those companies will go to great lengths to make sure they raise the money – heightening the risks and information asymmetry for investors.

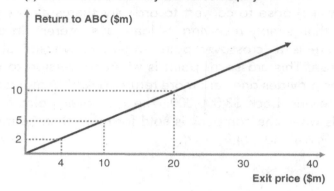

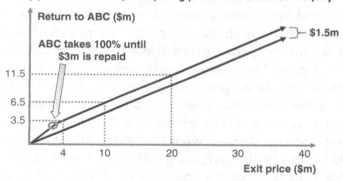

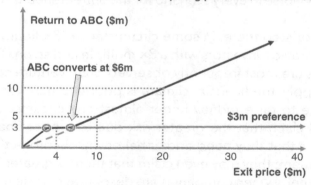

Figure 6.4 Ordinary shares, preferred shares and preference shares.
The figures represent the differences between ordinary shares, double-dipping preferred shares and non-participating preference shares. Part (a) illustrates the return to ABC Ventures if it holds ordinary shares and part (b) illustrates the impact of the double dip at low valuations, with the $1.5 million preference gap at all valuations thereafter. Part (c) shows the milder effects of the non-participating preference share before the return profile becomes identical to that of ordinary shares after the $6 million conversion point.

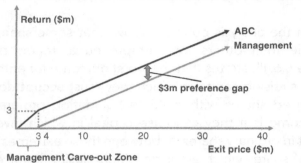

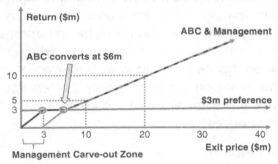

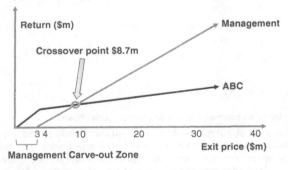

Figure 6.5 ABC Ventures versus the management team.
The figures represent graphically a comparison of the returns between ABC Ventures and 'Management' (the entrepreneurial team plus the option pool combined). Part (a) illustrates the return to ABC Ventures with double-dipping preferred shares and emphasises that it always stays $3 million ahead of management, even at high valuations. Part (b) illustrates the effects of the non-participating preferred share when the return profile becomes identical to that of management after the $6 million conversion point. Part (c) illustrates that if management negotiated ABC Ventures down to a lower equity percentage, even with double-dipping preferred shares, there is a crossover point at which the management team overtakes ABC Ventures in its share of the return. The conclusion is clear: entrepreneurial teams confident of successfully delivering a high-value exit should focus on the percentage equity rather than preferences.

A HIERARCHY OF OUTCOMES

It is clear from the analysis outlined above that some shares are more desirable than others for entrepreneurial teams raising finance. Figure 6.6. illustrates that the worst outcome for entrepreneurial teams is raising capital in which they must accept double-dipping preferred shares with multiple liquidation preferences. The best outcome is if they can raise capital in which investors agree to invest in ordinary shares. In between these extremes there are a variety of shares which are increasingly desirable for entrepreneurial teams. Double-dipping preferred shares with a 1× liquidation preference are better than those with a multiple liquidation preference. Non-participating shares are better still, unless ordinary shares can be negotiated. The question for entrepreneurial teams in a negotiation with VCs or other investors is whether they should expend their energy negotiating away preferred or preference shares or focus more on the pure equity percentage they retain; in other words, a greater share of the equity for the team versus accepting preferences.

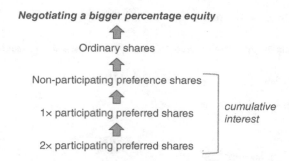

Figure 6.6 A hierarchy of outcomes for the entrepreneurial team.
When management teams set about responding to a term sheet and negotiating with VCs, there may be a trade-off between banishing preferred shares from the term sheet or accepting a lower valuation, in other words a smaller share of the equity. There is a hierarchy of desirable outcomes for management in which participating preferred shares with multiple liquidation preferences represent the least desirable deal, and they should try to push the negotiation as high up the hierarchy as they can, ideally arriving at a deal in which the investment is made in ordinary shares. If they can achieve this and at the same time negotiate a bigger percentage equity for themselves, then they have achieved the best possible outcome – a greater share of the upside whilst minimising the impact upon them if things do not go quite to plan. It is more usual for entrepreneurial teams to climb part way up this hierarchical ladder, perhaps shifting from participating preferred shares with a multiple liquidation preference to non-participating preference shares, and perhaps along the way negotiating a lower cumulative interest rate. All of these outcomes are an improvement on what might be an aggressive first offer from VCs.

Figure 6.5 illustrates how percentage equity is more important for ordinary shareholders at high valuations. In the example, if the founders can negotiate a better share of the equity (in this case retaining 55% compared to 40%) assuming a 10% option pool, and leaving the double-dipping preferred shares in place, they benefit greatly if the business is successful. Therefore, if an entrepreneurial team is confident in their potential success, they should care less about leaving double-dipping preferred shares in place and more about negotiating a better share of the equity. If they are nervous about the ultimate performance of their venture and more worried about the downside consequences, they may have greater concerns about the presence of double-dipping preferred shares. Where they focus their negotiating energy is a personal choice...

If founders and management teams are confident, they focus on percentage not preference...

PREFERENCE CASCADES

All the examples discussed above refer to a single investment round, that of ABC Ventures investing $2,000,000 in a start-up followed by an exit. But it is clear from previous chapters that start-ups do not cross the Valleys of Death with one financing round and there are usually multiple financing rounds based on achieving milestones prior to an eventual exit. What happens to preference and preferred shares during multiple financing rounds will be discussed in more detail in Chapter 9 but suffice to say that throughout a series of financing rounds, layers of preferred or preference shares will be created. This is referred to as a *preference cascade* or waterfall, in which the most recent investors – who have probably paid the highest share price – will also have the most senior preferred or preference shares. They will get their money back first before investors in the previous round, and so on. Ordinary shareholders may then find themselves sitting underneath a preference cascade that requires a substantial exit valuation before the ordinary shares make a return for them.

The complexities of preference cascades can be significant, and sometimes the preferred or preference rights of previous investment rounds will be negotiated away by new incoming investors. They will argue that their new investment at a higher price removes the need for investors in previous rounds to retain preferred status as the risk has been decreased. They will also argue that for those previous investors the information asymmetry argument no longer exists, since they are insiders with a seat on the board, and therefore should not be able to claim information asymmetry as a rationale for maintaining their pre-existing preferred status. This can be helpful for the ordinary shareholders, as simplifying the preference cascade and removing layers from it will incentivise them further. This is very much part of the argument that new incoming investors will make. They are interested in maximising the performance of the management team, not the returns for existing investors.

IF AN INVESTOR ASKS...

What if, at the end of a successful pitch to investors, they ask an entrepreneurial team for their expected pre-money valuation? Is the best answer to lay out an analysis of achievements and a walk through the venture capital method for valuing early-stage businesses? The answer is no. Although it is perfectly acceptable to share with potential investors an outline of the cash raised to date, and the post-money valuation of the most recent round if there has been one, the best answer is to point out that the business is talking to a wide variety of potential investors, and the *market* will decide the answer to the question.

An entrepreneurial management team will gain great credibility by pointing out that they're seeking the right investor for the business, and talking to all the relevant parties who might potentially invest. By pointing out that they are sensible and rational and will listen to what investors tell them, they're more likely to generate a sense of competition and an idea that they know what they're doing. The market decides, and they will raise money based on what the market tells them. This is how it is done, and it is never wise to state an expected pre-money valuation.

Only when entrepreneurial teams receive a term sheet from a VC or other investor are they able to fully evaluate an offer to invest. Term sheets are discussed in detail in the next chapter, and it is important to understand that offers to invest must be viewed holistically and not simply as a function of valuation; this is only one aspect of a VC's offer to invest.

The best answer is don't answer...

THE RULE OF THUMB...

The question posed at the beginning of this chapter was the million-dollar question: How much equity do entrepreneurial teams need to sell to raise investment? It may be disappointing, therefore, to have reached the end of the chapter without a clear answer. Valuation of start-ups and early-stage ventures is an *art* not a science, and it shifts according to the changing financial landscape in which companies find themselves. Geopolitical, financial and even natural events elicit great changes in the supply of and demand for venture capital finance, and valuations shift according to the supply–demand equation.

This is further complicated by several varieties of preferred or preference shares, which alter the exit payouts for different classes of shareholders in a non-linear fashion, meaning that economic gain is not directly related to equity shareholding. Consequently, numerical valuation alone does not give a finite indication of the economic returns for shareholders based on their equity holding; the class of shares may have the greater impact at some exit valuations.

But is there a broad guideline for valuation and the spectre of dilution that shareholders face when raising capital? Is there a rule of thumb for dilution of existing shareholdings when start-ups or early-stage ventures are raising capital? The answer is... yes, kind of. Having outlined all the factors and mechanisms that influence valuation, broadly speaking – when entrepreneurial ventures raise new capital, existing shareholders can expect dilution of about one-third of their shareholding if they do not invest in the round.

Empirical observation and experience suggest this is just the way it tends to play out after all the negotiations and the dust settles, as if there is an unwritten understanding in the venture industry that there is a one-third dilution every round that approximates to a 'fair deal'. Shareholders seem to accept this as the price they must pay for recruiting new investors with fresh capital, and as a guideline this is the best approximation to an answer that is on offer...

> *Existing shareholders should expect a dilution of about one-third...*

SUMMARY OF CHAPTER 6

Rather than providing a deeply numerical analysis of the venture capital method and other approaches, this chapter has sought to explain how valuations in start-ups and early-stage ventures are market-driven; the market for early-stage equity being the VCs, angels and other investors who are prepared to buy into high-risk ventures. The interplay between external factors like the financial climate with internal factors such as the progress made in achieving milestones is one important aspect of this imprecise art. Reputation, timing and other qualitative factors feed into the early-stage valuation conundrum. Figure 6.3 illustrates that valuation can only be a science when there is something to measure, and when companies are delivering reliable performance metrics such as revenue and profitability, corporate finance techniques will deliver a more precise and sophisticated view of the valuation. In the period prior to that, entrepreneurs and VCs rely to some extent on the alignment of interests and motivations towards delivering an exit as the common factor that binds them together.

The substantial impact of different classes of shares used by VCs and other investors, such as double-dipping preferred shares and non-participating preference shares, alters the valuation equation in ways that may be surprising for the inexperienced or uninitiated. But these are standard tools used within the venture capital industry to account for the information asymmetry that exists when investors back risky, early-stage ventures. Considering the preferred status of shares bought by VCs, it is important for entrepreneurial teams to work through the impact of these shares at a range of exit valuations. Having someone on the team who is good at building financial models is an important resource, as understanding the precise impact is the best way to negotiate undesirable terms away. Preferences have a big impact in poor exits, but stellar exits mean they become somewhat irrelevant. Where a management team spends its negotiating energy will depend on their confidence in delivering a high-performing exit.

The next chapter takes a detailed look at how term sheets issued by VCs to entrepreneurial teams are used as a platform for negotiating the final deal. The key theme running through the next chapter is that VC deals must be viewed holistically, and how different terms within the term sheet interact with each other is an important part of the process. Looking at the overall deal is better than looking at valuation alone.

REFERENCE

Gompers, P. and Lerner, J. (1999). *The Venture Capital Cycle*. MIT Press.

Chapter 7

Inside the Deal

TERM SHEETS

The previous chapter outlined the art of valuation, and the complexities of various forms of preferred and preference shares, which modify both the return to different groups of shareholders and the control they might exert over the company's strategic direction.

This highlights that the deal negotiation between VCs and entrepreneurial teams is not just about a simple split of the equity and sharing out the proceeds from a future exit, but also the decision-making process within the business and who wields control over important decisions. The class of shares each shareholder holds not only determines their rights to appoint a director to the board but also any *veto* they may have as shareholders over important matters, as well as their rights to receive information about the company's performance.

Being clear about the economic proceeds of an eventual exit, and who controls what at the beginning, is crucial in enabling investors and entrepreneurial teams to agree on a common set of goals for the investment. This is usually captured in a document issued by VCs to the entrepreneurial team outlining all the terms and conditions of their proposed investment in the business. This document is called a *term sheet* and serves as an outline of the commercial deal that will underpin the investment in the company. Usually, term sheets are *not* legally binding but are a precursor to appointing lawyers who will produce binding shareholders agreements based on the outline in the term sheet. Term sheets outline the investment offer as a whole and must be viewed in their entirety, considering not only the valuation and the class of shares, but also corporate governance and other management issues – such as what happens when things go wrong.

Receiving a term sheet outlining a proposed investment from a VC is a transformational moment in the entrepreneurial financing journey for any start-up or growing venture. Up until that point in the journey, for entrepreneurial teams it may seem like meeting after meeting, a lot of talk from various investors expressing interest, requesting a never-ending stream of information but never quite committing. Receiving a term sheet changes everything. It is a moment of crystallisation when the terms of a potential venture capital investment are laid out in black and white. It signifies real engagement and is a document around which the final deal can be constructed.

Not only does a term sheet serve as the basis for a negotiation of the final deal, it also serves as a document around which an additional *syndicate* of investors may be built. A term sheet is usually issued by an investor to a company, and that investor is one who is prepared to take the lead on negotiating terms and conducting detailed and extensive due diligence required to complete the investment. Such an investor is referred to as a *lead investor*, one who will lead the deal. Part of that commitment to *lead* may also be to recruit additional investors into a larger investment syndicate, perhaps because the size of the round is too large for the lead investor alone, but also for a range of additional reasons. Lead investors will often recruit syndicate partners to the investment round because they want to access additional capital in the *future*, or the complementary skills and non-financial resources that a syndicate partner may bring – such as access to networks, specific industrial knowledge or technical skills, or access to overseas markets. Money plus works for syndicate partners too...

Building syndicates will be discussed in more detail later in this chapter, especially how the makeup of a syndicate is defined and how syndicate partners are selected. This is a crucial process for both lead investor and entrepreneurial team, as the correct construction of a syndicate may mean the difference between success and failure for the venture. Introducing what turns out to be an unreliable investor into the syndicate can spell disaster for future governance within the business and its ability to grow. This plays directly into the notion of corporate governance and the dynamics of the board of directors, which will be discussed in Chapters 8 and 9.

WHO AND WHEN?

Term sheets are issued *by* investors *to* entrepreneurial teams. That is the direction of the investment offer in virtually all investment deals, and it is rare that entrepreneurial teams issue their own term sheet to investors inviting them to invest on certain terms. In some unusual cases with more established growing ventures, so-called 'hot deals' – in which there is competition from numerous VCs to invest, an entrepreneurial team might be in the fortunate position of writing their own terms.

Term sheets can take various forms and may be issued at different stages of the venture capital process. The best form of term sheet is a detailed outline of the core principles of the deal, including valuation, class of shares, milestones and tranches, board governance, share rights and importantly *deal management*. The latter point is particularly important, as it should outline the clear steps and information required to turn the term sheet into a legally binding agreement. It should outline the information the VC requires to complete its due diligence and engage lawyers to create the shareholders agreement and update the articles of association.

Ideally, lead investors issue term sheets when they have completed the bulk of their evaluation and made a definite fund-level decision that, barring unforeseen circumstances, they are committed to the principle of investing in the business, even if it is not legally binding at this stage. It is a sign that they are willing to put considerable resources in the form of time and energy into completing the investment. The term sheet should be issued because of a considered decision based on the due diligence so far and the buy-in of all the key decision-makers within the VC's organisational structure. The term sheet should, therefore, be a commitment to working with the entrepreneurial team to make the investment happen by laying out a roadmap to signing the legally binding investment documents and cash flowing into the company's bank account.

A term sheet that is unduly brief or issued early in the venture capital process should arouse suspicion. It might indicate to an entrepreneurial team that the VC is fishing for information about valuation expectations and the valuation stated in the term sheet is less likely to be the valuation finally negotiated. One-page term sheets from VCs are generally not a good sign; it does not suggest they have put considerable time and energy into shaping the deal but that this is only a first stab at seeing what the team is prepared to accept. It is more likely to be followed by further negotiations as the evaluation and due-diligence process progresses, and there is no doubt the terms of the deal will 'slide' in favour of the VCs as the process continues. Entrepreneurial teams confronted with an early, brief term sheet should see it for what it usually is and should be prepared to push back hard against the investors who issued it. They should question how a VC has reached conclusions about valuation and governance when they hardly know the business at all.

Receiving a term sheet early, however brief, is not all negative though; there are ways in which an entrepreneurial team can use it to its advantage. Making it known that it has received a term sheet can be a key trigger point for creating competitive tension and eliciting further term sheets from other VCs. An entrepreneurial team walks a fine line at this stage: subtly letting it be known it is in possession of a term sheet, without giving away its contents and from whom prior to signing it, is a delicate dance. VCs hate to lose deals to a rival and for an entrepreneurial team, creating the smell of competition is key.

Only by maximising competitive tension can entrepreneurial teams truly negotiate.

PURPOSE

The purpose of a term sheet is to lay out the commercial framework of the deal terms before getting expensive corporate lawyers involved. Experienced lead investors know how to write a term sheet; they are familiar with the key terms of standard venture capital deals and they will usually prepare a term sheet without the assistance of legal advisors. Private equity and corporate lawyers are expensive, and executing the legal agreements for a venture capital deal can run into tens of thousands of dollars. So, it is in everyone's interests to iron out a commercial understanding of the deal before starting to pay the lawyers' bills, and even the lawyers will confirm this – it makes for a smooth transaction if the terms are established prior to their engagement.

Term sheets also serve as a unifying document around which a syndicate of additional investor followers can be built. When a lead investor builds a syndicate of VCs or other investors in a financing round, everyone invests on the same terms. The lead investor does not get cheaper shares than the rest of the syndicate, nor special rights, and VCs who wish to join the syndicate agree to the same terms spelled out in a term sheet that is signed by all parties. Any departure from the terms agreed in the term sheet should relate only to smaller details relevant to specific requirements of individual investors, such as regular reporting of specific information required by individual funds. There should be no wholesale renegotiation of substantial terms such as valuation, class of shares, governance or milestones. Therefore, signing a term sheet aligns all the parties around a common set of terms and ensures that entrepreneurial teams do not have to negotiate unilaterally with a range of different investors in the same round. Everyone follows the lead.

For VCs there are also specific advantages to signing a term sheet with an entrepreneurial team. VCs commit considerable time and resources to completing the transaction, and signing the term sheet creates a period of exclusivity and confidentiality for them to

154 Inside the Deal

do so. Once an entrepreneurial team signs a term sheet, it is bound to that investor for a period, usually 6 weeks to several months, during which time the investor has the exclusive right to further negotiate with the team and conclude the transaction. During this time, the nature of the transaction must also be kept confidential, and the entrepreneurial team is forbidden to market their venture further or engage with other potential investors. The exclusivity and confidentiality clauses are the only legally binding clauses in the term sheet and VCs will enforce them vigorously.

Competitive tension can only be generated before the moment of signing...

The process of negotiating a term sheet also allows a VC to observe how an entrepreneurial team negotiates in real time, and this is an essential part of the due-diligence process. How the team negotiates the term sheet is a good indication of how it will manage and negotiate deals going forward. It would be a bad sign if the team simply accepted the terms of the term sheet, signed it and sent it back with no objections. VCs expect a tough negotiation! A management team that responds emotionally and irrationally to a term sheet (or perhaps even angrily) is a red flag for a VC. Is this how the team will behave going forward, every time there is a disagreement? On the other hand, a team that responds assertively but logically during negotiation gives a clear indication that this is how it does business: it is tough but fair and understands exactly how to negotiate.

For this reason, it is important for an entrepreneurial team to understand the key terms of venture capital term sheets and the business model underpinning those terms to demonstrate its ability to negotiate logically, clearly and fairly. The previous chapter argued that entrepreneurial teams confident about delivering a valuable exit should consider focusing on their equity share rather than expending energy negotiating away classes of preferred shares. On the other hand, negotiating away preferred shares by demonstrating their knowledge of how preferred shares work, and how they misalign investors' and entrepreneurs' goals, will serve to bolster a VC's perception of their experience and credibility. In conclusion, negotiating hard but negotiating logically is an important part of the VC due-diligence process.

CORE PRINCIPLES

There is some irony in the fact that amongst the shared optimism of an entrepreneurial team and the VCs aiming to back it, the greatest portion of any term sheet they will sign is concerned with what happens if things go wrong. Only a minor portion of the term sheet appears to relate to what happens if things go right. In fact, only the clause spelling out the equity split between the existing shareholders and the new incoming investors relates to how they will eventually divide the spoils of a successful exit. The remainder of a term sheet has more to do with who controls what, and who decides when to act if things do not go to plan.

There are several core principles running through all venture capital term sheets, and which are fundamental to the venture capital business model. The following items discuss these principles and will explain why they exist and how they manifest themselves in a venture capital term sheet.

1. A VC Always Has a Right to Maintain Its Stake

When a VC invests in a new business, it not only buys a specified share of the equity but also buys an option to maintain its stake through further investments. This means that every time the venture raises a new equity finance round the VC will have the right, but not the obligation, to subscribe for its *pro-rata* percentage of the round. In other words, if a VC buys 35% of the equity in a start-up it will have the right to subscribe for 35% of any future equity financing rounds conducted by the growing venture. This is an important point because when a VC believes it has found a good thing, it wants to hold onto it and deploy more capital to a potential winner in its portfolio. It does not want to be the first investor in a company that then gathers momentum without having the right to invest further. VCs want to find a good deal, nurture it and then deploy further capital to it.

It is important to note that this is a right, not an obligation. The VC is not *obliged* to invest further if it chooses not to. This is important for the VC's business model, as it allocates capital *dynamically* across its portfolio – continuing to allocate capital to the winners and declining to put further cash into poor performers. Term sheets will always make clear that VCs have the right to reinvest a pro-rata share in future financing rounds.

2. A VC Always Gets Its Money Back First and Foremost in All Scenarios

In Chapter 6, the concept of information asymmetry was introduced as a rationale for VCs' request that their investments are made via preferred or preference shares. A fundamental component of both preferred and preference shares is that the investors who own them will always receive their payout from any exit or liquidation event in priority to all other shareholders. They get their money back *first and foremost in all scenarios*. The term sheet will spell this out and VCs will hold onto this aspect of the deal vigorously, as they defend one of the key tools they possess for guarding against information asymmetry.

3. Everyone Is Tied Together Until Exit

A question often asked by those with little experience of the venture capital business is: Can I sell my shares at any time? The answer is a resounding 'no'. A key principle of all venture capital deals is that all shareholders are tied together until there is an exit for all. Nobody gets to sell their shares early and if they attempt to do so, there will be severe penalties, sufficient to make it economically unattractive to even try. This principle is important in making sure that everyone is aligned with the same goal: delivering an exit that is profitable for all. It disincentivises groups of shareholders from acting in their own interests, although this can never be entirely avoided. By tying all shareholders together, no one gets to jump ship early, especially if the ship is sinking... The effect of this is clear to see: everyone is forced to stick together until the end, whatever that end may be...

4. Founders and Managers Cannot Leave Without a Penalty

A crucial component of the value in any start-up is the entrepreneurial team. The knowledge and skills possessed by the founders and key executives within the team makes up a significant component of the investment decision to back the company, and therefore every effort is made to retain that team. Part of that effort is making sure the founders and managers are incentivized properly with a decent share of the equity and proper salaries, in other words a positive incentive. But of course, negative incentives are deployed as well in the form of penalties should those founders or managers leave the business, which could be disastrous for the investors who put their faith in the team to deliver an exit. These penalties can include losing all or some of the equity they own in the business.

From the perspective of a VC this makes sense, as it would be grossly unfair if, having raised money from a VC on Monday, a founder walks away on Tuesday whilst retaining their equity share in the business and leaving others to build the value of the business in which they retain a share. Equally, stripping founders and managers of equity they own in the business which they created can seem grossly unfair to entrepreneurs! Why should a new investor have the right to remove the equity they owned before if they choose to walk away from their own company? But it is also important to look at this question not from the perspective of a founder who is leaving, but also one who is *staying behind*. If two founders launch a business and one of them leaves, why should the other continue working for the same share in the business whilst a departing co-founder leaves them with all the responsibility? Looking at penalties for leaving from the perspective of the co-founder who is *staying* is just as valid as looking at them from the perspective of a founder who is *leaving*.

5. A VC Controls Who the Founders and Managers Give Shares To

VCs need to know who owns the shares in the company they are backing. Using the same principle outlined above, a key component of the intrinsic value of the business lies in the founders and managers. Almost as bad as founders and managers leaving, is founders and managers passing or selling their shares to other parties in an uncontrolled fashion. Locking the value into the business is important and if a founder passes their shares to a family member, the VC wants to know about that. In addition, the financial regulators in many countries will enforce the duty of VCs to know who they are investing in and who they are investing alongside to prevent the possibility that fraudsters, criminals or other unsuitable shareholders receive investment from regulated and authorised investment funds.

6. A VC Will Always Want the Right to a Board Seat

'Money plus' has been discussed throughout this book. It is an essential component of a venture capital investment and one which is expected not only by the entrepreneurial teams receiving investment but also by the LPs who invest in venture capital funds and pay a substantial management fee for doing so. They expect value for money and they want the VCs they back to play an active role in building businesses. The venture capital term sheet will enshrine this 'money plus' by requiring the right to appoint a nominee director to the board of the company. This director will usually be a partner within the venture capital firm but could also be an external industry expert who the VC decides it will appoint instead. The VC's right to appoint a board director will usually be outlined in the term sheet and any conditions attached to that will be further spelled out, such as who gets the right to remove that director under certain circumstances, and whether that director has any special powers to approve certain decisions at board level.

7. A VC Has the Power to Veto Shareholder Decisions

Control is not only exercised by VCs at the level of the board, and in fact control via a shareholder veto can be more powerful. Directors must act in the interests of all shareholders, not the interests of the fund which nominated them to the board. For investor directors this imposes constraints upon them to prevent them doing anything in the interests of their own fund which could harm other shareholders. If they did so they could be liable to a civil lawsuit, or even a criminal prosecution, resulting in them being disqualified from acting as a director in future companies. Investor directors must, therefore, be very careful about decisions to ensure they are in the interests of all shareholders. But what happens when the fund itself must make decisions solely in its own interest as a shareholder? This is where a shareholder veto is more powerful, since a shareholder is allowed to make decisions in its own interests and is not obliged to consider other shareholders too.

For this reason, a VC's term sheet will usually spell out an extensive array of shareholder-level vetoes, which enable it to wield power to protect its investment regardless of the harm done to other shareholders. One conclusion from this is that entrepreneurial teams negotiating with VCs should always seek to shift shareholder vetoes to board-level decisions. A single shareholder having the right to block a decision – such as whether to raise more money or sell the company – is dangerous, and having too much power in the hands of a single shareholder or a concentrated group of shareholders should be avoided. One of the solutions to this is to move those decisions from the level of shareholder vetoes to a collective board decision, or failing that at least to a decision of the investor director who again is bound by the obligations to all shareholders.

Later in this chapter these core principles will be discussed again during a guided tour of a term sheet issued by ABC Ventures. The chapter will seek to highlight and illustrate where clauses may or may not be negotiated with ease. VCs will cling onto these core principles as they lie at the very heart of the venture capital business model, and it is important for entrepreneurial teams to understand where they can press hard and where VCs simply cannot surrender their position because of the terms imposed upon them by the LP agreements they have signed with their own investors. They have a duty of care to their LPs and they are contractually obliged to protect their investments by whatever means they can; seeking out aspects of the VC deal that can more easily be negotiated is important.

A DELICATE DANCE

When entrepreneurial teams set out to raise finance for their start-up, they begin a process that can be lengthy and all consuming. From the first pitches to VCs and other investors, a picture of the entrepreneurial financing market begins to emerge. The team will receive feedback from investors it pitches to, there will be certain questions that come up time and time again and a pattern begins to emerge about where the team can make improvements to the plan and items they should consider revising before they pitch to the next VC. Eventually it will become clear that a subset of all VCs the team has pitched to is becoming interested in the business and they will enter more detailed due diligence. They will begin to examine every aspect of the business, from the size of the market to the technology platform to the business model.

As the process moves on, one or more of those VCs might issue a term sheet. The ideal scenario for the entrepreneurial team is to receive more than one term sheet at around the same time, for only then can they truly negotiate the terms – when they have an alternative. Competition is key, a point made time and again throughout this book.

HOW TO CHOOSE A VC?

An entrepreneurial team finding itself in the ideal situation of receiving more than one term sheet at around the same time is in the best position it can ever hope to be in: it has a choice and can negotiate the best set of terms by playing one investor off against the other. It is important to note that entrepreneurial teams can only do this *before* a term sheet is signed. Once a term sheet is signed, exclusivity and confidentiality clauses are enforced and the team is prevented from engaging in conversations with other investors.

By comparing term sheets from alternate investors, an entrepreneurial team can attempt to construct the best deal possible by using competitive tension to negotiate away undesirable terms. But the contents of a negotiated term sheet are not the only parameters on which a decision is made to accept an investment proposal – sometimes the intangibles, which are not represented in a term sheet, are just as important.

Earlier chapters have discussed money plus in detail and it is difficult to capture elements of money plus in a written term sheet. Valuation and the class of shares are easy to write down, but reputation and credibility are not. The final decision over which term sheet to sign from competing investors lies not only within the contents of term sheets that have been negotiated as far as possible, but also in the nature of those investors themselves. It is not only reputation and credibility but also financial reserves (the ability to invest in further rounds), experience in the sector, connections with other investors, assistance with routes to market, technological expertise and perhaps above all personal chemistry that will decide which term sheet is finally agreed upon.

Personal chemistry seems like a vague and nebulous term. It is hard to capture that concept in a term sheet or put a value on it, but valuable it is. The statement 'don't invest in an entrepreneur unless you want to have dinner with them' may seem like a flippant remark but turns out to be remarkably accurate. It also works in reverse for entrepreneurial teams. Accepting a term sheet from a VC with whom little personal chemistry exists is probably doomed to fail. Getting along through the difficult existential crises that will face any growing venture is essential and a good working relationship is the foundation of that.

The contents of the term sheet are not the only basis on which a decision is made.

BUILDING INVESTOR SYNDICATES

Having signed a term sheet with a lead investor, if the investment round is too big for the lead investor alone, they may seek other VCs to form a syndicate – the members of the syndicate will be expected to sign the same term sheet. How other VCs are chosen to form part of that syndicate depends on a number of factors related to the money plus concept discussed earlier.

VCs will only syndicate deals with other VCs if they believe they can bring additional value. That value might be in the form of purely financial resources – especially if they operate a large fund – which may be essential for supporting future investment rounds. But additional value may relate to other money plus factors such as reputation, credibility, networks and perhaps a geographic focus that is complementary to the lead investor. They must bring something in addition to the money and it is well established that VCs will not syndicate deals with other VCs they regard as of lower quality or inferior to themselves. This is an important point, because forming a syndicate also allows for a second opinion on a risky new venture with uncertain technologies and unpredictable future revenues. A second opinion from a potential syndicate partner is a tremendous resource for the lead VC: perhaps they missed something, or perhaps another VC will come up with a new angle or idea to refine the investment decision or suggest new strategic directions.

Sometimes those syndicate partners may even be the other VCs who were bidding against the lead VC in the term-sheet process. This is not unusual and can often expedite the process because they will already be up to speed and keen to invest in the business. Sometimes the lead VC will become aware of who else was looking at the deal after the term sheet is signed. However they come into contact, it is not unusual for VCs who lost out in a term-sheet process to rejoin as a syndicate partner or follower if they are happy to sign up to the lead VC's term sheet. Sometimes entirely new VCs are invited to join the syndicate, perhaps one that has worked with the lead investor in a previous deal. This process will usually be carried out in consultation with the entrepreneurial team. Perhaps they will already have spoken to those VCs in the past and the lead investor needs to be made aware of that.

ONLY ONE TERM SHEET...

The paragraphs above paint a very rosy picture of the term sheet process in which the entrepreneurial team is in receipt of more than one offer to invest, can make choices and therefore negotiate the best possible terms, but this is very much an ideal-world scenario. It is more common for entrepreneurial teams to receive only one term sheet, and this weakens their negotiating position considerably. How can entrepreneurial teams negotiate when they have no alternatives?

The first instinct of inexperienced entrepreneurs might be to bluff. They might decide that to 'create' competitive tension, they will pretend to have term sheets from other investors and use this to leverage their position in a negotiation. But this is a dangerous game to play, as a VC might at some point during the negotiation simply walk away leaving the entrepreneurial team with no alternative. Bluffing may eventually be exposed, and the entrepreneurial team may find itself going back to the VC in a weaker negotiating position: it becomes crystal clear that the team has no alternative and the poor attempt to create competitive tension by failing to be truthful has blown up. This serves to decrease the credibility of the management team and may well play into further decision-making by the VC to alter the terms of the deal or replace members of the management team they believe are commercially weak. The venture capital market is, in the end, small – entrepreneurial teams need to be very careful about spinning stories about who wants to invest in their business, because invariably news gets around and their misplaced attempt to negotiate by deception might be uncovered.

Entrepreneurial teams must not lie about interest in their business...

A subtlety in this process relates to how to communicate competitive tension (see Figure 7.1). Entrepreneurial teams should not state that they have multiple term sheets if that is untrue, but it is probably acceptable to state, quite truthfully, that there are several investors showing an interest in the business and that for the potential lead VC, failure to reach suitable terms within a specified period may allow those other investors to catch up. It is a tough challenge to negotiate successfully when there is only one term sheet on the table but negotiating logically, calmly and with a clear understanding of the business of venture capital is the best an entrepreneurial team can hope for under these circumstances.

A GUIDED TOUR OF A TERM SHEET: ABC VENTURES

To negotiate logically, it is important to understand all the elements of a venture capital term sheet, and to understand why they are there. The previous chapter considered the example of ABC Ventures investing in a start-up at a specified pre-money valuation.

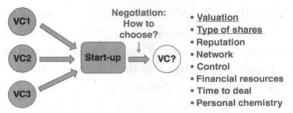

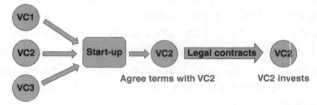

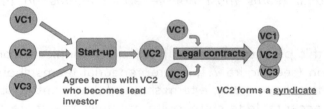

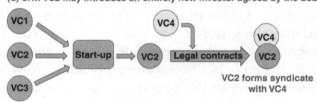

Figure 7.1 The best way to negotiate? Create competitive tension.

The ideal scenario for any entrepreneurial team is to generate sufficient interest in the start-up to result in multiple offers to invest in the business. By securing competing term sheets from VC1, VC2 and VC3 in (a) the team can negotiate between the alternatives. In (b) signing a term sheet with a lead investor (VC2) is a pivotal moment in the deal-making process. It establishes a framework and an exclusivity period within which lawyers can prepare and agree legally binding shareholders agreements allowing completion of the deal and cash to flow from VC to start-up. Signing a term sheet also facilitates syndication. In (c) VC2, in discussion with the start-up's board of directors, agrees to invite VC1 and VC3 to take a second look at the investment opportunity under the terms and conditions outlined in VC2's signed term sheet. If the terms are acceptable to them, they may form a syndicate for several reasons – including sharing risk, increasing the size of the investment round or to bring additional skills and networks to the investment. Alternatively, and probably more common, is when VC2, in discussion with the start-up's board, invites a new investor to join a syndicate as illustrated in (d). VC4 may not have seen the opportunity but having been introduced to the start-up may choose to sign up to VC2's term sheet and offer more investment. This syndication process may be lengthier than in (c) as VC4 may not be familiar with the start-up and has some catching up to do.

The example was subsequently developed to illustrate the impact of preferred and preference shares at an exit and introduced the notion of 'fully diluted valuation', with the addition of an option pool into the capital structure. The ABC Ventures investment will now be used to further illustrate the nature of venture capital terms by considering a term sheet issued by ABC Ventures outlining the overall terms of its proposed deal.

The following pages discuss the clauses within ABC Ventures' term sheet and the principal clauses of the term will be examined via a brief guided tour of the points to look out for. By doing so, the intention is to enable entrepreneurial teams, and VCs alike, to understand why certain terms exist, why some will be very difficult to change and why others are more flexible. The complete term sheet is included at the end of this chapter, but selected sections are reproduced below to illustrate important points regarding valuation, milestones and the class of shares ABC Ventures is proposing to purchase.

Amount and Form of Investment

The first section of any term sheet usually spells out the basics. It will outline the investment, including the amount to be invested and the pre-money valuation of the investment, sometimes accompanied by a precise number of shares and the share price for the investment. Whichever way this is done, the goal is to make clear what percentage of the equity the investor expects to own when the transaction is concluded.

The sections in bold text in Figure 7.2 are important. What is the true pre-money valuation for the founders John Smith and Anne Brown? The answer is not $2 million as it first seems. This is not ABC Ventures trying to catch out the founders but is, in effect, a statement of intent that there needs to be an unissued stock option pool in place after the deal is completed to build what will be the company's greatest asset – its management team. A central theme for VCs is the belief that the best management team possible must be recruited and retained to build future value and this requires equity to align motives towards an eventual exit. The VC usually makes the (perhaps unfair) assumption here that Smith

Investor	The Investor ABC Ventures Fund I LP will invest $2 million in XYZ Tech Ltd in two phases as outlined below
Founders/Managers	Mr John Smith & Ms Anne Brown
Amount of financing	**$2 million**
Pre-money valuation (fully diluted)	**$2 million (includes 10% stock option pool)**
Post-money valuation	**$4 million**
Use of proceeds	The funds raised by this round of investment shall be used for operational capital expenditures and general working capital purposes.
Form of investment	The Investment will take place in **two phases**, the second phase being **conditional upon certain key business milestones ('The Milestones')** by the Company: Phase 1: On completion of the Investment ('Initial Completion'), the Investor will subscribe a total of $1 million for new Preferred shares in the Company. Phase 2: In the event the Company completes **The Milestones described below within 12 months of Initial Completion**, the Investor will subscribe a further $1 million for new Preferred shares in the Company.

Figure 7.2   Amount and form of investment.

This section of a term sheet defines who the investors are, names the founders and then spells out the amount of investment and the pre-money and post-money valuation, therefore indicating the percentage share of equity. Some term sheets leave nothing to chance and will DEFINE the number of shares and the share price they will pay if they have been given access to the capitalization table of the business in advance. Any phases or tranches of the investment will be spelled out here too – outlining the amounts and stages of how the investment may flow into the company.

and Brown already know that and have incorporated a 10% stock option pool into their existing ownership structure. If they have not, then Smith and Brown are going to have to pay for it and this is what is meant by 'fully diluted' (including the 10% stock option pool). The valuation assumes the stock option pool is in place and will be fully issued.

The calculation of the 'true' pre-money valuation from the perspective of the founders is as follows:

- 10% of the $4,000,000 post-money valuation is to be reserved for options.
- These shares will sit in a pool ready to be awarded to new employees.
- The VC receives 50% of the equity based on $2,000,000 pre-money.
- 40% of the equity remains for the founders, valued at $1,600,000.

The Milestones

Milestones form an essential part of the entrepreneurial finance journey, but the milestones outlined in the ABC Ventures term sheet are not milestones between *independent* financing rounds. They are milestones *within* the same financing round, a form of 'mini milestone' referred to as *tranches*. A tranche is a French word meaning 'portion' and this is exactly the case here. The investment round is split into portions or phases, which are contingent upon the entrepreneurial team hitting defined mini milestones: the price of the round is agreed upfront, but the cash is released according to pre-agreed mini milestones. This will appear unattractive to entrepreneurial teams, who would much rather have all the cash invested in the company up front – it is better for them to have all the cash in the bank immediately and therefore not subject to any conditions and without the risk that it may not appear. For the VC the opposite is true, they use tranches as a means of mitigating their risk of investing in the venture. What if things go wrong very early on? What if the technology fails just a few months after the investment is made? It would be a very embarrassing outcome for a VC, locking up a large amount of capital in a start-up that fails soon after.

The problem with structuring investments in tranches based on pre-agreed milestones lies in defining precisely what those milestones should be. In the ABC Ventures term sheet, the second phase of the investment is only triggered when the company achieves a mix of technical, commercial and team-related milestones, some of which are difficult to measure. Crucially, in all the milestones defined in this term sheet, as we will see in Figure 7.3, achieving those milestones only occurs when the investor is *satisfied* they have been achieved. This is a huge red flag for the entrepreneurial team: What if the investor is never satisfied? It is impossible to enforce the satisfaction of an investor and any time an entrepreneurial team sees the words 'to the satisfaction of the investor' it should negotiate this term robustly. Milestones should be defined in an objective and measurable format; they should avoid subjectivity and avoid being subject to the approval of the investor.

The ideal negotiating position for an entrepreneurial team should be to get rid of tranches entirely. To some extent the use of tranches in recent years has declined, purely because of the difficulties of defining and enforcing milestones, although European VCs continue to use this approach more frequently than those in the United States. Perhaps because of the difference in risk perception and availability of large pools of capital in the United States, American VCs tend to use tranches less than their European counterparts.

If entrepreneurial teams are confronted with an investment based on tranches, they should focus on minimising the number of tranches and maximising the objectivity of the milestones underpinning them. If any subjective judgement around those milestones remains, it should be in the hands of the board of directors to adjudicate whether they have been achieved. The board of directors must act in the interests of the company and therefore presents a more balanced view of progress. However, if an investor truly disagrees that a milestone has been achieved, a legal fight will ensue and this could be an existential moment for the

A Guided Tour of a Term Sheet: ABC Ventures   **169**

company. A start-up embroiled in a legal dispute with its investors is unlikely to survive.

The ABC Ventures term sheet also has a surprising phrase in the milestones clause (see Figure 7.3): *'The Investor may agree to defer or delay any Milestone deadline, or to waive any Milestone in its absolute discretion'*. At first glance this appears to be a positive outcome for the entrepreneurial team, as it simply states that the investor might choose just to put the money in even if

---

The relevant milestones for the second phase of the financing are:

1. Achieve technical proof of concept to the **satisfaction of the Investor**:
   - Demonstration of working prototype at laboratory scale
   - Measurement of defined set of parameters **to be agreed**
   - Build 3 sets of prototypes for use in customer trials.

2. Chief Executive with relevant commercial experience in the sector to have been appointed to the **satisfaction of the Investor**.

3. Agreement with two potential customers to test prototype instruments, and installation of prototype instruments at their factories.

The Investor may agree to defer or delay any Milestone deadline, or to waive any Milestone in its absolute discretion.

Figure 7.3   The milestones.

This section of a term sheet defines any milestones for triggering the tranches of investment in the company and may describe a range of technical, commercial or team-related milestones. Note that these mini milestones are distinct from the major milestones that will trigger the next independent financing round, which will be led by a fresh set of new, incoming investors – hopefully at a higher valuation.

the team doesn't hit its milestones. Although it is great to have that flexibility, there is also a more sinister outcome. What if a large corporate comes along and offers to buy the business for a large sum of money before the investor puts in the second tranche? Before ABC Ventures puts in its second tranche it only owns half of the shares it originally agreed to buy. By having the right to waive the milestones and invest the additional tranche at any time, ABC Ventures could in this unusual circumstance double its return simply by putting in the second tranche just before the business is bought via an M&A process. Although this is an unlikely scenario, it would be an unfair outcome and the entrepreneurial team needs to spot this and remove it from the term sheet.

Share Rights: The Impact of Preferred Shares

This section of the term sheet is normally where the class of shares is specified and any liquidation and sale preferences, such as double-dipping preferred shares or non-participating preference shares, are described. The language used to spell this out is sometimes opaque and entrepreneurial teams need to look closely at the sequence and hierarchy of payments at exit, and what conditions must be satisfied before ordinary shareholders are paid out.

In the case of the ABC Ventures term sheet this is a straightforward double-dipping preferred share in which ABC Ventures will receive any dividends that have accumulated on the balance sheet of the company and its initial subscription price before being treated as an ordinary shareholder along with everyone else. In other words, ABC Ventures benefits from the double dip of being repaid first and foremost in all circumstances and then participating as an ordinary shareholder. The impact of these rights has been explained in detail already and will not be covered again here, but these clauses are where the eyes of the entrepreneurial team should be directed first when they receive a term sheet. Valuation is always the headline act in any term sheet but the share rights – and specifically the impact of preferred shares – is often as important if not more so, and entrepreneurial teams should study this clause in detail, model the outcomes and

A Guided Tour of a Term Sheet: ABC Ventures **171**

be prepared for a tough negotiation based on their calculations of the impact on them at an exit.

It is also worth noting that this section of the term sheet outlines the right but not the obligation of investors to reinvest in the future according to their pro-rata shareholding (see Figure 7.4). Indeed, under pre-emptive rights the shareholder will always have the right to buy shares issued in the future prior to those shares being offered elsewhere.

Dividend	The Preferred shares shall rank *pari passu* in all respects as to dividend with the ordinary shares in the capital of the Company ('Ordinary Shares'). The Preferred shares shall be entitled to receive a **cumulative fixed dividend of 8 per cent (8%) per annum** on the subscription price of the Preferred shares payable on redemption and compounding monthly.
Liquidation and sale preference	A mechanism will be included to ensure that upon the liquidation (or other return of capital) or sale of the Company, the holders of the Preferred shares **will first be entitled to receive** an amount equal to all arrears of dividends on the Preferred shares and the subscription price for its Preferred shares in priority to any distribution to holders of any other class of shares. Any balance shall then be distributed proportionately between the holders of the Preferred shares and the holders of the Ordinary Shares (**pro rata to shareholdings and on an as-if converted basis**).

Figure 7.4   Share rights.
This section of the term sheet defines the types of shares to be purchased by the investor, in this case double-dipping preferred shares. The words used to describe share rights can vary and need to be studied closely to understand the impact on ordinary shareholders.

Share Issues and Transfers

Listed under the section 'share issues and transfers', clauses generally relate to the protection of the investor's shareholding. One of the core principles outlined earlier stated that everyone is tied together until exit, and no one can sell their shares before the moment at which everybody sells their shares. This is the purpose of so-called *tag-along* and *drag-along* clauses. The tag-along clause seeks to prevent an individual shareholder selling out early by obliging them to find a buyer for all the shares owned by other shareholders too, or an equivalent proportion of them. In other words, if you want to sell your shares you have to find a buyer for mine too, otherwise there will be penalties. This is usually sufficient discouragement for any shareholder to attempt to sell, consistent with the concept that everyone is tied together until everyone sells at exit.

Drag-along clauses provide the opposite perspective: they prevent individual, small shareholders from refusing to sell when everybody else thinks it's a good idea. For example, if there is a good offer on the table to buy the company and most shareholders believe this is a good deal, the drag-along clause allows them to enforce the sale of shares owned by minor shareholders who otherwise might block the deal for reasons of self-interest, perhaps to extract more of the proceeds for themselves just for signing the deal. Drag-along clauses are meant to enforce the majority view that if now is a good time to sell, then all must sell. Again, it is consistent with the notion that everyone is tied together until and at exit.

The anti-dilution clause enables investors buying shares in this round to be compensated if the company – at any point in the future – raises money by selling shares at a cheaper price. It is as the name suggests, protection against dilution because of the company selling 'cheap shares'. This can appear as if ABC Ventures is attempting to have the best of both worlds. They arrived at a valuation for the business, a share price based on their own due diligence, but now they appear to be saying that if they got it wrong, and in the future another investor invests more cheaply, then they should be compensated. This does appear unfair, after all they are the ones who proposed the valuation in the first place. But the presence of anti-dilution clauses in venture capital term sheets is almost ubiquitous; they are always there in one form or another but are often not used. If a company is forced to raise capital at a lower share price in the future, its existing investors will always have the right to invest at that lower share price and if they choose not to, anti-dilution clauses might become invalidated through so-called pay to play provisions, under which they must invest to be protected by their anti-dilution rights.

Clauses on compulsory transfer are all to do with one of the other core principles of a venture capital term sheet, that founders and managers cannot leave without a penalty. As stated earlier, a substantial part of the value in any start-up relates to the founders and the entrepreneurial team. If they leave, there is substantial damage to the value of the business and therefore there must be a penalty for doing so. It is a means of encouraging managers to stay, and this is spelled out under these sections of the term sheet. The main negotiation point here is not that this principle should be removed, but rather around the definitions of a 'good leaver' or a 'bad leaver'. A good leaver will keep a greater proportion of their shares and might be defined as someone who had to leave the business because of ill health or perhaps because they were asked to leave by the board (if the role had outgrown them). That is a point of debate and probably will be debated again at the time of any founder's departure. Bad leavers are usually easier to define – surely anyone who has been dismissed for gross misconduct such as fraud or acting against the interests of the company is clearly defined as a bad leaver and may stand to lose all their equity in the business. It is worth considering again that this clause should be read not only as the founder who might be *leaving* but also as the founder who might be *staying*. In the case of the latter, it does not feel unfair to penalise someone who leaves the business early and before a successful exit is generated.

The Board and Control

A substantial part of any term sheet deals with control and control is exercised both at the level of the board of directors and at the shareholder level by investors, who may act independently and without regard to fiduciary duty observed by the board. Control is therefore a two-layered mechanism: (1) control at board level via the appointment of a nominated director and (2) control exercised via shareholder vetoes.

The term sheet will normally spell out the size of the board and the initial directors appointed to that board, normally comprised of a small number of executives or founders, the investors and ideally some independent industry experts. In the case of ABC Ventures' proposed investment in XYZ, the board initially is comprised of only four directors: one of the founders, an investor director, an independent chairman who appears to have been identified and the CEO of the business when appointed.

There are subtle issues to observe here, which may present challenges. Note that only one of the founders is nominated to the board, and this may create tension within the founding team that might need to be addressed. It is not wrong of ABC Ventures to specify only one founder on the basis that one founder should be able to speak for both, and there is a symmetry to having one founder and one investor director. The fact that an independent chair is to be appointed is welcome news, as this recognises the importance of an independent chair who knows the industry and can bring substantial value and credibility.

The appointment of the CEO to the board when hired is also not unusual, but there is a note of caution here: the appointment of a CEO is one of the milestones triggering the release of the second tranche of investment and as written in the term sheet this is very much in the hands of ABC Ventures to approve. It may be the case that the company feels compelled to appoint a CEO to fulfil the milestones for the second tranche, and that CEO may be a candidate very much under the influence of ABC Ventures. It appears as if ABC has the power to appoint or approve the CEO, and that individual will then automatically be on the board of directors. This puts a considerable amount of power over the board in the hands of (or influenced by) ABC Ventures, and this is an area the founders will want to question. Perhaps there is a compromise in which the decision regarding the appointment of the CEO must be approved by the founders jointly. Whatever the solution, here a balanced board that is not unduly influenced by one or a group of investors is very important and entrepreneurial teams should strive to negotiate a balanced board.

But power is not only wielded by the board; shareholders too can exert a great degree of power directly via the use of shareholder vetoes, in which certain actions must be approved by investors. In the ABC Ventures term sheet (Figure 7.5) this is spelled out as a list of specific activities requiring the approval of the investor (i.e. ABC Ventures). The investor can act entirely in its own interests, for example, it could block actions which might save the company but diminish their own shareholding. There is a divergence between the interests of the company and the interests of individual shareholders, and entrepreneurial teams should always seek to minimise the number and range of shareholder vetoes and instead try to shift that power to something controlled by the board. At least when such issues are controlled by the board, the directors have a responsibility to act in the interests of the company – including all shareholders. This would be a preferable outcome to putting control in the hands of a small number of investors directly.

Deal Management

The only legally binding sections of the term sheet are often the cause of the greatest debate and could have the most immediate impact on the start-up. The deal management clauses spell out the timing, costs, preconditions to closing and issues of confidentiality and exclusivity.

The timing required to complete a venture capital investment in an early-stage venture varies but, overall, a reasonable expectation is that the transaction should be completed over the course of 6 to 8 weeks from signing the term sheet. This provides the VC with sufficient time to complete due diligence and lawyers with ample time to turn the term sheet into legally binding agreements. If the timing proposed by a VC runs beyond a couple of months, then suspicions should be aroused as to whether they have the funds to invest or whether they have the competence to back the company. Lengthy periods of exclusivity indicate that they might be fishing for information, or not yet sufficiently up to speed to properly issue

ABC Ventures LLP Term Sheet

The Term Sheet below represents the outline proposal from ABC Ventures Fund I LP to invest in XYZ Tech Ltd, a company developing new software for controlling robots in the car manufacturing industry. ABC Ventures is committed to working with XYZ Tech to build a successful venture and we very much hope you will accept these terms. Please respond directly to our Managing Partner Elizabeth Gray with any questions you may have.

Amount and Form of Investment

Investor	The Investor ABC Ventures Fund I LP will invest $2 million in XYZ Tech Ltd in two phases as outlined below.
Founders/Managers	Mr John Smith & Ms Anne Brown
Aggregate amount of financing	$2 million
Pre-money valuation (fully diluted)	$2 million (includes 10% stock option pool)
Post-money valuation	$4 million
Use of proceeds	The funds raised by this round of investment shall be used for operational capital expenditures and general working capital purposes.
Form of investment	The Investment will take place in two phases, the second phase being conditional upon certain key business milestones ('The Milestones') by the Company:
	Phase 1: On completion of the Investment ('Initial Completion'), the Investor will subscribe a total of $1 million for new Preferred shares in the Company.
	Phase 2: In the event the Company completes The Milestones described below within 12 months of Initial Completion, the Investor will subscribe a further $1 million for new Preferred shares in the Company.

	The relevant milestones for the second phase of the financing are:
	
	1. Achieve technical proof of concept to the satisfaction of the Investor:
	
	    • Demonstration of working prototype at laboratory scale
	
	    • Measurement of defined set of parameters to be agreed
	
	    • Build 3 sets of prototypes for use in customer trials.
	
	2. Chief Executive with relevant commercial experience in the sector to have been appointed to the satisfaction of the Investor.
	
	3. Agreement with two potential customers to test prototype instruments, and installation of prototype instruments at their factories.
	
	The Investor may agree to defer or delay any Milestone deadline, or to waive any Milestone in its absolute discretion.

Share Rights	
Dividend	The Preferred shares shall rank *pari passu* in all respects as to dividend with the ordinary shares in the capital of the Company ('Ordinary Shares'). The Preferred shares shall be entitled to receive a cumulative fixed dividend of 8 per cent (8%) per annum on the subscription price of the Preferred shares payable on redemption and compounding monthly.
Liquidation and sale preference	A mechanism will be included to ensure that upon the liquidation (or other return of capital) or sale of the Company, the holders of the Preferred shares will first be entitled to receive an amount equal to all arrears of dividends on the Preferred shares and the subscription price for its Preferred shares in priority to any distribution to holders of any other class of shares. Any balance shall then be distributed proportionately between the holders of the Preferred shares and the holders of the Ordinary Shares (pro rata to shareholdings and on an as-if converted basis).

(Continued)

(Continued)

Redemption	The Investor may elect to cause the Company to redeem the Preferred shares in three equal tranches commencing on the fifth anniversary of issue of such shares at a price equal to all arrears of dividends and the subscription price for such shares. Upon default of redemption, the unpaid balance will accrue interest at a rate of 8 per cent (8%) per annum payable quarterly in arrears and the Investor shall be entitled to appoint such further number of directors to the board so as to constitute a majority of the board.
Conversion	The Investor will have the right to convert its Preferred shares at any time into Ordinary Shares on a one for one basis. The Preferred shares will automatically convert on a Qualifying Offering or on the written election of the holders of a majority of the Preferred shares. A 'Qualifying Offering' shall mean a listing which is at a public offering price per Ordinary Share of not less than five times the subscription price for each Preferred shares and which raises a total of not less than $20 million after underwriting expenses and commissions.
Voting rights	The Ordinary Shares and Preferred shares will carry one vote per share.
Pre-emptive rights on issue and transfer	If new shares are issued or a shareholder proposes to sell any shares (excluding shares issued in connection with the 'Option Pool' or pursuant to any agreed permitted transfers), these shares will first have to be offered to the existing shareholders on a pro-rata basis. Any transferee or new shareholder shall be required to enter into a deed of adherence to any shareholders' agreement.
Transfer restrictions	The Founders may not transfer their shares in the capital of the Company except with the consent of the Investor or to immediate family members or family trusts.

Share Issues and Transfers	
Tag rights	At the option of the Investor, upon any sale of shares by a shareholder (not being an agreed permitted transfer), the selling shareholder will have to ensure that the purchaser acquires an equivalent proportion of shares from the Investor on the same terms.
Drag rights	At any time after 3 years from completion of this Investment, if no sale or IPO has occurred, the Investor shall have the right to initiate and conduct a formal sales process in which the Company and all shareholders will co-operate and the Investor shall have the ability to force all members to sell their shares to a bona fide third party offeror on terms no less preferential in all material respects than are available to them.
Compulsory transfer	In the event that a Founder/Manager leaves the Company in circumstances involving his being summarily dismissed by reason of fraud, dishonesty or gross misconduct of such Founder/Manager (a 'Bad Leaver'), such Founder/Manager will be required to transfer all of his/her shares to the Company at the lower of the Subscription Price (being the amount paid up or credited as paid up on a share, including the full amount of any premium at which such share was issued) of such shares.

In the event that a Founder/Manager leaves the Company but is not a Bad Leaver (a 'Good Leaver'), a proportion of his/her shares may, if the Investor so determines, be subject to transfer or repurchase by the Company at the Subscription Price of such shares at such time.

The shares of Founders/Managers who are Good Leavers will vest on the following schedule: 25% upon Initial Completion, 25% on the first anniversary of Initial Completion, and thereafter will vest on a quarterly basis starting on the date which is 3 months after the first anniversary of Initial Completion and on each 3-month date thereafter to a maximum of 100% vested (on the third anniversary of Initial Completion). |

(Continued)

(Continued)

Anti-dilution	If the Company issues additional shares (excluding shares issued to employees in the form of share options or shares issued on the conversion of Preferred A shares) at a subscription price less than that paid by the Investor in this Investment (a 'Down Round'), the number of shares acquired by the Investor in this Investment will be adjusted on a weighted average basis. Any such further shares shall be issued to the Investor by way of a bonus issue or by way of a cash subscription at par.
The Board and Control	
Board composition	The Board will comprise of a maximum of 4 directors in the first instance. The composition of the board upon Initial Completion will be: 1. Christopher Jones (Industry Expert) (Chairman) 2. Dr John Smith (Founder) 3. Elizabeth Gray (ABC Ventures) We anticipate that the CEO, when employed, will also be appointed to the Board.
Investor director/observer	The Investor shall have the right to appoint one member of the board and a non-voting observer to attend board meetings for so long as it holds an interest in the Company. The Company will not be required to remunerate directors/observers appointed by the Investor or reimburse expenses incurred in the normal course of attending board meetings.

Veto rights	The Investor will have the right to consent in relation to specific matters having a material effect on the value or structure of the Investment and/or having a material effect on the operation and/or management of the Company. Such matters shall include, but will not be limited to (i) any further issue of shares; (ii) any amendment to the Company's constitutional documents or the rights attaching to any shares; (iii) any sale or listing; (iv) any liquidation or winding up of the Company; (v) borrowings which in aggregate exceed $250,000; (vi) acquisitions and disposals; (vii) varying or making any binding decision on the terms of employment of any of the Founders or any other senior employee or increasing or varying the salary or other benefits of any such person; (viii) the appointment or removal of any person as a director; (ix) the conduct of material litigation; and (x) the implementation of or variation to any share option or pension scheme.
Information rights	The Investor will be entitled to receive monthly management accounts within 10 days of the month end, audited annual accounts within 90 days of the year end, an annual budget within 30 days prior to the next financial year, board agendas, minutes and related board papers and any other information reasonably requested by the Investor.
Employment and restrictions on Founders/Managers	The Founders/Managers will enter into service agreements with the Company, to be agreed with the Investor prior to Initial Completion, which will contain appropriate protections in favour of the Company including restrictive covenants and provisions dealing with the Company's ownership of intellectual property. In addition, the Founders/Managers will in the shareholders' investment documentation give 12-month non-competition and non-solicitation undertakings in favour of the Investor.

(Continued)

(Continued)

Option pool	Ten per cent (10%) of the fully diluted equity shares at Initial Completion will be reserved for issue to new employees pursuant to a share incentive plan to be adopted as soon as practicable following Initial Completion and as approved by the Investor.
Deal Management	
Costs	The Company will be responsible for the Investors' reasonable expenses in connection with the Investment on Initial Completion or will be so responsible if during the exclusivity period the Company withdraws without reasonable cause, or the Investor withdraws for reasonable cause.
Timing	The Company, the Founders/Managers and the Investor agree to use their best efforts to sign definitive legal documentation to complete this round of investment within 8 weeks of signing this term sheet.
Confidentiality	The terms of this term sheet and the fact that the Investor is considering making an investment in the Company shall remain strictly confidential and may not be disclosed to any other parties except to respective professional advisers under terms of confidentiality.
Exclusivity	In consideration of the Investor committing time, money and resources to conduct its due diligence on the Company and draft, and negotiate the definitive legal documentation, the Company agrees not to discuss any potential investment in the Company or to continue or initiate any such discussions with any other potential investors. This right shall expire 8 weeks from the date of signing this term sheet.
Preconditions to completion	Completion of due diligence on patents and other IP to be conducted by a patent attorney appointed by ABV Ventures.

Warranties and indemnities	The Investor shall be entitled to receive warranties and indemnities from the Company and the Founders/Managers on a joint and several basis, as are customary in a transaction of this nature. There will be individual caps on liability for the Founders/Managers, capped at $250,000 each and the Company, capped at the aggregate amount of the Investment together in both cases with the costs of recovery.
Governing law	None of the terms in this term sheet are legally binding except for clauses on costs, exclusivity and confidentiality.
Signed on behalf of ABC Ventures LLP the General Partner of ABC Ventures Fund 1 LP by	Elizabeth Gray Managing Partner DATE
Signed on behalf of XYZ Tech Ltd by	Mr John Smith Founder DATE	Ms Anne Brown Founder DATE

Figure 7.5   The ABC Ventures term sheet.

The preceding pages contain the entire term sheet proposed by ABC Ventures. All term sheets should be read holistically with a view to understanding the entire deal proposed.

a term sheet and this is just a first stab in what might be a protracted negotiation.

Lengthy periods of exclusivity could also lock the start-up into a period of inactivity and leave it dangerously close to running out of cash. If the deal negotiation process drags on, the entrepreneurial team should be very cautious about locking itself into such an arrangement. It may even be a negotiating tactic for the investor to keep the business locked into an exclusivity arrangement whilst it runs low on cash, to soften it up for a tough renegotiation near the end of the process. This would be disappointing from a venture capital fund intent on providing money plus to build the business; they should be fully on board with helping the entrepreneurial team achieve their goals, but it would be naive to believe this type of behaviour does not happen. VCs and other investors will sometimes exert the toughest pressure near the end of the negotiation when the entrepreneurial team is tired, exhausted and close to running out of cash. Teams need to avoid this scenario and therefore should keep exclusivity periods short and sufficient to do the deal but nothing more. Exclusivity periods can be extended but entrepreneurial teams should extract a price for doing so, perhaps loosening other terms in exchange for an extension.

The question of who pays for the lawyers in a venture capital investment provides an interesting and somewhat surprising answer. It is obvious that the lawyers appointed by the start-up and acting on behalf of the start-up are paid by the start-up. The surprising discovery is that venture capital term sheets usually insist that the start-up also pays for the VC's lawyers too. How can this be? How can investors putting money into a start-up insist that the same impoverished start-up pays for their fancy lawyers to negotiate against them? This is a surprising and vexing concept for entrepreneurs, but the argument put forward by VCs for this situation is as follows: upon successful completion of the investment, cash flows from the venture capital fund into the start-up's bank account and it is from this cash that all legal bills for the transaction are paid, both for the start-up and the VC, so ultimately the venture capital fund pays both legal bills. Note that it is the venture capital *fund* paying the legal bills and not the venture capital *firm* from its 2% management fees. This is a way of avoiding expensive lawyers' bills being paid from the VC's management fee, which has to cover running costs, including salaries, travel, office space and day-to-day running. VCs do not want to absorb expensive legal bills within the running costs, and they would much rather charge these fees to the fund itself and *capitalise* those costs by including them within the amount invested into start-ups. Clearly this gives the start-up less money to build its venture; it goes against the notion that the venture capital fund should be utilised for value creation and not deal with the costs of the transaction, but VCs see the transaction costs as something to be borne by the fund and not something they are prepared to absorb from their own budget.

When the transaction completes and cash flows from the fund to the start-up there is no harm done, the VC argues that the fund pays for everything anyway and the start-up and entrepreneurial team are no worse off. The problem arises, however, if the transaction does not complete, perhaps because of some issue that arises late in the legal process, or an investor changes its mind. The question is then, who should pay? It would be grossly unfair if an investor pulled out of an investment for no good reason and expected a start-up to pay a legal bill for potential investors who, in the end, did not invest. But what about if investors pull out because they uncover some new fact or perhaps believe they have been misled as to the potential of the business and decide not to proceed? Who pays the legal bills here is less clear and it might be argued that if the start-up had been open at the beginning, it would not be saddled with a legal bill for an investment that didn't happen. These points about failed or aborted transactions are often some of the most fiercely negotiated terms in a term sheet because the impact of a failed or aborted transaction on a cash-strapped start-up can be immediate and severe. Being landed with a large legal bill as a start-up with no cash to pay it could instantly kill the company.

The solution to this is that in failed transactions, where investments do not complete, each party often ends up bearing its own legal costs. This is often a compromise position reached after some tough discussions. The VC knows that if the start-up is expected to pay all the legal bills, the further the transaction progresses the less able the start-up is to withdraw and therefore the easier it is for the VC to negotiate. The potential fear of the transaction not completing if they are on the hook for large legal bills often means that entrepreneurial teams weaken in their resolve the closer they get to the finish line of a completed transaction. Entrepreneurial teams need to be aware of this and fight hard to minimise their exposure to large and immediate legal bills should investors walk away. It is an existential risk they must manage carefully.

In any investment transaction such as this, investors will always require the entrepreneurial team to provide warranties as to the validity and genuine nature of the business the investors are investing in. This does not mean that founders must guarantee everything in the business plan will come true; everyone knows business plans are only as good as the paper they are written on and are usually out of date the day after. Investors therefore are not seeking a guarantee of performance. Warranties simply state that the facts on which the investment decision is made are correct as far as the entrepreneurial team is aware. They are putting their names to the factual elements underpinning the business, such as owning the intellectual property or that the accounts at the time of the investment are correct and up to date. There can be severe penalties for breaches of such warranties and often these penalties can amount to the total investment for the company, and sometimes a year's salary for the entrepreneurial team. Negotiating the warranties and indemnities is usually intricate work for the lawyers and usually a middle ground is found. Entrepreneurs can never be asked to guarantee things they could not possibly have known, and likewise VCs should only expect the entrepreneurs to put their names to clear information regarding the basis of the company, not unknowns such as the likely behaviour of potential competitors. These can never be guaranteed and should never form part of the warranties.

NEGOTIATING WITH VCs:
A PRACTICAL EXAMPLE

There is nothing like being in the hot seat of a negotiation to illustrate the key learning points. Written articles about term sheets can often be very dry and it is hard for entrepreneurial teams and potential investors alike to envision what this all means on the pages of a book. It is best to experience this in real life and understand how the principles of venture capital term sheets can be applied and altered to achieve certain negotiating aims. The following pages attempt to address that by providing a practice case study. The case is fictional but contains accurate elements of venture capital term sheets specifically created to highlight where and how certain aspects of a deal may or may not be negotiated.

It is best to read the case from the perspective of an advisor to the board of Gabriel.AI and assume that you have been recruited as an advisor because of your knowledge and understanding of how to negotiate venture capital deals. What would you do?

The ProVenture term sheet is structured a little bit differently to the ABC Ventures term sheet discussed above. This serves to illustrate the variation in term sheet structures that might be observed; they may be organised differently, under different headings, and arrange their clauses in different ways but essentially the core principles of venture capital term sheets are exhibited nonetheless. Entrepreneurial teams need to recognise that term sheets will look different but will usually be outlining similar core principles.

The answers to the case are presented at the end of this book. Of course, as with all business scenarios, there is never one clear-cut answer. There is never one ideal solution, but the core framework applied will guide the reader towards the key terms to be negotiated and other terms where it is best not to expend negotiating energy.

Case Study

Gabriel.AI: Raising the First Round

Gabriel.AI had not even been incorporated as a company when the two founders decided to pitch their start-up idea at a technology showcase event attended by angel investors and venture capital funds. John Spiegel and Jenny Wainwright were software engineers and avid sports fans, and they had developed a ground-breaking AI platform for professional sports teams to model on-field tactics.

Despite having little business experience, they impressed several investors with the quality of their pitch and the progress they had made. The partners of one venture capital fund that attended the event, ProVenture, showed great interest and had spoken in detail with the founders afterwards. ProVenture was a well-known venture capital fund with a good reputation in AI and some experience in sports data.

After several further meetings at ProVenture's offices, the founders were taken aback to receive a term sheet with an offer to invest in Gabriel. The founders had never dealt with VCs before, and this was an entirely new experience.

The founders of Gabriel.AI have approached you for advice. Put yourself in the role of mentor for the founders and help them to formulate a response to ProVenture.

Background

By collecting performance data on player movement and performance, John Spiegel and Jenny Wainwright were able to model responses to real-life game situations allowing sports coaches to make split-second decisions. The platform was robust and could be applied across a variety of professional team sports. The idea for starting a company had started as a semi-serious conversation in a pub but as they began to test their platform with local amateur teams, they realised the commercial impact this could make. In the high-value professional sports arena, finely balanced decisions in the dying seconds of a game could make the difference between success and failure and that could mean millions in financial rewards.

AI and machine learning had become a hot sector for the venture capital industry, with numerous examples of start-ups raising

Negotiating with VCs: A Practical Example

money at high valuations. VCs were starting to chase deals and entrepreneurs talked of bidding wars to invest in their companies, based on nothing more than a good business plan, a passionate team and early traction.

It felt to John and Jenny that this was their moment, an opportunity to raise money and move quickly with a reputable VC who could propel Gabriel.AI into the big league, quite literally.

The Term Sheet

Venture capital term sheets were generally of a standard format outlining the split of equity, board rights, shareholder control and the terms and conditions for the founders' shares. These variables were often dependent on market conditions, the supply versus demand for venture capital finance from start-ups. Around the time ProVenture issued its term sheet to Gabriel, the market for AI deals was hot – VCs were moving quickly in a 'land grab' for AI applications in high-value sectors such as sports data.

The term sheet sent by ProVenture spelled out the key terms of the investment. The term sheet was detailed and daunting for the founders. It seemed to be a very dry, pedantic and turgid document that did not reflect the positive interactions John and Jenny had with ProVenture so far. Those meetings had emphasised the 'money plus' benefits that an investment from ProVenture could bring to a start-up such as Gabriel. Was ProVenture showing its 'true colours' and were they going to be tough investors to deal with?

Within the context of a hot investment market for AI, your role is to advise the founders (John Spiegel and Jenny Wainwright) on how to proceed.

- Calculate the pre-money and post-money valuation. What percentage of the equity will be owned by the founders immediately after all three tranches are invested.
- Comment on the phases (tranches) of the proposed investment and the risks to the founders due to these tranches. Make

suggested changes to the milestones to enable the founders to manage these risks.

- Comment on the class of shares specified by ProVenture in the term sheet. Explain how these shares may affect the founders at exit. What are the alternatives?
- What do you think about the structure of the board proposed by ProVenture's term sheet?
- Discuss what information the founders should find out about ProVenture before signing the term sheet. Suggest how they could go about gathering this information.
- If the founders asked you to take the lead on negotiating with ProVenture, what approach would you take to get the best deal?

ProVenture (II) LP: SUMMARY OF TERMS FOR PROPOSED FINANCING (1 MARCH 2024)

ProVenture II LP (PVII LP) proposes, subject to contract, due diligence, investment committee approval and the following terms and conditions to invest £2,000,000 in Gabriel.AI Limited (the 'Company') as part of a total equity investment round of £3,000,000 (the 'Investment').

The investment:

Investor Syndicate	**PVII LP** £2,000,000 with the remaining £1,000,000 from additional '**syndicate investors**' identified by ProVenture.
Amount of financing	£3,000,000 in newly issued Series A Preferred Shares.
Pre-money valuation (fully diluted)	£2,000,000 to include a 10% available stock option pool post-investment for granting to new and existing management.
Post-money valuation	£5,000,000
Use of proceeds	The funds raised by this round of investment shall be used for operational capital expenditures and general working capital purposes directed towards the launch of Gabriel.AI's first product.

Form of investment	The Investment will take place in three phases, the second and third phases being conditional upon certain key business milestones ('The Milestones') by the Company:

Phase 1: On completion of the Investment ('Initial Completion'), the Investors will subscribe a total of £1,000,000 for new Preferred A shares in the Company.

Phase 2: In the event the Company completes The Milestones described below within 12 months of Initial Completion, the Investors will subscribe a further £1,000,000 for new Preferred A shares in the Company.

Phase 3: In the event the Company completes The Additional Milestones described below within 24 months of Initial Completion, the Investors will subscribe a further £1,000,000 for new Preferred A shares in the Company.

The Milestones

The **Milestones** for the second phase of financing are:

- Gabriel.AI's first product commercially available and having achieved revenues of at least £1,000,000.
- Gabriel.AI to have established a partnership with a leading sports team to develop a second product that is acceptable to PVII LP.

The **Additional Milestones** for the third phase of financing are:

- Recruitment of a commercially experienced CEO acceptable to PVII LP to lead the company.
- Identification of additional investors acceptable to PVII LP who have expressed an interest in leading a Series B financing round of at least £10,000,000 in Gabriel.AI.

PVII LP may agree to defer or delay any Milestone deadline, or to waive any Milestone in their absolute discretion.

(Continued)

(Continued)

Share rights:

Dividend	The Preferred A shares shall rank *pari passu* in all respects with the ordinary shares in the capital of the Company ('Ordinary Shares').
Liquidation and sale preference	A mechanism will be included to ensure that upon the liquidation or sale of the Company, the holders of the Preferred A shares will first be entitled to receive 2.0× the subscription price for their Preferred A shares together with an amount equal to 8% per annum on the subscription price of the Preferred A shares in priority to any distribution to holders of any other class of shares. Any balance shall then be distributed between all shareholders (*pro rata* to shareholdings and on an 'as-if converted' basis).
Conversion	The Investors will have the right to convert their Preferred A shares at any time into Ordinary Shares on a one for one basis. The Preferred A shares will automatically convert on a Qualifying Offering. A 'Qualifying Offering' shall mean an Initial Public Offering which is at a price per Ordinary Share of not less than five times the subscription price for each Preferred A share and which raises a total of not less than £100,000,000.
Voting rights	Ordinary Shares and Preferred A shares will carry one vote per share.
Pre-emptive rights on issue and transfer	If new shares are issued or a shareholder proposes to sell any shares (excluding shares in the 'Option Pool'), these shares will first have to be offered to PVII LP.
Transfer restrictions	The Founders may not transfer their shares in the capital of the Company except with the consent of PVII LP.
Tag rights	At the option of the PVII LP, upon any sale of shares by a shareholder (not being an agreed permitted transfer), the selling shareholder will have to ensure that the purchaser acquires an equivalent proportion of shares from PVII LP on the same terms.

Drag rights	At any time after 3 years from completion of this Investment, if no sale or IPO has occurred, PVII LP shall have the right to initiate and conduct a formal sales process in which the Company and all shareholders will co-operate and the PVII LP shall have the ability to force all members to sell their shares to a bona fide third party on terms no less preferential in all respects than available to them.
Compulsory transfer	If a Founder leaves the Company in circumstances involving being summarily dismissed by reason of fraud, dishonesty or gross misconduct (a 'Bad Leaver'), such a Founder will be required to transfer all their shares to the Company at the Subscription Price.
	If a Founder leaves the Company but is not a Bad Leaver (a 'Good Leaver'), the unvested proportion of their shares will be subject to repurchase by the Company at the Subscription Price. The shares of Founders who are Good Leavers will vest on the following schedule: 25% upon Initial Completion; 25% on the first anniversary of Initial Completion; 25% on the second anniversary of Initial Completion and 25% on the third anniversary of Initial Completion (100% vested four years from Initial Completion).
Anti-dilution	If the Company issues additional shares (excluding shares issued to employees in the form of share options) at a subscription price less than that paid by the PVII LP in this Investment (a 'Down Round'), the number of shares acquired by the Investor in this Investment will be adjusted on a weighted average basis. Any such further shares shall be issued to the Investor by way of a bonus issue or by way of a cash subscription at par.

(Continued)

(Continued)

Board position:

Board composition	The Board will comprise a maximum of 5 directors in the first instance. The composition of the board upon Initial Completion will be:

1. One Founder of Gabriel.AI
2. One director nominated by PVII LP
3. The CEO of Gabriel.AI when appointed
4. One director appointed by the founders and approved by the PVII LP director
5. One director selected as an industry expert to be approved unanimously by the remaining directors.

Investor director/observer	PVII LP shall have the right to appoint (1) one member of the board and (2) a non-voting observer to attend board meetings for so long as it holds an interest in the Company. The Company is expected to remunerate directors/observers appointed by investors and reimburse expenses incurred when attending board meetings.
Veto rights:	PVII LP will have the right to consent in relation to specific matters having a material effect on the value or structure of the Investment and/or having a material effect on the operation and/or management of the Company. Such matters shall include, but will not be limited to (i) any further issue of shares; (ii) any amendment to the Company's constitutional documents or the rights attaching to any shares; (iii) any sale or listing; (iv) any liquidation or winding up of the Company; (v) borrowings which in aggregate exceed £250,000; (vi) acquisitions and disposals; (vii) varying or making any binding decision on the terms of employment of any of the Founders or any other senior employee or increasing or

	varying the salary or other benefits of any such person; (viii) the appointment or removal of any person as a director; (ix) the conduct of material litigation.
Information rights:	The Investors will be entitled to receive monthly management accounts within 10 days of the month end, audited annual accounts within 90 days of the year end, an annual budget within 30 days prior to the next financial year, board agendas, minutes and related board papers.
Founders:	
Employment and restrictions on Founders/Managers	The 'Founders' (John Spiegel and Jenny Wainwright) will enter into service agreements with the Company, to be agreed with the PVII LP prior to Initial Completion, which will contain provisions dealing with the Company's ownership of intellectual property. In addition, the Founders will give 12-month non-competition and non-solicitation undertakings.
Option pool	Ten per cent (10%) of the fully diluted equity shares will be reserved for issue to new employees pursuant to a share incentive plan to be adopted as soon as practicable and as approved by the PVII LP.
Warranties and indemnities:	The Investor shall be entitled to receive warranties and indemnities from the Company and the Founders on a joint and several basis, as are customary in a transaction of this nature. This will include, but not be limited to, warranties relating to the business plan, accounts, litigation and intellectual property. There will be individual caps on liability for the Founders of £100,000 each and the Company, capped at the aggregate amount of the Investment together in both cases with the costs of recovery.

(Continued)

(Continued)

Pre-conditions to completion:	This Investment shall be conditional upon the following conditions being met prior to Initial Completion:

- External expert review of intellectual property to the satisfaction of PVII LP.
- Development of an appropriate strategy and short list of sports teams for the product collaboration outlined in milestone 2 to the satisfaction of PVII LP.
- Execution of definitive legal documentation to be drafted by PVII LP legal counsel Marcher & Fellows LLP according to the terms of this term sheet.
- Appropriate commercial, legal and accounting due diligence to be completed to the satisfaction of PVII LP.

General:

Costs	Gabriel.AI will be responsible for PVII LP's reasonable expenses in connection with the Investment on Initial Completion or will be so responsible if during the exclusivity period Gabriel.AI withdraws without reasonable cause or PVII LP withdraws with reasonable cause, subject to a maximum of £50,000.
Timing	The Company, the Founders and PVII LP agree to use their best efforts to sign definitive legal documentation to complete this round of investment on or before April 30th, 2024.
Confidentiality	The terms of this term sheet and the fact that PVII LP is considering making an investment in the Company shall remain strictly confidential and may not be disclosed to any other parties except to respective professional advisers.
Exclusivity	In consideration of PVII LP committing time and resources to conduct due diligence and negotiate the definitive legal documentation, the Company agrees not to discuss any potential investment in the Company or to continue or initiate any such discussions with any other potential investors.

Legal effect	This term sheet is not legally binding save the sections regarding costs, exclusivity, confidentiality, and governing law will be binding immediately upon the Company countersigning this term sheet.

We agree to the terms and conditions set out above:

....

for and on behalf of PVII LP

....

Date

....

for and on behalf of Gabriel.AI Ltd

....

Date

SUMMARY OF CHAPTER 7

Reading about term sheets can be a dry affair, but this chapter has attempted to outline the seven core principles underpinning venture capital deals and how they manifest themselves in the clauses of a term sheet. The delicate dance of securing a term sheet from a lead investor by generating and maintaining competitive tension until the point of signature enables entrepreneurial teams to maximise valuation and negotiate the terms put forward by VCs.

The model term sheet put forward by ABC Ventures and discussed during this chapter was used to illustrate where entrepreneurial teams should push the hardest and where they should not. Certain terms are 'must haves' for VCs, the right to receive information and the right to reinvest pro rata are key among them. Issues of control – such as the appointment of directors to the board – are often non-negotiable but should also be desirable, under the right conditions, both for the VC and the entrepreneurial team. Having an experienced VC on the board can be highly beneficial, and research has shown that start-ups with VCs on the board tend to do better than those without. However, the conditions for appointment of an investor director should be negotiated and specified, for example when a VC fails to reinvest in a future round and falls below a specified percentage equity, they could lose the right to appoint a board member.

Control is not only wielded at the level of the board of directors. Substantial shareholder veto provisions in most venture capital term sheets enable investors to exert their power through their shareholding. Shareholder vetoes are not subject to fiduciary duty and therefore shareholders are able to act solely in their own interest. It is generally beneficial for entrepreneurial teams to shift shareholder vetoes to issues that must be approved by the board, sometimes including the approval of the investor director specifically. Even if an investor director's approval is required, this is preferable to shareholder vetoes because the investor director is bound to act in the interests of all shareholders, and this places constraints upon their ability to vote only in favour of their own fund's interests.

It is important for entrepreneurial teams to understand and appreciate the different forms of preferred and preference shares discussed in the previous chapter, and how they are expressed in a term sheet is essential. Looking out for the key terminology used to define classes of shares in a term sheet will enable teams to model the potential impact of preferred and preference shares upon their returns at exit. Doing so enables them to negotiate hard with VCs who may be asking for substantial preferential rights. By confronting VCs with a well-laid-out argument supported by illustrations of exit valuations and proceeds to the shareholders, the entrepreneurial team may argue that the interests of shareholders are misaligned by the introduction of preferred shares and the best way to drive a high-performing exit is for all shareholders to be totally aligned through ordinary shares. VCs will always push back against this notion, claiming that information asymmetry requires the use of preferred or preference shares to protect them from the downside risk if things do not go according to the plans devised by the entrepreneurial team.

The practical example provided in the Gabriel.AI case study provides an opportunity to practice some of these skills: the term sheet put forward by ProVenture has specific points that entrepreneurial teams should negotiate and the suggested answers to the case are provided at the end of this book. Negotiating term sheets only really comes to life in a real scenario when both entrepreneurial teams and VCs alike understand their business intimately and understand what the key pressures are that must be dealt with via the construction of the best deal. Anyone reading this book should try to reflect on their own business or their own investment portfolio and look at how best to apply the core principles of term sheets outlined in this chapter. Only then does it truly make sense – but hopefully the case study is a good start.

Ultimately, it is the market that determines the level of flexibility of venture capital terms. If venture capital is in plentiful supply and numerous investors are chasing relatively few investment opportunities, then negotiating power rests with entrepreneurial teams and they stand a much better chance of getting rid of undesirable terms like preferred shares. But in tough times, when VCs are holding onto their cash, it is far less likely that desperate entrepreneurial teams eager to fund their businesses from the scarce resources available will be successful in negotiating a great deal. In the end, supply and demand determines the outcome, and competition to invest is the entrepreneurial team's best friend. Likewise, for VCs attempting to select good investments in a sea of unpredictability, the best they can hope for is that under tough market conditions, when entrepreneurial teams are more flexible and need the money, they are sitting on a pile of cash. In other words, VCs who have raised a new fund but have not deployed it before a market downturn can often find themselves able to pick up a bargain. They rule the roost and entrepreneurial companies, which may have grown beyond their means and are now desperate for cash, will be more open to accepting investment on any terms they can get. VCs with a new fund ready to deploy in a down market will generate great returns because they have been able to negotiate great valuations.

The next chapter turns its attention to this issue. It will focus on the specific pressure entrepreneurial teams and their shareholders face in raising further rounds of capital. Many books and articles on entrepreneurial finance tend to focus on raising the first round as if it is the single greatest challenge faced by an entrepreneurial team, but experienced entrepreneurs will confirm that this is only the beginning of a wild ride. Funding the business as it grows presents unique challenges – such as managing diverse sets of investors appointed to the board, who may not share the same views about how best to fund growth. For growing ventures, time is of the essence, and when a real company has been built with employees, facilities and bills to pay, leaving it too late to raise the next round of capital can be a fatal mistake.

Chapter 8

Raising the Next Round

Start-ups do not raise all the capital they need to cross the Valleys of Death in one go. Previous chapters have explained how start-ups cross the valleys in stages, perhaps best envisioned as baby steps then strides as they raise successive rounds of investment in larger amounts and at higher share prices. As start-ups begin to mature into growing ventures, the challenges they face in assembling these investment rounds do not necessarily become easier, they just change. Inexperienced entrepreneurs would be forgiven for believing the first round is always the hardest – surely getting off the ground is the hardest step in the growth of any new venture – but this is not always true.

As new ventures grow, they become more complex, not only in their business strategies and interactions with the market, but also in terms of the mix of shareholders who own the company and who are represented to varying degrees around the board table. Managing a range of investors with different goals, different timelines and different expectations can be one of the greatest challenges for the CEOs of growing ventures, and all of this must be managed whilst running a business, exploring new markets and developing new innovations. Being the CEO of a growing venture is a constant juggling act, and anyone who has run such a business will confirm it can be a 24-hour, 7-day per week role, and one that demands more than their full attention.

The CEOs of growing ventures are in constant fundraising mode, even when they are not raising capital. An earlier chapter concluded that the best time to raise money is when you don't need it, and this is a philosophy that experienced entrepreneurial CEOs will know well – even when they are not fundraising, they are warming up potential investors for a future investment whenever that occurs. Building the business, keeping existing investors happy and constantly being on the lookout for new investors go hand in hand on a daily basis. Pitching the business at conferences, investor events and other networking get-togethers to create a buzz of excitement and competitive tension for when an investment round is launched is all part of laying the groundwork to securing future financing rounds. But telling a good story is not enough, and it is essential that growing ventures continue to hit compelling, tangible milestones and keep delivering value.

BUILDING VALUE BEFORE LAUNCHING THE NEXT ROUND

A key theme of this book is that building value does not necessarily mean generating revenue and often doesn't mean generating profits. Growing ventures backed by VCs build value, and consequently achieve high valuations, by establishing their dominance in a variety of ways. This can vary depending on the industry within which they operate; in the field of biotechnology, for instance, value is built through the development of intellectual property, the ownership of assets that could lead to the next great blockbuster drug or product. Similarly, data from clinical trials showing that a new pharmaceutical or medical device delivers a clinical benefit to patients will be reflected in the valuation of the company. Investors back value, they need to perceive that future revenues and profits will flow from the solid foundations of value being created now in the growing venture.

Demonstrating that the business has built value since the last financing round is essential in raising capital from new investors at a higher share price than the previous round (see Figure 8.1). Showing that the business has developed intellectual property, or clinical trials data, or has significantly increased user numbers for a piece of software or has secured exclusive deals with clients would all qualify as tangible, value-adding steps. Going out with a fundraising pitch that demonstrates this momentum and shows how the business has built value is the fundamental building block of putting together a new round. All of this must be achieved well before the business runs out of cash; it is no use delivering valuable milestones just as the business reaches the end of its cash runway, because being out of cash will have a far greater influence on valuation than any achievements the business may have concluded. Raising money when you don't need it means just that: raise the money well before you ever get to the stage where you really, really need it.

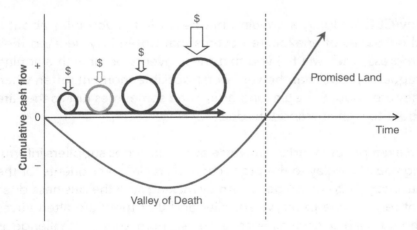

Figure 8.1 Raising the next round.
The CEOs of growing ventures are in constant fundraising mode – and are alert to the possibility of warming up potential investors. The best time to raise money is when the company does not need the cash, and experienced CEOs are skilled at creating a perception of scarcity around their business. The clock is ticking, and CEOs need to ensure they raise capital having hit value-adding milestones but before cash runs low. Keeping an eye on the second round is key…

This seems straightforward to understand but it is incredibly difficult to execute when the senior management team of the growing venture must contend with the daily challenges that any business will throw up, especially ones operating in new and untested markets.

Keeping on top of the day-to-day tasks at the same time as thinking about the strategy for building value is no mean feat. CEOs and the leadership teams of growing ventures have employees to hire and salaries to pay, they have equipment, supplies, offices and travel to take care of and the inevitable human resource challenges that confront all businesses – let alone those under pressure to perform for VCs. There are meetings with boards of directors every 6 to 8 weeks and there are investors who may already be focused on the timeline to delivering an exit. For CEOs, the clock is always ticking and getting ready to raise the next financing round at a higher share price – well in advance of running out of cash and all at the same time as managing the business – is the challenge they face

ADVERSE EVENTS AND THE VALLEYS OF DEATH

Any CEO building a growing business will tell you tales about a whole series of unexpected events that potentially derailed their progress. They will tell you that these events occur with alarming frequency, usually at the very worst possible moment, often when they are about to begin fundraising and sometimes just as they are about to sign an important deal.

An example of mundane adverse events includes suppliers informing you of a delay to the production of crucial components for the business. This can be dealt with by making sure the business does not rely on one exclusive supplier and that there are alternatives should such a circumstance arise. A more serious challenge is posed when, for example, a competitor emerges and announces a new product launch that would materially impact your ability to compete in the market. The seriousness of this adverse event is redoubled if their product infringes the venture's intellectual property rights and the company needs to mount a legal defence. This is a costly and unwanted message that you might have to give to both existing and new investors.

More serious again are adverse events relating to the core team within an entrepreneurial venture. What happens if your co-founder decides to leave the business, or a senior member of the management team begins to underperform badly and needs replacing? What happens if there is a stock market crash or one of your investors defaults on their commitment to the second tranche of a pre-agreed investment round? If such an event occurs very close to the point when you are seeking new investment, then there might be precious little time to recover, pivot and rebuild before cash runs out…

Far more likely, and more common, is a realisation that you may have underestimated costs and will need to raise more investment sooner than anticipated. Breaking that news to the board of directors and investors is a common challenge faced by many CEOs. Entrepreneurs are, by their very nature, optimistic – and sometimes that overoptimism leads to the business falling short in terms of financial resources. Managing that communication is a delicate process that CEOs need to navigate.

The life of a start-up CEO involves juggling whilst staring at the distant horizon…

CONDUCTING THE ORCHESTRA

A key difference between entrepreneurs starting a completely new business and the management team of a growing venture not only relates to the juggling act of managing near-term crises whilst searching for the next value inflexion point. Far from being a happy band of entrepreneurs, maybe working out of a garage, management teams building ventures that have raised finance previously now have multiple shareholders and those shareholders are often represented on the board of directors. They have voices, and those voices may not sing in unison. A board of directors means a variety of views expressed around the board table and although this is a healthy ideal, it also presents one more challenge for an entrepreneurial team to navigate. Listening to and acting upon the advice of a variety of voices around the board table requires a new skill, a skill that was not necessary when starting the business.

Investor directors will have a powerful voice when they hold the key to unlocking new investment in the business. Venture capital investors who are expected to follow on from their initial investment will have specific requirements as to what needs to happen before they do so. The views of some investors will vary compared to others, sometimes depending on what price they invested at and when. A new investment round at a specific pre-money valuation may be good for early investors but less positive for investors who participated in the most recent round; perhaps it threatens their shareholding, or even the status of their preferred shares. Of course, we know the directors must always act in the interests of all shareholders – that is their duty and they are bound by law to do so – but balancing the twin pressures of fiduciary duty to both portfolio company and investment fund is a challenge investor directors must struggle with and this, in turn, may pose a problem for entrepreneurial management teams.

CEOs of growing businesses need to conduct an 'orchestra' around the board table, and in some cases the musicians are not even working from the same sheet music. More seriously, some musicians may be working to a secret tune that nobody else is aware of and which relates closely to the performance of their own funds! The conflicts of interest that arise can be damaging and a skilful chair of the board will be adept at managing such issues.

This could paint a bleak picture of the challenges facing entrepreneurial teams raising further rounds of finance, but there are also substantial advantages to having a group of VCs around the board table.

WHAT ARE THE DIFFERENCES?

When entrepreneurial teams are raising later stages of investment, they have the advantage of existing investors who are supportive and who will guide them (see Figure 8.2). Existing investors usually

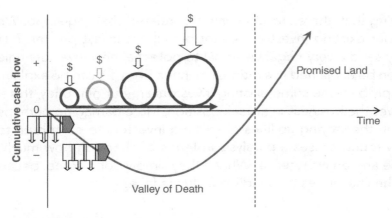

Figure 8.2 Raising later rounds.
When entrepreneurial teams raise the second round of finance, they usually shortcut the usual venture capital deal-flow process discussed earlier. Warm introductions from their existing investors and board of directors provide them with greater credibility and will result in a higher rate of acceptance for first meetings with VCs, and a likely higher rate of success from those meetings. This is where the money plus aspect of VCs really comes to the fore – especially if they are highly reputable. Reputation goes a long way to raising the next round of finance…

take the lead in deciding what a realistic fundraising target is and, once agreed, they will access their networks to provide warm introductions to further investors who they believe may invest in the business. This is probably the most valuable aspect of money plus discussed in previous chapters. A warm introduction to potential investors from a trusted VC with a strong reputation will shortcut the typical venture capital investment process. The early stages of that process – such as screening – are effectively bypassed because investors know each other well enough to know who is more likely to invest and the first meeting may be a more detailed affair with a greater chance of success. Existing investors will also share more openly their expectations of pre-money valuation for the new round. Investors sometimes talk to each other off the record and an investor-to-investor conversation will be more open about a realistic share price for the new round, making the valuation negotiation smoother and more constructive.

For members of the entrepreneurial team, they have been through all of this before. They know how to build a successful pitch; they know how to deliver it and answer difficult questions, and more importantly they will know what to look for in any term sheet they receive with an offer to invest in the business.

Saying that, there are some investor-related challenges too. What if your existing investors cannot or will not invest pro rata? This may send a very negative signal to potential new investors unless it can be explained in a rational manner. Even if it can be explained simply because some existing investors are out of money, this still leaves the business in a weak position. More damaging perhaps is when the varying abilities of existing investors to contribute to a new round causes a paralysis in terms of choosing how much to raise and on what terms. What if they simply don't agree, because of the challenges their individual funds face?

HOW TO BEGIN THE PROCESS

The process of raising new capital usually starts when the 'cash out' date begins to appear to the board of directors over the horizon – a shortening cash runway prior to the moment the company runs out sharpens the discussions about how much and when to begin a fundraising process. Regular board meetings and reports about the financial status of the company will make it obvious that a new financing round must occur. Planning might begin for this up to a year before the company runs out of cash, and experience suggests it can indeed take up to a year to raise larger, later rounds. The first step in this process might involve the board asking the management team to work on a plan for a new financing round and to make recommendations about the size of the round and what it will deliver for new, incoming investors. Just as in previous chapters, delivering tangible value-adding milestones with a new investment round is an essential component of an investment pitch, and the board will help the management team to arrive at their fundraising story.

Getting everyone around the board table to agree on the size and timing of a new investment round is not always easy, but once that is done, the next step in the process is to agree what proportion of that new round will be covered by the existing investors. Previous chapters highlighted the importance of investing pro rata to maintain a stake in the business and the confidence this demonstrates to the external world is essential. It is not necessary for all investors to invest pro rata, some may be out of money whilst others can take up the slack, but the *net* effect must be that the overall group of existing investors invest at or around their pro-rata share or some other pre-agreed proportion that is sufficient to show a clear level of confidence in the business. A decision to raise, for example, a $10 million investment round, of which the existing investors will contribute $4 million, means that new investors must be sought for the balancing sum of $6 million. In other words, $6 million of new money is required in a $10 million round supported by the existing investors. From a marketing point of view, it is often useful to target an amount that is slightly less than existing investors have recommended, on the basis that oversubscribing a round looks better than not reaching a larger target. This type of optical illusion – oversubscribing a round – may even play into the final valuation of the round by creating a perception of scarcity. New, incoming investors don't like to miss out and a scramble to fit into an undersized round may ultimately result in that round being bigger and at a higher price.

Having agreed the size and timing for a round, the process usually begins with the development and refinement of a high-impact pitch and the creation of a data room that contains all the digital information required to evaluate the company. The next step will involve going around the board table and existing investors to understand who knows whom in the investment community, to decide which investors will be approached. Certain board members having good contacts with external VCs may be given the task of making the first approach and hence start the process with a warm introduction. This is where the money plus really comes in…

THE CONVERTIBLE LOAN

Inevitably, despite all the warning signs and advice from experienced VCs and other directors on the board, sometimes growing ventures find themselves running out of cash just as they are in the process of raising new investment, and usually just as they are in the process of negotiating the terms of that investment. As discussed in an earlier chapter, nothing harms the valuation of a growing venture more than running out of cash. Even if the business has achieved fantastic technical or commercial milestones prior to the next financing round, if it has close to zero in the bank account during a negotiation the valuation will be seriously harmed.

It is at this point that the existing investors will need to step in and support their company just that little bit more to give it some more time and breathing space to secure the best investment terms. It would not make sense to provide such a financial injection in the form of a new equity round just prior to external investors arriving on the scene, as this would muddy the waters and add confusion to the agreement of a new share price. Existing investors cannot and should not set the share price of an investment round, as they are conflicted due to their current shareholdings. Therefore, they will usually inject finance into the business in the form of a specialised loan referred to as a *convertible loan* (colloquially known as a *bridge loan*, as it forms a short-term bridge between the last equity round and the anticipated new round).

Bridge rounds in the form of convertible loans avoid the thorny question of setting a new share price, as the loan will ordinarily convert into equity on the same terms and conditions as the anticipated equity round that hopefully is just around the corner. There is a caveat, however, as the existing investors who agree to participate in a convertible loan will require some kind of additional reward for putting their money at risk in a venture that may, in the end, fail to secure its next equity round. In normal conditions there are a commonly used set of terms for convertible loans with the loan converting into equity at a 20% discount to the share price of the next round, therefore giving the loan holders a reward for taking the risk in the form of extra shares. In other words, if the price of the new round is $100 per share, set by the new, incoming investors, then the convertible loan will convert at $80 per share.

Convertible loans will usually also yield an interest rate agreed by the loan holders and the company, which itself will also convert into shares at the completion of the next round. The question is, what happens if the next round does not occur because the company is unsuccessful? In those cases, the loan will sit at or near the top of the sequence of creditors who will need to be paid if the company subsequently fails. Shareholders make convertible loans partly for this reason: it offers an extra level of protection in the event the company fails.

There are many other, more complicated terms that often creep into convertible loans, and these are driven by market conditions. In very tough financial climates, the discount at which the loans converted to equity can climb from the industry standard 20% to 30% – or in some cases 40% if the risks are deemed very high. Similarly, the accrued interest rates on the loan may climb from an industry standard 8% to levels of 12% or more. The higher the discount upon conversion, the more incentive it provides for the existing investors to provide a loan, and those who do not participate in the loan are therefore punished by additional dilution. Convertible loans with a conversion discount at the next round serve to encourage existing investors to participate and punish those who do not. The higher the discount, the more the punishment.

In extreme circumstances, where a convertible loan is deemed to be the only source of saving the company, perhaps when time is very short or the business is in real danger of failure, convertible loans might even be accompanied by a restructuring of the shareholding of the company such that those who do not participate, or are unable to participate, are punished by a recapitalisation of the share structure, diluting them to a very small level and removing them from a position of influence – either as a shareholder or as a director. These restructurings are often referred to as *cram downs* when non-participants in an important convertible loan are diluted close to zero.

This does serve to illustrate a very important theme that runs throughout this book. The first investment round raised by a company – or indeed invested by a VC in a company – is never going to be the last one and it is very important for investors who back start-ups to be able to see the job through to the end. Being unable to invest in the very last round prior to an exit, or specifically in a convertible loan that is crucial to saving the business, is likely to wipe out their shareholding through a restructuring initiated by those who are willing or able to save the business. This is a nasty lesson for entrepreneurial teams and VCs alike, when all that hard work and investment is wiped out just before the finishing line comes into sight.

Knowing quite when the finishing line will come into sight is, however, the problem; it is why convertible loans may sometimes contain what appear to be rapacious terms. What happens if a convertible loan put in place as a bridge to the next financing round turns out to be more of a 'pier', half a bridge that ends somewhere out to sea. Bridge loans need to reach the other side, not just halfway, and predicting that is difficult and is the justification for why those who participate must be rewarded. A bridge disappearing into the clouds might turn out to be a pier and the rewards for setting out across it need to be consistent with the risk.

RAISING THE NEXT ROUND: A PRACTICAL EXAMPLE

The remainder of this chapter is devoted to a realistic, practical case study which illustrates many of the challenges facing management teams and boards of directors in raising further rounds of finance and choosing between potentially competing term sheets. There is nothing like real experience and – within the confines of a book – a realistic case study is as good as it gets. The pressures of timing, different investor perspectives, conflicts of interest in term sheets from competing investors that appear to offer subtle, yet substantial, differences are the subject of the case study contained in the following pages. Anyone who has been the CEO or served on the board of a growing venture seeking to raise a large round of capital, having already embarked upon its growth phase, will be familiar with some of the scenarios contained within this case. It is a fictional case but is realistic in the decisions that must be made. Readers are encouraged to read the case study and assume the role of an advisor to the board of SolidEx. What would you advise the board to do and how should they handle the negotiation?

The case develops the themes of valuation, preferred and preference shares and potential conflict between existing investors when presented with term sheets for new investment rounds. For the board and the existing investors in such a venture, the clock is often ticking during the Series B or later rounds, as the responsibility to secure funding and pay employees is substantial. Failure to raise capital could see a mass exodus of employees from the company and lead to possible failure. Boards need to be aware of the time it takes to raise fresh VC finance and the terms on which that may be achieved.

SolidEx has raised a seed (angel) round and a Series A (first venture capital round) and is now raising a Series B under time pressure. The case presents two different venture capital term sheets, with the overall challenge of deciding which term sheet to accept and which terms to negotiate to complete the Series B. The competing term sheets each offer advantages and disadvantages.

As with the previous term sheets from ABC Ventures and ProVenture discussed in this book, it is worth noting that the term sheets from Skappa Ventures and Hippogriff Ventures are again variations around a common set of themes. They are structured, organised and written in slightly different styles but, broadly speaking, cover the same general themes. Again, it is important for entrepreneurial teams to cut through these variations and identify the really important issues at hand, and those terms that may affect them significantly if not negotiated firmly. It is important to remember that not all of the factors for deciding between VCs lie within the term sheets, and it is important to understand the background and philosophy of different VCs. Which one will make the biggest money plus impact and which one will be the best to work with?

Readers are advised to study the case and answer the questions set at the end to gain an in-depth understanding of real-life venture capital deal terms before returning to read the summary of Chapter 8. The case answers can be found at the end of the book.

Case Study

SolidEx: Raising Capital to Grow

SolidEx Inc. was poised to raise a substantial Series B financing round to develop its solid-state battery technology for electric vehicles (EVs) from lab scale to commercial prototyping. The Series B would allow the company to test its battery platform over the next 2 years and position the business for a strategic partnership with one or more EV manufacturers. SolidEx management had put in place a first-rate technical team and had equipped the business with the best testing facilities available in order to move forward aggressively. The payroll and overheads had grown to match SolidEx's ambition and cash reserves were starting to dwindle. With 6 months of cash remaining in the bank, the SolidEx board launched an ambitious £40,000,000 financing round to finance its ambitious strategy.

Background

SolidEx was the brainchild of David Chamberlain, Professor of Physics at a leading university. Fifteen years of research with three colleagues had resulted in SolidEx spinning out as an independent company in 2021.

The solid-state battery technology they had developed was intended to provide EVs with ranges up to 800 miles and the ability to recharge within 15 minutes at rapid charging stations. Chamberlain and many others believed that range and speed of charge were key to the universal adoption of EVs. Chamberlain's research had already spawned a series of licensing deals with EV manufacturers keen to place their bets on the future of solid-state batteries and the university had filed a wide range of patents in the field.

At 55, David Chamberlain's intellectual star shone brightly, and his commercial acumen had guided SolidEx to a position of strength in this burgeoning industry. As part-time CEO of SolidEx he knew, however, that he was going to have to step aside for a professional CEO to be hired, one who could grow the business and jump the many hurdles that undoubtedly lay ahead. As he put it: 'I created a racehorse, but we need a jockey to run the race.' He felt that the Series B round was the right moment for the process to hire a new CEO to begin.

Spin Out, Seed Funding and Series A

David Chamberlain and three colleagues had developed the core technology for SolidEx over the course of 15 years. They were all named inventors on the patents filed by the university and assigned to the company at its launch in January 2021. The five academic founders received equity in the new venture (with Chamberlain receiving the lion's share) amounting to 59% of the equity. They were awarded the collective right to appoint a director onto the board of SolidEx and Chamberlain had been nominated as the Founder Director. More importantly, as part of the spin-out deal he stepped into the role of part-time CEO and worked tirelessly to promote opportunities for the company whilst retaining his position at the university.

The 2021 spin-out process had been closely followed by an £800,000 seed funding round led by Circadian Capital, with a £200,000 investment from its latest £80,000,000 venture capital fund (launched the previous year). This was a tiny investment for Circadian's fund, which could invest up to £8,000,000 over the life of any single portfolio company, but the VCs at Circadian wanted an early stake in SolidEx in the anticipation that they could invest pro rata over a series of rounds. The five founders had also invested (£100,000 from Chamberlain and £50,000 from each of the other founders). It was unusual for academic founders to invest so much of their own cash into spin-outs, and this had been a factor in Circadian's decision to invest so early.

The University Seed Fund (launched 3 years previously to back spin-outs) also invested £250,000 in the seed round. This figure was the university's maximum commitment to a single financing round and half the total it was permitted to invest over the life of any individual spin-out. The remaining £50,000 in the seed round was invested by business angel and former automobile executive Roger Agan, who regularly attended university technology show-case events. He was well known by the university hierarchy and had received an Honorary Doctorate for his work developing innovations in the auto industry. The investment from Agan had been an important factor in persuading the university to invest its maximum allocation in the company's seed round.

On completion of the seed investment round, the university appointed a Nominee Director – Thomas Cooper. Calvin Hughes joined the board as the Nominee Director of Circadian Capital. Hughes was an experienced VC who had plenty of early-stage experience. He understood the complex personal dynamics that sometimes swirled around early-stage boards and had seen many of the pitfalls that SolidEx would undoubtedly face.

Summary of £800,000 seed round	
University Seed Fund	£ 250,000
David Chamberlain	£ 100,000
Founders	£ 200,000
Circadian Capital III LP	£ 200,000
Roger Agan	£ 50,000
All Ordinary Shares	
Post-money valuation of round	*£2,500,000*

Just over a year later, SolidEx had pulled off the unexpected coup of raising its next significant financing round earlier than antici-pated. Chamberlain had been active on the conference circuit, telling the SolidEx story wherever and whenever he could. His talk had caught the eye of Vivien Smith, a trained engineer now work-ing as a Junior Partner at Vertigon Ventures, a large generalist investment fund primarily investing the family wealth behind a long-established industrial conglomerate. Vertigon took a long-term view and during her first year in the role, Smith had been given the freedom to make some early-stage bets in the battery and energy storage field. Having been specifically recruited to find opportunities such as SolidEx, she saw this as her opportunity to make an impact and quickly engaged Chamberlain in discussions.

Over the course of 2 months, SolidEx and Vertigon negotiated the terms of the Series A round (the first 'serious' venture capital round after the seed round). The round was to be £5 million – led by Vertigon and supported by follow-on investments on the same terms from Circadian, the University Seed Fund and Roger Agan. This investment took the University Seed Fund to its maximum commitment level and Agan to the highest amount he had ever invested in a single company. Chamberlain had negotiated a good step up in the pre-money valuation to just over £11.6 million, thus protecting the founders' initial shareholding – a remarkable achievement for a part-time CEO.

Summary of £5,000,000 Series A round	
Vertigon Ventures	£3,000,000
Circadian Capital III LP	£1,650,000
University Seed Fund	£ 250,000
Roger Agan	£ 100,000

Series A shares: all non-participating preference shares

In return for agreeing to this step up in valuation, however, Vertigon insisted on two conditions:

1. The Series A round would be in non-participating preferred shares, giving Vertigon some 'down-side protection' given the substantial step up in share price from £2.50 in the seed round to £10.00 in Series A.

2. A stock option pool equivalent to 10% of the total shares in SolidEx post-Series A investment would have to be created *prior* to the round. This means the pre-money valuation was effectively reduced to £10 million. Vertigon's argument, which the existing shareholders ultimately accepted, was that an option pool should have been in place from the beginning and Vertigon and other Series A investors should not suffer dilution if it was created after the round. The option pool was intended to recruit and retain management for an aggressive growth strategy proposed by Vertigon and aimed at positioning SolidEx to develop a commercially viable battery by 2023.

Vivien Smith joined the SolidEx board on completion of the funding round in April 2022 and, with cautious support from the other directors, developed a more aggressive stance towards growth. This included the board giving Chamberlain the mandate to set about hiring numerous key management positions for an accelerated product launch.

	Ordinary Shares					
	Spin out	Seed[a]	Option Pool[b]	Series A[c]	Total	(%)[d]
Vertigon-	-			3,000	3,000	18
Circadian	-	800		1,650	2,450	14.7
University	2,800	1,000		250	4,050	24.3
D Chamberlain	2,000	400		-	2,400	14.4
Roger Agan	-	200		100	300	1.8
Founders	2,000	800		-	2,800	16.8
Option Pool	-	-	1,675	-	1,675	10
Shares Issued	6,800	3,200		5,000		
Total Shares	6,800	10,000	11,675	16,675	16,675	100

[a]Seed round share price £2.50 per share.
[b]Option pool created in ordinary shares immediately pre-Series A.
[c]Series A share price £10 per share in non-participating preference shares.
[d](%) is fully diluted assuming all options are issued.

Building for Success

SolidEx was now growing faster than the founders (including Chamberlain) had ever anticipated. The chance to 'win big' was consistent with the risk profile of VCs such as Vertigon and Circadian but it had risks too. Indeed, 'win big… or fail early' was a mantra often used by VCs who adopted a portfolio approach to investments. They pushed hard for success and often structured investments to minimise losses to their funds in the event of individual company failure, and this made the ordinary shareholders nervous.

Regardless of differences in philosophy between the founders and the VCs, the entire board agreed that a rapid expansion of the management team was required if the first product was to be launched. An early decision following the completion of the Series A round was the recruitment of a new director to the board with experience in the battery industry. There had for some time been an opening on the board and Sarah Klein was a long-standing friend of David Chamberlain who had advised him through the spin-out process. Chamberlain had put her forward to fill the vacant spot just prior to the Series A completion and with the agreement of Vertigon and Circadian she joined the board on the day of completion. It was hoped by Roger Agan and Tom Cooper that she would provide a sense of balance to the board, perhaps reigning in the ambitions of the Investor Directors Vivien Smith and Calvin Hughes. In return for joining the board she was awarded 0.25% of the equity via the newly created option pool.[1]

A further 4.75% was awarded to incoming new management, including a Chief Engineering Officer, a Director of Intellectual Property and a Chief Operating Officer. This left 5% of the pool available for future hires.

Building towards its commercial prototypes, SolidEx had grown to 25 full-time employees by August 2022 and was rapidly approaching a cash burn rate that would see it requiring a new financing round early in 2023. During the dying days of summer 2022 Chamberlain worked hard with the management team to develop a comprehensive budget to hit its targets within 2 years. The draft budget was presented to the board at the September board meeting...

September 2022

A collective gasp went around the boardroom as Chamberlain presented his business plan, which called for a £40,000,000 funding round. This was more than anyone expected and a lengthy, at times ill-tempered, debate followed. Subsequent follow-up calls over the next 10 days and a series of modifications to the budget eventually led the board to approve the broad plan. Chamberlain had the go-ahead for £40,000,000 fundraising to deliver commercially viable prototypes within a 2-year time frame. But this was a much bigger round than the board and investors had expected. Even Vivien Smith and Calvin Hughes, the Investor Directors from Vertigon and Circadian, were surprised and questioned whether their own funds could invest pro rata in such a large fundraising. Their funds would likely be expected to reinvest their share of the financing round and for Vertigon this meant 18% of the round (£7,200,000). Similarly for Circadian 14.27% of the round meant £5,700,000 and this would push Circadian close to its maximum commitment for any single investment. Worse still, if the company failed to raise sufficient external investment in time, Vertigon and Circadian may be expected to fill the gap which would be near impossible.[2]

By this stage, SolidEx's burn rate meant the company had 6 months of cash remaining in the bank, and the financing process would have to begin immediately.[3]

SolidEx board composition at the launch of Series B	
Academic Founder/CEO:	Prof. David Chamberlain
University Nominee Director:	Thomas Cooper
Series A Nominee Director:	Vivien Smith, Vertigon Ventures
Seed Round Nominee Director:	Calvin Hughes, Circadian Ventures
Non-Executive Director:	Sarah Klein
Non-Executive Director:	Roger Agan

Chamberlain wasted no time. He set about approaching contacts in the venture capital industry introduced by his existing investors and other board members.

In the following weeks there were regular board updates during which Chamberlain would report on progress and board members would offer new ideas on VCs to approach or focus on. During a series of particularly tense weekly calls, the board urged Chamberlain to have at least one term sheet offering to invest in the company by Christmas or steps would have to be taken to conserve cost – and that meant reducing SolidEx's headcount and reversing the aggressive strategy that Chamberlain and the board had agreed. The company would run out of cash by the end of April 2023 at the very latest and, given the time taken to complete venture capital financing rounds, Christmas was becoming a deadline by which decisions would have to be made. Chamberlain was not used to failure and redoubled efforts to raise the round.

Christmas 2022

David Chamberlain, leading physicist and part-time CEO, did not disappoint. By mid-December, following approaches to more than 25 venture capital funds and extensive discussions with several of them, two term sheets were duly received by Chamberlain from VCs who were prepared to lead the round (see Annex I and Annex II). Chamberlain had been skilful in creating just the right amount of competitive tension amongst the VCs he talked to, and this had prompted rival term sheets from Skappa Ventures and Hippogriff Capital, two well-known VCs who were different in both style and scale (see Annex III).

Chamberlain reviewed the term sheets and circulated them to the board by email with a request for feedback in a board meeting via Teams scheduled for 5pm on 17th December 2022.

It all seemed to come down to a set of clear decisions for the board. Chamberlain prepared for the call with a set of recommendations, but ultimately the board had to be aligned on the course of action. As 5pm approached, Chamberlain activated the Teams meeting and began to speak...

Put yourself in the position of an advisor to the Board of SolidEx and consider the following questions:

1. What are the key differences between the Skappa and Hippogriff term sheets?
2. How should SolidEx respond to the offers and what issues does the board need to consider in fulfilling its duty to all shareholders?

3. As written, which term sheet (if any) do you feel SolidEx should accept?
4. What key points do you believe you could negotiate? How would you go about the negotiation process?
5. If you could negotiate some of your key points successfully, how would that change your attitude towards the best investors for the SolidEx Series B?

Annex I: Skappa Term Sheet sent 16th December 2022

SKAPPA VENTURES (IV) LP

SUMMARY OF TERMS FOR PROPOSED FINANCING (16TH DECEMBER 2022)

Skappa Ventures IV LP (SKVIV LP) proposes, subject to contract, due diligence, investment committee approval and the following terms and conditions to invest a minimum of £50,000,000 in SolidEx Limited (the 'Company') as part of a total equity investment round of up to £60,000,000 (the 'Investment').

Amount and form of investment:

Investor Syndicate	SKVIV LP £50,000,000; existing SolidEx investors £10,000,000 (together 'the Investors').
Aggregate amount of financing	£60,000,000 in newly issued Series B Preferred Shares.
Pre-money valuation (fully diluted)	£80,000,000 to include a 10% available stock option pool post-investment for granting to new and existing management.
Post-money valuation	£140,000,000
Use of proceeds	The funds raised by this round of investment shall be used for operational capital expenditures and general working capital purposes directed towards the launch of SolidEx's commercially viable prototype.

Form of investment	The Investment will take place in two phases, the second phase being conditional upon certain key business milestones ('The Milestones') by the Company:

Phase 1: On completion of the Investment ('Initial Completion'), the Investors will subscribe a total of £30,000,000 for new B Preference shares in the Company.

Phase 2: In the event the Company completes The Milestones described below within 12 months of Initial Completion, the Investors will subscribe a further £30,000,000 for new B Preference shares in the Company.

The Milestones	The relevant milestones for the second phase of the financing are:

1. SolidEx to demonstrate a commercially viable prototype battery to the satisfaction of SKVIV LP within 12 months from the Initial Completion.

2. SolidEx to have established a commercial partnership with an automobile manufacturer generating at least £5,000,000 in revenue via upfront payments within 12 months from the Initial Completion.

3. The Board to have appointed an experienced CEO to the satisfaction of SKVIV LP within 12 months from the Initial Completion.

The Investors may agree to defer or delay any Milestone deadline, or to waive any Milestone in their absolute discretion. If relevant milestones for the second phase are not achieved, the Investors have the right to withhold all or a portion of the investment and/or renegotiate the terms of that investment.

Share rights:

Dividend

The B Preference shares shall rank *pari passu* in all respects as to dividend with the ordinary shares in the capital of the Company ('Ordinary Shares').

Liquidation and sale preference

A mechanism will be included to ensure that upon the liquidation (or other return of capital) or sale of the Company, the holders of the B Preference shares will first be entitled to receive an amount equal to all arrears of dividends on the B Preference shares and 2.0× the subscription price for their B Preference shares together with an amount equal to 8% per annum of the subscription price of the B Preference shares compounded in priority to any distribution to holders of any other class of shares. Any balance shall then be distributed first to the holders of the Preferred A shares who shall be entitled to receive the subscription price for the Preferred A shares (together with any accrued or unpaid dividends) and thereafter equally between all shareholders (pro rata to shareholdings and on an as-if converted basis).

Conversion

The Investors will have the right to convert their B Preference shares at any time into Ordinary Shares on a one for one basis. The B Preference shares will automatically convert on a Qualifying Offering or on the written election of the holders of a majority of the B Preference shares. A 'Qualifying Offering' shall mean a listing which is at a public offering price per Ordinary Share of not less than five times the subscription price for each B Preference share and which raises a total of not less than £200,000,000 after underwriting expenses and commissions.

Voting rights

The Ordinary Shares and B Preference shares will carry one vote per share.

Share issues and transfers:

Pre-emptive rights on issue and transfer	If new shares are issued or a shareholder proposes to sell any shares (excluding shares issued in connection with the 'Option Pool' or pursuant to any agreed permitted transfers), these shares will first have to be offered to SKVIV LP. Any transferee or new shareholder shall be required to enter into a deed of adherence to any shareholders' agreement.
Transfer restrictions	The Founders may not transfer their shares in the capital of the Company except with the consent of the Investor or to immediate family members or family trusts.
Tag rights	At the option of the Investors, upon any sale of shares by a shareholder (not being an agreed permitted transfer), the selling shareholder will have to ensure that the purchaser acquires an equivalent proportion of shares from the Investor on the same terms.
Drag rights	At any time after 3 years from completion of this Investment, if no sale or IPO has occurred, SKVIV LP shall have the right to initiate and conduct a formal sales process in which the Company and all shareholders will co-operate and the Investor shall have the ability to force all members to sell their shares to a bona fide third-party offeror on terms no less preferential in all material respects than are available to them.
Compulsory transfer	In the event that a Founder/Manager leaves the Company in circumstances involving his being summarily dismissed by reason of fraud, dishonesty or gross misconduct of such Founder/Manager (a 'Bad Leaver'), such Founder/Manager will be required to transfer all of his shares to the Company at the lower of the Subscription Price (being theamount paid up or credited as paid up on a share,

(Continued)

(Continued)

including the full amount of any premium at which such share was issued) of such shares.

If a Founder/Manager leaves the Company but is not a Bad Leaver (a 'Good Leaver'), a proportion of his shares may, if the Investor so determines, be subject to transfer or repurchase by the Company at the Subscription Price of such shares at such time.

The shares of Founders/Managers who are Good Leavers will vest on the following schedule: 25% upon Initial Completion, 25% on the first anniversary of Initial Completion, and thereafter will vest on a quarterly basis starting on the date which is 3 months after the first anniversary of Initial Completion and on each 3-month date thereafter to a maximum of 100% vested (on the third anniversary of Initial Completion).

If the Company issues additional shares (excluding shares issued to employees in the form of share options or shares issued on the conversion of B Preference shares) at a subscription price less than that paid by the Investor in this Investment (a 'Down Round'), the number of shares acquired by the Investor in this Investment will be adjusted on a weighted average basis. Any such further shares shall be issued to the Investor by way of a bonus issue or by way of a cash subscription at par. The number of further shares shall be calculated in accordance with the mechanism currently in place, updated to reflect the terms of this investment.

The Board:

Board composition

The Board will comprise of a maximum of 5 directors in the first instance. The composition of the board upon Initial Completion will be:

1. CEO of SolidEx (initially David Chamberlain).
2. One Director nominated by SKVIV LP.

(Continued)

(Continued)

3. One Director nominated by Series A investors.

4. One Director nominated by the Founders of SolidEx (it is intended that David Chamberlain will be appointed in this role following recruitment of a CEO).

5. One Director selected as an industry expert by the remaining members of the Board subject to the approval of the SKVIV LP Director.

Investor director/observer

SKVIV LP shall have the right to appoint (1) one member of the board and (2) a non-voting observer to attend board meetings for so long as it holds an interest in the Company. The Company will not be required to remunerate directors/ observers appointed by investors or reimburse expenses incurred in the normal course of attending board meetings.

Veto rights:

SKVIV LP will have the right to consent in relation to specific matters having a material effect on the value or structure of the Investment and/or having a material effect on the operation and/or management of the Company. Such matters shall include, but will not be limited to (i) any further issue of shares; (ii) any amendment to the Company's constitutional documents or the rights attaching to any shares; (iii) any sale or listing; (iv) any liquidation or winding up of the Company; (v) borrowings which in aggregate exceed £250,000; (vi) acquisitions and disposals; (vii) varying or making any binding decision on the terms of employment of any of the Founders or any other senior employee or increasing or varying the salary or other benefits of any such person; (viii) the appointment or removal of any person as a director; (ix) the conduct of material litigation; and (x) the implementation of or variation to any share option or pension scheme.

Information rights:	The Investors will be entitled to receive monthly management accounts within 10 days of the month end, audited annual accounts within 90 days of the year end, an annual budget before 30 days prior to the next financial year, board agendas, minutes and related board papers and any other information reasonably requested by the Investor.

Founders/Managers:

Employment and restrictions on Founders/Managers	The Founders/Managers will enter into service agreements with the Company, to be agreed with the Investor prior to Initial Completion, which will contain appropriate protections in favour of the Company, including restrictive covenants and provisions dealing with the Company's ownership of intellectual property. In addition, the Founders/Managers will in the shareholders' investment documentation give 12-month non-competition and non-solicitation undertakings in favour of the Investor.
Option pool	Ten per cent (10%) of the fully diluted equity shares at Initial Completion will be reserved for issue to new employees pursuant to a share incentive plan to be adopted as soon as practicable following Initial Completion and as approved by the Investor.
Warranties and indemnities:	The Investor shall be entitled to receive warranties and indemnities from the Company and the Founders/Managers on a joint and several basis, as are customary in a transaction of this nature. This will include, but not be limited to, warranties relating to the business plan, accounts, management accounts, litigation, employees and intellectual property.

(Continued)

Skappa Ventures (IV) LP **229**

(Continued)

There will be individual caps on liability for the Founders/Managers, capped at £200,000 each and the Company, capped at the aggregate amount of the Investment together in both cases with the costs of recovery.

Pre-conditions to completion:

This Investment shall be conditional upon the following conditions being met prior to Initial Completion:

- Commercial due diligence on all aspects of SolidEx's business plan to be completed to the satisfaction of SKVIV LP.

- Development of an appropriate strategy and short list of partners for the pharmaceutical collaboration outlined in milestone 2 to the satisfaction of SKVIV LP.

- Execution of definitive legal documentation to be drafted by SKVIV LP'S legal counsel Marcher & Fellows LLP according to the terms of this term sheet.

- Appropriate legal, tax and accounting due diligence to be completed to the satisfaction of SKVIV LP.

General:

Costs

SolidEx will be responsible for SKVIV LP's reasonable expenses in connection with the Investment on Initial Completion or will be so responsible if during the exclusivity period SolidEx withdraws without reasonable cause or SKVIV LP withdraws as a result of the pre-conditions to completion failing to be met, subject to a maximum of £50,000.

Timing

The Company, the Founders/Managers and SKVIV LP agree to use their best efforts to sign definitive legal documentation to complete this round of investment on or before 30th April 2023.

Raising the Next Round

Confidentiality

The terms of this term sheet and the fact that SKVIV LP is considering making an investment in the Company shall remain strictly confidential and may not be disclosed to any other parties except to respective professional advisers under terms of confidentiality.

Exclusivity

In consideration of SKVIV LP committing time, money and resources to conduct its due diligence on the Company and draft, and negotiate the definitive legal documentation, the Company agrees not to discuss any potential investment in the Company or to continue or initiate any such discussions with any other potential investors. This shall not preclude the Company entering into agreements in the ordinary course of business with potential commercial partners to be agreed with SKVIV LP. This right shall expire at 12:00 am on 30th April 2023.

Governing law

This term sheet and the definitive legal documentation required to effect the Investment shall be governed by and are to be construed in accordance with the laws of England and Wales the parties hereby agree to submit to the exclusive jurisdiction of the English courts.

Legal effect

This term sheet is not legally binding save that this section and the sections regarding costs, exclusivity, confidentiality and governing law will be binding immediately upon the Company countersigning this term sheet.

We agree to the terms and conditions set out above:

....

for and on behalf of SKVIV LP

....
Date

....

for and on behalf of SolidEx

....
Date

Annex II: Hippogriff Term Sheet sent 17th December 2022

HIPPOGRIFF CAPITAL (II) LP

TERM SHEET FOR PROPOSED INVESTMENT (17/12/2022)

Hippogriff Capital II LP (HCII LP) proposes, subject to contract, due diligence, investment committee approval and the following terms and conditions to invest up to £12,000,000 in SolidEx Limited (the 'Company') as part of a total equity investment round of up to £40,000,000 (the 'Investment').

Amount and form of investment:

Investor Syndicate	HCII LP £12,000,000; Additional Investors £16,000,000 to be identified and agreed by Hippogriff and SolidEx; Existing SolidEx investors £12,000,000 (together 'the Investors').
Aggregate amount of financing	£40,000,000 in newly issued B Preference shares.
Pre-money valuation (fully diluted)	£60,000,000 to include a 10% available stock option pool post-investment for granting to new and existing management (it is the understanding of Hippogriff that SolidEx currently has 5% of its equity available as unissued options).
Post-money valuation	£100,000,000
Use of proceeds	The funds raised by this round of investment shall be used for operational capital expenditures and general working capital purposes directed towards the launch of SolidEx's first prototype.

Share rights:

Dividend	The B Preference shares shall rank *pari passu* in all respects as to dividend with the ordinary shares in the capital of the Company ('Ordinary Shares').

232   Raising the Next Round

Liquidation and sale preference

A mechanism will be included to ensure that upon the liquidation (or other return of capital) or sale of the Company, the holders of the B Preference shares will first be entitled to receive an amount equal to all arrears of dividends on the B Preference shares and the subscription price for their B Preference shares together with an amount equal to 6% per annum on the subscription price of the B Preference shares in priority to any distribution to holders of any other class of shares. Any balance shall then be distributed to the Ordinary shareholders in proportion to their shareholding.

Conversion

The Investors will have the right to convert their B Preference shares at any time into Ordinary Shares on a one for one basis. The B Preference shares will automatically convert on a Qualifying Offering or on the written election of the holders of a majority of the B Preference shares. A 'Qualifying Offering' shall mean a listing which is at a public offering price per Ordinary Share of not less than five times the subscription price for each B Preference share and which raises a total of not less than £100,000,000 after underwriting expenses and commissions.

Voting rights

The Ordinary Shares and B Preference shares will carry one vote per share.

Share issues and transfers:

Pre-emptive rights on issue and transfer

If new shares are issued or a shareholder proposes to sell any shares (excluding shares issued in connection with the 'Option Pool' or pursuant to any agreed permitted transfers), these shares will first have to be offered to the Investors on a proportionate basis. Any transferee or new shareholder shall be required to enter into a deed of adherence to any shareholders' agreement.

Hippogriff Capital (II) LP   **233**

Transfer restrictions	The Founders may not transfer their shares in the capital of the Company except with the consent of the Investor or to immediate family members or family trusts.
Tag rights	At the option of the Investors, upon any sale of shares by a shareholder (not being an agreed permitted transfer), the selling shareholder will have to ensure that the purchaser acquires an equivalent proportion of shares from the Investor on the same terms.
Drag rights	At any time after 3 years from completion of this Investment, if no sale or IPO has occurred, HCII LP shall have the right to initiate and conduct a formal sales process in which the Company and all shareholders will co-operate and the Investor shall have the ability to force all members to sell their shares to a bona fide third party offeror on terms no less preferential in all material respects than are available to them.
Compulsory transfer	In the event that a Founder/Manager leaves the Company in circumstances involving his being summarily dismissed by reason of fraud, dishonesty or gross misconduct of such Founder/Manager (a 'Bad Leaver'), such Founder/Manager will be required to transfer all of his shares to the Company at the lower of the Subscription Price (being the amount paid up or credited as paid up on a share, including the full amount of any premium at which such share was issued) of such shares.
	If a Founder/Manager leaves the Company but is not a Bad Leaver (a 'Good Leaver'), a proportion of their shares may, if the Investor so determines, be subject to transfer or repurchase by the Company at the Subscription Price of such shares at such time.

(Continued)

(Continued)

The shares of Founders/Managers who are Good Leavers will vest on the following schedule: 25% upon Initial Completion and thereafter will vest on a quarterly basis starting on the date which is 3 months after the first anniversary of Initial Completion and on each 3-month date thereafter to a maximum of 100% vested (on the fourth anniversary of Initial Completion).

Anti-dilution

If the Company issues additional shares (excluding shares issued to employees in the form of share options or shares issued on the conversion of B Preference shares) at a subscription price less than that paid by the Investor in this Investment (a 'Down Round'), the number of shares acquired by the Investor in this Investment will be adjusted on a weighted average basis. Any such further shares shall be issued to the Investor by way of a bonus issue or by way of a cash subscription at par. The number of further shares shall be calculated in accordance with the mechanism currently in place, updated to reflect the terms of this investment.

Board position:

Board composition

The Board will comprise of a maximum of 7 directors. The composition of the board upon Initial Completion will be:
- CEO of SolidEx.
- One Director nominated by HCII LP.
- One Director nominated by Vertigon Ventures.
- One Director nominated by Circadian Capital.
- One Director nominated by the University.
- One Director nominated by the Founders.
- One Director selected by the remaining members of the Board based on their industry experience.

Investor director/ observer	HCII LP shall have the right to appoint (1) one member of the board and (2) a non-voting observer to attend board meetings for so long as it holds an interest in the Company. In addition, the Additional New Investors will have the right to appoint a non-voting observer as long as they hold an interest in the Company. The Company will reimburse directors and observers for reasonable expenses incurred in the normal course of attending board meetings.
Veto rights:	HCII LP will have the right to consent in relation to specific matters having a material effect on the value or structure of the Investment and/or having a material effect on the operation and/or management of the Company. Such matters shall include, but will not be limited to (i) any further issue of shares; (ii) any amendment to the Company's constitutional documents or the rights attaching to any shares; (iii) any sale or listing; (iv) any liquidation or winding up of the Company; (v) borrowings which in aggregate exceed £100,000; (vi) acquisitions and disposals; (vii) varying or making any binding decision on the terms of employment of any of the Founders or any other senior employee or increasing or varying the salary or other benefits of any such person; (viii) the appointment or removal of any person as a director; (ix) the conduct of material litigation; and (x) the implementation of or variation to any share option or pension scheme.
Information rights:	The Investors will be entitled to receive monthly management accounts within 10 days of the month end, audited annual accounts within 90 days of the year end, an annual budget before 30 days prior to the next financial year, board agendas, minutes and related board papers and any other information reasonably requested by the Investor.

Founders/Managers:

Employment and restrictions on Founders/Managers	The Founders/Managers will enter into service agreements with the Company, to be agreed with the Investor prior to Initial Completion, which will contain appropriate protections in favour of the Company including restrictive covenants and provisions dealing with the Company's ownership of intellectual property. In addition, the Founders/Managers will in the shareholders' investment documentation give 12-month non-competition and non-solicitation undertakings in favour of the Investor.
Option pool	Ten per cent (10%) of the fully diluted equity shares at Initial Completion will be reserved for issue to new employees pursuant to a share incentive plan to be adopted as soon as practicable following Initial Completion and as approved by the Investor.

Warranties and indemnities:

The Investor shall be entitled to receive warranties and indemnities from the Company and the Founders/Managers on a joint and several basis, as are customary in a transaction of this nature. This will include, but not be limited to, warranties relating to the business plan, accounts, management accounts, litigation, employees and intellectual property.

There will be individual caps on liability for the Founders/Managers, capped at £100,000 each and the Company, capped at the aggregate amount of the Investment together in both cases with the costs of recovery.

Pre-conditions to completion:	This Investment shall be conditional upon the following conditions being met prior to Initial Completion: • SolidEx shareholders to agree that all existing Preferred Shares in SolidEx are converted to Ordinary Shares at Initial Completion. • A new commercially experienced CEO for SolidEx to be hired to the satisfaction of HCII LP. • Appropriate commercial, legal, tax and accounting due diligence to be completed to the satisfaction of HCII LP. • Execution of definitive legal documentation to be drafted by HCII LP'S legal counsel Masters and Smith LLP according to the terms of this term sheet.

General:

Costs	SolidEx will be responsible for HCII LP's reasonable expenses in connection with the Investment on Initial Completion or will be so responsible if during the exclusivity period SolidEx withdraws without reasonable cause or HCII LP withdraws because of the pre-conditions to completion failing to be met, subject to a maximum of £70,000.
Timing	The Company, the Founders/Managers and HCII LP agree to use their best efforts to sign definitive legal documentation to complete this round of investment on or before 14th July 2023.
Confidentiality	The terms of this term sheet and the fact that HCII LP is considering making an investment in the Company shall remain strictly confidential and may not be disclosed to any other parties except to respective professional advisers under terms of confidentiality.

238   Raising the Next Round

Exclusivity	In consideration of HCII LP committing time, money and resources to conduct its due diligence on the Company and draft, and negotiate the definitive legal documentation, the Company agrees not to discuss any potential investment in the Company or to continue or initiate any such discussions with any other potential investors. This shall not preclude the Company entering into agreements in the ordinary course of business with potential commercial partners to be agreed with HCII LP. This right shall expire at 12:00am on 14th July 2023.
Governing law	This term sheet and the definitive legal documentation required to affect the Investment shall be governed by and are to be construed in accordance with the laws of England and Wales the parties hereby agree to submit to the exclusive jurisdiction of the English courts.
Legal effect	This term sheet is not legally binding save that this section and the sections regarding costs, exclusivity, confidentiality, and governing law will be binding immediately upon the Company countersigning this term sheet.

We agree to the terms and conditions set out above:

....

for and on behalf of HCII LP   Date

....

for and on behalf of SolidEx   Date

Annex III: Background to Skappa Ventures and Hippogriff Ventures

Skappa Ventures

Skappa Ventures was a London-based venture capital firm established in 1998 specialising in the technology sector. Skappa Ventures Fund I (launched in 2006) and Fund II (launched in 2012) were successful profitable funds and the firm developed a reputation for driving portfolio companies rapidly to high-value IPOs.

Skappa had developed a reputation for having the golden touch based on Fund I and Fund II and its portfolio companies had benefited from the halo effect this created. Customers, investors and competitors alike tended to sit up and listen once a company had been blessed by an investment from Skappa. Skappa Ventures Fund III was launched in 2017 and had delivered a number of exits but was too early in its lifecycle to have delivered positive returns to its investors.

The firm, however, also had the reputation for being aggressive and reshaping the management teams and boards of its investee companies early in the investment process. The Skappa partners had a belief in their own way of doing things and aimed to be the dominant shareholder. There were a few examples within Skappa's portfolio of underperforming companies being cut adrift early and starved of further investment. They were not patient investors and fully subscribed to the 'aim big… fail early' philosophy. Although Skappa was a partnership comprising 8 partners and 15 associates, the founding partner Graham Bourne was believed to be the real decision-maker and had a reputation for making decisions on gut feel, which occasionally varied from week to week. Nothing was a certainty with Skappa.

Despite Skappa III not yet making any returns to investors, Skappa managed to raise Skappa Ventures IV LP, a £500,000,000 10-year LP fund. The fund, launched in 2021, was Skappa's largest to date and had significant funds to deploy in the sector. Skappa IV, being a 2021-vintage fund, was only 1 year into its 5-year investment period at the time it issued a term sheet to SolidEx. This meant it had 9 years of fund life remaining to deliver an exit.[4]

The Skappa partner in charge of the SolidEx deal had been with the firm 4 years, being made up to partner at the beginning of Fund IV. He had a background in investment banking within the energy sector and this would be his second investment as a Skappa partner (although he had worked on more than 10 deals as an associate supporting the other partners). He was aiming to build his reputation within the firm and was championing the SolidEx deal within the partnership.

Hippogriff Capital

Hippogriff Capital was a relatively young UK-based venture capital firm but with relatively old managing partners. The two co-founders of Hippogriff were experienced energy industry veterans (one from the United Kingdom and the other from the Netherlands) who raised their first £50,000,000 venture capital fund in 2007. Hippogriff Capital I LP had achieved modest success so far.

Against a backdrop of market turbulence related to the financial crisis of 2009 and Brexit in 2016, Hippogriff had still managed to raise its second fund, a £160,000,000 10-year LP launched in 2018, although the fund was smaller than the partners had initially hoped (having aimed for a £200,000,000 fund). Hippogriff had the reputation of being relatively patient but with a fund that was a little too small and which may struggle to support its portfolio companies all the way to exit.

At the time Hippogriff issued its term sheet to SolidEx, Fund II was a few months away from the end of its investment period. The Hippogriff portfolio was almost complete and SolidEx would be the last investment prior to moving into the management period. This would give SolidEx 5 years to deliver a financial exit for Hippogriff and other investors.

The partners at Hippogriff had good connections within the energy industry and were liked and respected within the venture capital industry for their straight-talking and honest approach to investing. They were seen as fair and easy to work with by entrepreneurs. They often worked as part of a syndicate with other VCs and were seen as good co-investors to have on board, even if they did not command the same reputation for success as some of the other VCs within the sector. The phrase 'reliable but not dazzling' had occasionally been whispered at venture capital conferences when the Hippogriff team entered the room.

SUMMARY OF CHAPTER 8

This chapter has focused on the unique challenges faced by entrepreneurial teams raising Series B investment rounds and beyond. Many articles and texts written about entrepreneurial finance will focus on raising the first round, as if it is the most challenging step and that further financing rounds will simply fall into place. This chapter has explained that this is usually not the case and that raising Series B and beyond can be just as challenging, albeit with a different set of challenges to manage.

The twin pressures of time and cash will conspire to cause many a sleepless night for the CEOs of growing ventures, never mind the investors who back them. Commitments to aggressive growth models, which result in high burn rates for investor cash, always start the clock ticking in terms of raising the next round. Getting this done in a timely fashion and without interference from external negative events – such as a financial crash – is usually on the wish list of all around the board table.

A large part of this chapter was devoted to a realistic case study, because learning about these unique challenges is best done in a real situation. The case study illustrated the subtle yet significant differences between two competing term sheets, each seemingly offering advantages over the other. Balancing what is good for the business versus the individual demands of existing shareholders is a delicate process and will require agreement from all shareholders who must sign a new shareholders agreement. The risks inherent in completing a new investment round when the board is aware of a diminishing cash balance come to the fore if a deal is derailed. In the case of SolidEx, investors pulling out of a deal when cash is already low in SolidEx's bank account could have proven to be a fatal event, rescued only by the agreement of existing investors to put forward a convertible loan. Convertible loans are used with surprising frequency to extend the cash runways of businesses when they are in the later stages of raising finance. The last thing existing investors and the board wants to see is a negotiation where the company is almost out of cash, for this will impact the valuation more than any other factor. A final lesson from the SolidEx case is that the deal is not done until it really is done, and a term sheet has been transformed into a legally binding shareholders agreement. For an entrepreneurial team in the fortunate position of having multiple term sheets with offers to invest in the business, how they say no to the unsuccessful bidders is important, as they may have to go back to them. This is a people business and positive working relationships with both existing and future investors is important for entrepreneurial teams working towards a successful exit for all.

The next chapter will discuss further challenges in growing the venture and delivering an exit and will include a detailed case study posing questions about how the board handles a potential exit and how it should go about balancing the interests of all shareholders. Exits can often be the most challenging path of the entrepreneurial journey and how the board handles this can be the difference between success and failure.

NOTES

1. Options in the option pool were granted and vested according to SolidEx's option scheme. This meant that options were granted in equal portions over 3 years with a 1-year cliff. The 1-year cliff meant that at the first anniversary of the option grant, a third of the total granted options 'vested' to the employee with the remaining two-thirds granting over the remaining 2 years. If the employee left within the first year of the grant they received no options – hence the 'cliff'. This was typical in the industry and was aimed at preventing early leavers from becoming shareholders in the company.
2. Smith and Hughes exchanged numerous emails and phone calls over the course of the week to share their thoughts on the risks of going for a £40,000,000 round but the numbers Chamberlain produced were irrefutable and clearly supported by evidence. Eventually they both agreed with the fundraising and began to work together on how they would position the investment round to their own colleagues at their respective venture capital funds. They both believed the SolidEx story

and were convinced that if the company could deliver close to its plan, then significant financial returns would follow.

3. Timelines for a typical venture capital fundraising process can easily exceed 6 months.

4. Within the vast majority of venture capital funds, the first 5 years of an LP agreement are typically referred to as the 'investment period', when VCs identify and invest in new opportunities; the second 5-year period is referred to as the 'management period' and is the period during which VCs aim to exit investments. The management period usually has a lower management fee for the venture capital firm.

Chapter 9

Towards the Exit

DEFINING THE EXIT

Perhaps a book on venture capital ought to begin with this chapter. One of the key themes of the venture capital process is that exit opportunities are a prerequisite of any investment. VCs may even be thinking about the exit before, during and after the first pitch from an entrepreneurial team; they must see at least an opportunity to exit before they consider going forward with their evaluation of an investment. As the company grows and raises a series of investment rounds from an increasing number of investors, hopefully at a higher share price than previously, the attention of the entire board begins to shift towards growing an exit.

An exit involves the liberation of value and its subsequent distribution to the shareholders. Start-ups raise cash and transform it into value. Value is generated via a series of value inflexion points dependent upon achieving tangible milestones, and these milestones may relate to a range of activities such as generating intellectual property, gathering data, achieving revenue growth or profitability. The value created, however, is locked inside the firm

245

until exit: the moment when value is unlocked and distributed as cash to investors, entrepreneurs and employees alike. Most often this occurs via a sale of all or part of the firm (the bedrock of the M&A industry) or by selling shares on the public markets following an IPO or some other means of achieving share liquidity.

Whilst entrepreneurs might dream of the riches generated by the sale of a rapidly growing tech company to a global corporate, there is also a darker side to exits. Exits are sometimes the moment when inequities, both real and perceived, may bubble to the surface; founders and key members of the entrepreneurial team might feel there is not enough 'in the deal' for them, layers of preference shares in the preference cascade might result in some groups of shareholders emerging from an exit better or worse off than others. The impact of preferred and preference shares on exits was discussed in detail using a range of examples earlier in the book, with the conclusion that they have a great impact on poor to moderate exits. When things have not gone to plan, emotions are high and in such febrile environments scores are settled and wrangling ensues between different groups of shareholders.

If we view the series of financing rounds raised by a start-up simply as cash inflows to the company, then the exit can be viewed simply as a reversal of that investment cash flow (see Figure 9.1). The cash invested in the growing venture by a series of optimistic investors is finally returned to them all at the same time (and hopefully at a premium), giving them a good return on their risky investment. Since the venture capital business model and the carried interest remuneration system depend on buying low and selling high, an exit is an absolute necessity to return cash and profits to those investors and to distribute carried interest to the venture capital fund managers who raised a fund from them with the promise of great returns.

Such a simplistic view of a single exit event returning cash to investors is, of course, somewhat removed from reality. Exits occurring via the sale of a business will sometimes involve a series of smaller, partial exit events, perhaps with an initial upfront payment and then a series of further payments (called 'deferred payments') based on achieving a set of commercial goals agreed as a condition of the sale.

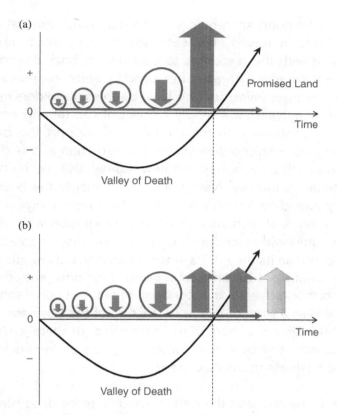

Figure 9.1 Exits are a simple reversal of investment cash flow.
Exits may be thought of as a reversal of the investment cash flows into start-ups as they complete their entrepreneurial financing journey across the Valleys of Death. In the simple example in (a), a single exit event (e.g. a trade sale via M&A) occurs, enabling the return of a healthy capital gain to those investors who invested at various stages of the company's growth. They are all repaid at the same time according to the shareholders agreement in which all shareholders are tied together until exit, observing the preference cascade that may alter returns to different groups of shareholders. A more common scenario is that exits like this occur via a series of payments shown in (b), in which there may be an upfront payment followed by a series of deferred payments contingent on the achievement of certain milestones such as revenue targets.

WHY IS AN EXIT NEEDED?

An exit is not just the liberation of value for equity investors. It serves another purpose entirely: enabling the business to grow. Whether an exit involves the sale of the business to another company, or involves floating the business on a stock market via an IPO, it is essentially just a change of ownership. The company is swapping out one set of shareholders for another and, usually replacing fatigued shareholders who may have exhausted their financial resources with a new set of investors, optimistic about the future and with the resources to continue to back the company. 'Investor fatigue' is a phrase often used by entrepreneurs and VCs alike. Sometimes investors who have been shareholders in a business for many years will simply run out of capital and emotional energy to continue with the journey and support the business. Swapping out shareholders via an exit can change this dynamic, providing both new money and new money plus for the business to continue its journey. New owners may enable the business to grow by providing financial resources, new technology, access to new international markets and vertical integration with the other business units within its domain. All of these may enable the venture to continue its growth trajectory in ways that its existing shareholders would not be able to support. First-time entrepreneurs, when confronted with the concept of an exit, can sometimes regard this as a form of failure or the end of the business, but it is neither. It is simply a financial exit for one set of shareholders, and their replacement by a new owner or group of owners who can take the business to the next stage.

Of note is the fact that the entrepreneurial team does not necessarily leave the business at an exit, especially if this is a trade sale to a corporate operating in a similar field. One of the key assets of any business is its people, and it is common that management teams are required to stay on for a period to integrate an acquired business into its new corporate parent. This may present both opportunities and challenges for entrepreneurial teams, who now find themselves part of the management operating a business unit within a larger entity.

An exit is not the end of the business – it is not 'failure'.

TAXONOMY OF EXITS

So far, the discussion of exits may have implied that they occur mostly via the sale of businesses to larger corporations operating in the same or similar fields. Indeed, this is the case, and the largest proportion of exits from VC-backed companies occur via trade sales. VCs will often describe the best and cleanest exit as a trade sale, all in cash and all paid on the date of signing the deal. A clean exit with no ties is always best but rarely, if ever, occurs.

The best exit for VCs is all in cash, all on day one.

Usually, trade sales (otherwise known simply as M&A) are structured in a more sophisticated manner to ensure that the acquirer is not taking on undue risk and that the business plan of the target company is delivered. Trade sales will often occur in stages with an upfront payment followed by a series of deferred payments contingent on a variety of milestones being achieved. Such exits usually require all or some of the entrepreneurial team to remain in place to deliver those targets, and are referred to as 'earnouts'. The terms of such deals require specialist legal and corporate advice, and the boards of venture-backed companies must make sure they take all the necessary guidance to conclude the best transaction.

Trade sales may also occur in return for cash or shares, or a mix of the two. In other words, a company may be acquired for a cash sum, or it may be acquired by swapping its shares for the shares of the company it is being acquired by. The latter is sometimes referred to as 'swapping paper', meaning that one set of illiquid shares is being exchanged for another, which may or may not be liquid. For example, if a large corporation with shares traded on a major stock exchange acquires a small business in return for shares, the shares may often be traded relatively freely on the stock exchange and may almost be as good as cash. On the other hand, if a trade sale is transacted all in shares and the acquiring company is smaller and perhaps has less liquid shares trading at small volumes on a stock exchange, it may take some time for the shareholders of the acquired business to eventually sell their shares in the new business.

Matters of liquidity are very important considerations for the board of venture-backed businesses when considering whether to accept an offer to buy their business. They must consider the liquidity of the shares they are accepting as part of the transaction, how long it might take shareholders to sell those shares over a period of time and whether share price movements during that time are likely to have an impact.

Sometimes these considerations are offset by transactions that occur in both cash and shares, in other words, a mix of the two. This provides exiting shareholders with an immediate upfront cash payment, sometimes covering their initial investment coupled with the future upside potential of holding shares in the new business that has acquired their own. Whether to hold onto those shares or sell them at the earliest opportunity is a matter for individual shareholders and by that stage is, of course, out of the hands of the board of the portfolio company, which will have been dissolved upon completion of the transaction.

There is a particularly important consequence of all-share trade sales for venture capital funds. Because most venture capital funds are structured as limited partnerships, sale of a business in return for shares usually means those shares are distributed directly to the LPs in the fund. The shares of the acquiring company are not held within the venture capital fund, but distributed in the relevant portions to each of the LPs within the fund – it is for them to decide whether they retain those shares and hope for future growth or whether they sell those shares as soon as they can in return for cash.

THE INITIAL PUBLIC OFFERING... AN EXIT?

This brings us to another major form of exit event: the flotation of a business on the stock market, otherwise known as an IPO. Reports in the press and media about very large and very successful IPOs, often associated with individual entrepreneurs becoming extremely wealthy, might give the impression that this is the most common form of exit, but it is not. In reality, an IPO is not even an exit. It is just another fundraising event in which the company issues new shares to investors who are prepared to back it. The only difference, in this case, is that the investors are the public markets. An IPO does not, therefore, deliver an *immediate* exit for most, but it does deliver liquidity – depending on the stock market, the regulations regarding the sale of shares and ultimately the trading

The Initial Public Offering... an Exit?

volume of the shares in the newly public company. The IPO presents shareholders with their first opportunity to *consider* the sale of portions of their shareholding.

Shareholders usually cannot immediately sell all their shares following an IPO, as this would result in the collapse of the share price, with major shareholders looking as if they are abandoning the venture. Therefore, IPOs are normally conducted with a so-called 'lockup period' in which the sale of shares by major shareholders is forbidden. These lockup periods usually last from several months to a year and are tightly controlled to ensure that the share price of the IPO is not compromised by large volumes of sales. Just as 'all-share' exits may distribute shares directly to LPs, the same process may apply following an IPO and individual LPs in a fund can hold the shares following an IPO, or decide to sell as soon as they can.

This does, however, raise an important point. As with any share traded on a public stock market, share prices after an IPO can go up or down (see Figure 9.2). This means there is room for additional gains to be made by LPs who choose to hold shares for longer. Equally, if the share price falls, the gains they thought they had may dissipate quickly, and they may decide to hold shares for even longer in the hope of a recovery. At the time of writing this book, a whole series of IPOs have not performed particularly well and the valuations of public stocks in companies that were venture capital-backed may be even lower than the valuations of the most recent private rounds they raised. Investors in the public markets might regard this as an opportunity to invest at venture capital prices in companies they believe will grow, and in some cases that has proven to be correct. In other cases, however, the losses after an IPO have been sustained and some shares have continued to perform badly. The conclusion is that following an IPO and the lockup period, investors must make their own decisions about what to do with the shares they hold. VCs usually adopt the philosophy that the best exit is all in cash all on day one period – they will often seek to sell shares in publicly listed companies simply to crystallise the exit, even if that means surrendering the possibility of some future upside in the course of share price growth.

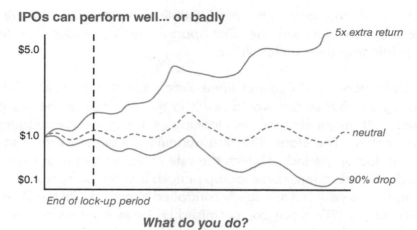

Figure 9.2 Share price movements after an IPO.
An issue of shares at an IPO is a fundraising event via which the company is raising capital from the public markets instead of private equity investors such as VCs. What happens beyond an IPO is out of the hands of those shareholders and share prices can rise or fall depending on the market's view of the company, and the wider financial environment. Shareholders normally cannot sell their shares until the end of a lockup imposed as a condition of the IPO. Once out of that lockup, they usually can only sell small portions in a periodic manner, depending on the liquidity of the stock. Share prices may continue to rise or fall and this might make a substantial difference to the returns the shareholders eventually receive once they sell their shares.

EXOTIC EXITS

In the years preceding the writing of this book there was a surge in the creation of special purpose acquisition companies (SPACs), which provided an alternative route for taking private companies public. SPACs are investment vehicles in which cash is raised into publicly listed entities (a form of cash shell) with the intention of acquiring a privately held high-growth business, hence turning it into a publicly listed company without an IPO. The formation of SPACs was a direct result of large amounts of cash being available for investment in risky assets following a decade of low interest rates across the world. Investors were prepared to back management teams in a SPAC to identify, acquire and then grow a privately held business with the idea that shares would soon be liquid. This, of course, provides a viable exit route for VCs and other equity investors in privately held businesses. The performance of many SPACs turned out to be mixed and they were an expensive way of raising money for venture capital-backed businesses, sometimes not providing the exit they hoped for. The surge of SPACs observed subsequently declined but may return and can be regarded as a viable if not optimal exit route for VCs.

Similarly, a viable but less than optimal exit route for VCs is the sale of their stake in a business to other private investors, sometimes selling the business to private equity funds who can take it to the next stage of growth. Often these forms of exit do not deliver maximum returns, as private equity funds are adept at negotiating deals and will usually structure such a transaction to be heavily dependent on continued high performance. Companies seeking an exit via a sale to a private equity fund are often not the best performing and may struggle to hit stretch targets forming part of the transaction.

THE DRAMA OF THE EXIT

If the entrepreneurial financing journey has, throughout this book, appeared to be a tortuous process, nothing compares to the drama that appears around the time of an exit. Raising money is one thing but delivering an exit is quite another. At exit, the financial stakes may be very high, with shareholders excited by the prospect of liberating the value created within the business and turning it into substantial cash rewards, but this does not come easy.

If, for example, a large corporate is buying a smaller business, it will conduct extremely thorough due diligence, crawling over every aspect of the business perhaps more meticulously than any of the VCs did in earlier rounds; the business will be examined in great detail and any one of those details may result in the offer price for the business changing, usually for the worse. If, on the other hand, there are competing buyers, then there might be a highly pressurised and exciting bidding war to acquire the business, resulting in even more returns to shareholders, but such deals are often difficult to compare directly to each other – meaning that different stakeholders will have different views on the exit and which deal is the best one to take.

Perhaps more important is the challenge of managing the flow of information about the potential transaction. What should the senior management team and the board tell the rest of the employees about a potential sale of the business? Maybe they shouldn't tell them anything at all but often news leaks, and careful consideration of how to communicate a potential sale of the business to important employees is fundamentally important. If employees get a sense that the business may be sold, they will start to worry about their jobs and may even leave. If important employees begin to leave the business on the rumours of a potential takeover, then there is a self-fulfilling prophecy that the valuation of the business will fall. Important people leaving does not preserve the value locked in the business, it will leak out and result in a lower-priced transaction.

How the board communicates to key employees about a potential sale is a delicate and difficult process and must be handled with the utmost care and respect. Keeping employees sufficiently informed and enthusiastic about the future is important and making sure they are looked after by the acquiring business is a key part of the negotiation. Often, key employees will hold equity in the business in the form of stock options and these are an important tool for retaining their services throughout the process of the transaction; only when the exit is concluded – and assuming they stay – do they get to realise the value locked within those options.

The exit is a moment of maximum drama.

WHEN?

There is usually not a single moment when the board of a venture-backed business decides to sell. There may, however, be a series of conversations around board meetings, considering the best strategic future for the business and how that might be funded. Sometimes, when investors who have nominated directors to the board make it clear that they are not able to or are unwilling to invest further in the business, a conversation about exits begins. The decision faced by the board may be whether to sell the business for the best price it can achieve or to attempt to raise external capital from new investors and continue growing the company independently.

These conversations may go on for some time but are determined by the cash runway within the business; in other words, how long the board has to figure out the future before the company runs out of cash. Getting perilously close to running out of cash does nothing to help the negotiation of the best exit, just as it would not help in a negotiation of raising more capital at a good valuation.

All these conversations may be cut short if the business is approached by a potential buyer, and this is often the trigger to begin a formal M&A process. The duty of the board here is not to accept the first offer that appears out of the blue, or indeed to negotiate that offer in the absence of others. The board ideally should seek alternate offers to generate competitive tension around the transaction and seek to maximise the return by being able to walk away from any deal. An opportunistic approach to buy the business from an interested buyer will often trigger the appointment of a specialist M&A advisor by the board (either an investment bank or an accounting firm) who can help them negotiate and structure the best transaction. Importantly, corporate advisors such as this are often adept at finding alternative buyers to create a competitive bidding process and are rewarded for doing so with a percentage of the value of the transaction.

The details of the M&A process are beyond the scope of this book but as a sector, the M&A business is huge and M&A advisors can vary from large global banks to boutique advisors who focus on particular industries. It is the role of the board to identify and select the most appropriate corporate advisors to help them negotiate a good transaction, and it is here again that the directors may look towards the VCs on the board for their money plus contribution via their financial networks.

Corporate finance advisors specialise in running structured bidding processes. Even if the trigger for such a process is an opportunistic offer from a single buyer, corporate advisors will attempt to slow that buyer down whilst bringing in other potential bidders and enforcing timelines by which bidders must submit offers for the company and give indicative valuations they are prepared to pay. Corporate advisors also specialise in getting those transactions to completion because they can (and do) fail at any time. Corporate advisors also maintain momentum in M&A transactions because there is a saying in this industry that 'time kills deals', meaning the longer they take to complete a transaction, the more reasons can be found by the buyer to either pull out completely or more commonly to negotiate a lower price. External events such as changes in the global financial climate, a war or the appearance of a pandemic will negatively affect the chances of a transaction completing and therefore doing it quickly is in the interests of the seller

> *Time kills deals... and momentum is key to getting over the M&A finish line.*

What features a company must possess to trigger an exit at a good valuation varies across industries, and investment banks and corporate advisors are good at describing what criteria a company must fulfil either to do an IPO or be acquired at a high price. This depends not only on regulations within specific stock markets but also on market conditions in the M&A sector. For example, a market that is hot for financial technologies, molecular diagnostics or a range of other hot sectors could trigger a surge in M&A activity or flotations in those areas and capturing that window of opportunity can depend on a mix of timing and luck. Sometimes companies that have developed a new technology are bought by large corporates early in their entrepreneurial journey, perhaps because of the intellectual property they hold or perhaps because the technology threatens the business of the incumbent corporate. In an earlier chapter, building value was described as 'Be needed by or feared by global corporations,' and this principle is most evident at the time of an exit. Sometimes large corporations pay vast amounts of money to own important technology, and exits can arrive for entrepreneurial teams long before they have crossed the Valleys of Death and long before the business is profitable.

> *Exits can occur long before a company is profitable...*

FORCED SALES: DRAG ALONG AND GRANDSTANDING

The prospect of an early and valuable exit is a tantalising dream for most VCs. Sometimes they and the entrepreneurial teams they back get lucky; they develop a great idea at just the right moment for a large corporation to come in and make a high bid to acquire the business. But the opposite may also be true.

Sometimes start-ups and growing ventures just take a long time to develop. So long in fact that their investors lose patience, become fatigued or run out of cash to keep supporting the business. In these cases, the investors and shareholders may seek a forced sale of the business to recoup their probable losses. All venture capital term sheets and subsequent shareholders agreements will contain provisions allowing an investor majority to force a sale of the business. These are commonly referred to as 'drag-along clauses' and can be found in the examples presented in this book. Usually, these clauses allow a defined majority of shareholders to force a sale of the business after a specified period (often 5 years) if an exit has not already been achieved. Although this legal clause exists, on a commercial level it is sometimes undesirable to enforce it. Forcing the sale of a business depends on its management team going along with the idea, as they will be the ones doing all the work to deliver such an exit. If a sale is forced, and there is little benefit to it for the entrepreneurial team, they will likely not cooperate or may even leave, causing substantial value to leak out of a business that may already be struggling. The conclusion is that drag-along clauses and forced sales may sometimes be little more than a threat and are used infrequently, perhaps only in circumstances where the only alternative is insolvency.

A variation of this notion occurs when instead of 'forcing' a sale, VCs push for or encourage a sale of the business through a mix of incentives and threats, the latter usually in the form of refusing to invest more money. The eagerness of VCs to exit is often a running joke in the entrepreneurial community, but exit they must and for some the sooner, the better. The VCs who are most eager to exit are usually those with a limited track record and consequently a desire to deliver exits from their fund to build their track record and enable them to raise a subsequent fund. This eagerness to exit is a clear conflict of interest for the director, who may be appointed to the board by such a fund. Investor directors in this precarious situation need to be very careful. This activity (pushing for early exits) is well known as 'grandstanding' and was described in the academic literature by Paul Gompers as far back as 1996

(Gompers 1996). More established, highly reputable VCs with a longstanding track record are far less likely to push companies towards an exit sooner than they are really prepared for. Younger VCs with less established funds are eager to build their track records and sometimes their interests diverge from those of the companies they back in doing so. Entrepreneurial teams need to watch out for grandstanding behaviour and the role of the board is to ensure the exits are in the interests of everyone and not an individual venture capital fund pushing for a grandstanding exit.

WHO DECIDES: THE ROLE OF THE BOARD?

We often joke that having made an investment and joined the board of directors, the first question a VC asks is 'OK, when is the exit?'. In an MBA class this usually raises a laugh, coupled with a few dismayed sighs, but there is a serious point to it: having raised venture capital finance, the board might well find it useful to work backwards from the exit to figure out what it needs to do to get there. By accepting venture capital investment, the board has accepted that generating an exit opportunity for equity investors (and consequently all shareholders) is the primary goal and is a necessity.

By the time a growing venture has raised several investment rounds, it will have assembled a board of directors containing a mix of investor directors, independent industry experts and representatives of the entrepreneurial team itself (usually the CEO). At what point the board begins to consider the realistic possibility of delivering an exit for shareholders will depend on many factors, including achievements the company has made and the external environment around it. This is not usually under the control of the board, but the board must evaluate the opportunities before it and sometimes make a choice whether to recommend an exit (e.g. a trade sale to a global corporation) or continue to grow a company as an independent venture, which usually requires further finance.

The board must act in the interests of all shareholders and in developing exit opportunities for the VCs who backed the company they must bear this in mind. The board can, however, only play the hand it is dealt and exits will sometimes benefit some shareholders more than others – according to the shareholders agreement. The board needs to make sure that it considers exit opportunities carefully and, if time allows, it should try to generate competitive tension to maximise the returns for shareholders (and it should evidence that it has done so).

The board recommends and the shareholders approve...

WHAT DO EXITS MEAN FOR FOUNDERS?

Some of the previous sections have indicated that the exit is a moment of maximum drama, when the stakes are high and conflict between groups of shareholders can occur. But it is also a moment delivering potentially life-changing wealth to the founders and entrepreneurial team behind the business. A successful exit from a high-value business can lead to untold riches and potential fame. Early members of the management team for successful tech companies in California can attest to the wealth and fame that such high-profile exits can bestow. Following the sale of the tech company PayPal to eBay in 2002, the founders of PayPal went on to become business angels and are widely regarded as creating an entire next generation of tech companies as both founders and investors. No doubt the future will produce yet more enormously wealthy tech entrepreneurs who have sold businesses and generated great wealth and fame for themselves and for others.

But what about the less high-profile exits? What is the impact on founders and entrepreneurial teams when their businesses are acquired for more modest sums, perhaps via transactions that require them to join the acquiring company? Becoming a manager of a division or a business unit within a larger corporation, perhaps under the terms of an earnout in which targets must be achieved, is a totally different experience for entrepreneurial teams used to building their own business. Playing to the tune of a larger corporation with different rules and regulations and a different business culture can be challenging, and there is a great deal of literature about the difficulties of integrating businesses following an M&A

transaction. How does it feel to be an entrepreneur now working as part of a larger organisation? There may be a sense of loss and longing for the freedom that entrepreneurial ventures provide, even if a role in the acquiring company is a temporary measure until the earnout is achieved.

What happens if, following a successful exit, an entrepreneurial team is now unemployed? What do they do next, either as a team or as individuals? How do they cope with the loss of structure to their day or a perceived lack of purpose following the intense period of building a company and negotiating an exit transaction. The PayPal founders are a great example of how entrepreneurs achieve an exit and then go on to do more great things, reinventing themselves as serial entrepreneurs or business angels and giving rise to the next generation of exciting businesses. Entrepreneurs who have sold businesses are often in great demand, either as investors or as directors on the boards of venture-backed businesses. Sometimes they even become VCs, joining venture capital firms as 'venture partners', advisors or full partners.

WHAT DO EXITS MEAN FOR VCs?

For the VCs who invested in the business, the philosophical impact of an exit is far simpler. It was always their goal, and this moment would always come. Quite simply, every exit generated from the portfolio moves the overall fund closer to a loan repayment point. When the loan repayment point is reached, the all-important carried interest is initiated, and the VCs begin to share in the profits they have generated for the fund. It is as simple as that: every exit generated within the fund moves it that step closer to the loan repayment point and the payment of carried interest to the VCs.

It is important to remember that carried interest from individual exits is usually pooled and shared by all partners in a venture capital firm, and individual partners are not usually rewarded individually for exits they have delivered. Carried interest pools are usually collective and therefore all partners should work in the interests of delivering the best exits they can. Everyone should pull together towards the loan repayment point.

For individual partners, however, delivering one or more successful exits may lead to personal reward in the form of promotion within the firm. The career progression of a venture capital fund manager within the firm, from associate to senior associate, partner and ultimately managing partner, is usually accompanied by a greater share of the carried interest, both in the current fund and in future funds they are likely to play a significant role in raising. The more successful they are, the more important they are to the future fundraising potential of the firm. LPs like to back winners, and individual VCs with a strong track record of delivering exits are highly prized by the firm.

PREFERENCE CASCADES AND THE MANAGEMENT CARVE-OUT

Chapter 6 explained how preferred and preference shares impact the returns for the ordinary shareholders at exit. Preferred and preference shares are paid out at exit in priority to any other shareholder, and the double-dipping preferred share receives a payout twice: first via a loan repayment and second via participation in the proceeds due to ordinary shareholders. The returns to groups of shareholders therefore may not reflect their percentage equity ownership and the impact will vary according to the size of the exit.

The example waterfalls in Figure 9.3 illustrate that in poor exits, certain groups of shareholders may receive a small portion of the exit proceeds, or perhaps even nothing at all as shown in the 'broken waterfall'. This is the consequence of the preference cascade that may have built up over the course of several investment rounds, with the impact of preferred and preference shares being compounded by the existence of multiple layers. In such cases, what happens to those who exist under the water level of the waterfall?

If those who are responsible for delivering the exit and managing the process feel aggrieved about their equity share, perhaps even

(a)

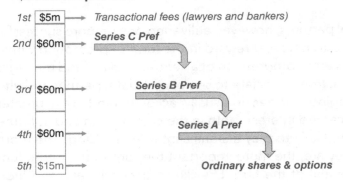

(b)

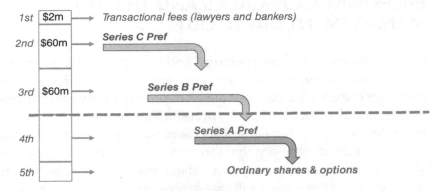

Figure 9.3 The impact of preference cascades at exit.

The examples above show how a cascade of preferred and preference shares may impact the ordinary shareholders when the business is acquired in cash for a defined sum. Although the numbers are fictional and for illustration only, when the business is acquired for $200 million in (a) the first group to be paid are the advisors and lawyers acting for the company, followed by the Series C Pref shares who will have likely paid the highest share price and invested most recently, followed by the Pref B and Pref A shareholders. The last group to be paid out are the ordinary shareholders, who in this example receive $15 million. If the acquisition price was higher, the ordinary shareholders would receive proportionately more of the proceeds as the impact of the Pref shares decreases, as explained in Chapter 6. There is an altogether different scenario in (b), where there are insufficient funds to pay out all shareholders and only the Pref C and Pref B shareholders receive a payout. The Pref A and ordinary shareholders are 'underwater' and according to the preference cascade above, will receive nothing. Clearly, if they have a sufficient shareholding to block the acquisition, they will do so until the Pref C and Pref B shareholders carve out some of the proceeds of the acquisition for them. When this is carried out for the management team, it is referred to as a 'management carve-out'.

receiving nothing, they will need to be 'made good' via a 'management carve-out' in which additional equity or cash bonuses are made available to the entrepreneurial team to deliver the transaction. Otherwise, why would they continue to work for the business? They would simply leave. It is an obvious trait of human nature that individuals rarely work for nothing, and that is certainly the case for entrepreneurial teams who have worked hard to build the business, even if it looks like it is close to failure or only a marginal success. To get an exit over the line, management teams must be rewarded, either with more stock options, equity or even cash bonuses for getting the deal done.

This may also be the case for groups of early investors, who may be required to sign agreements to enable the exit to occur. Even if drag-along clauses in the shareholders agreement can legally enforce the sale of their shares, legal advisors for acquiring companies usually advise against this. An acquiring company does not want to take on a potential lawsuit from small shareholders who believe they were not rewarded fairly, and will require that 100% of the shareholders in the target company willingly sign up to the transaction, thus waiving the chance of any future lawsuit. In these cases, small groups of shareholders may have to be rewarded to sign the deal. This raises the spectre of small constituencies of shareholders holding the company to ransom at the moment of maximum leverage (the exit), when everyone senses the finish line. The finish line, however, needs to be the same finish line for everyone, and sufficiently attractive for all who want to cross it at the same time. Management or shareholder carve-outs are not uncommon, highlighting that the splits of equity agreed at the beginning are not entirely cast in stone and may be revisited if needed.

TERRIBLE EXITS

There are exits that nobody wants to see. When a business fails or is close to failing, the board of directors needs to act and their responsibility changes from acting in the interests of the shareholders to acting in the interests of the creditors, in other words suppliers, employees, customers, anyone who has provided a loan and most importantly the tax authorities.

Start-ups fail and they fail a lot, so this has to become central to the thought process of any entrepreneurial team. What happens to investments when businesses fail? Even if shareholders own double-dipping preferred shares or non-participating preference shares, they are unlikely to see any return of their capital in the event of an insolvency.

Businesses become insolvent when they cannot meet their obligations to repay debts, or if their liabilities outweigh their assets. The tests for insolvency vary slightly between different countries but the core principle is that when the board of directors believes the company is unable to continue trading solvently and meet its financial obligations, it must call in administrators, specialised firms who take over the running of the business and attempt to seek a buyer or liquidate the assets to repay creditors as best they can.

Before getting to the point of insolvency, the board of directors may seek to sell the business via a sale of its assets, often referred to as a 'fire sale' — as if the company has burned to the ground and the leftovers are being sold to recoup some losses. This is quite different from selling the business via the sale of 100% of its share capital, as the buyer is only buying the assets and therefore not the liabilities. Asset sales are far less likely to occur if the business has been a success. Successful businesses are sold, lock stock and barrel, and the buyer takes on both assets and liabilities, buying the business as a functioning, going concern. Asset sales occur when businesses are close to failure and a buyer is found to buy assets such as intellectual property, machinery, real estate, valuable contracts or any other form of tangible asset the company may own. The sale of these assets may go to repaying creditors, with any leftovers being distributed among the shareholders according to their shareholding (and perhaps the preference cascade). Directors need to take care in these circumstances that they follow the rules precisely, and taking advice from experienced insolvency practitioners is essential to make sure that the board carries out its fiduciary duties in accordance with good corporate governance practices.

Beyond the strictly procedural aspects of filing for insolvency, there are an entire range of human issues associated with this unfortunate event. Although we don't think of it as an exit, it is just that, an exit – just not one that anybody ever wanted or predicted when that optimistic investment was made in a promising start-up. The emotional impact of failing in business is a deep human response, the extent of which varies between cultures. It is often said anecdotally that entrepreneurs need to fail a few times before they are successful, and VCs will look for that. There is a perception that in the United States failure is accepted more readily within the entrepreneurial community and in Europe it is looked on less kindly, with a long-lasting stigma that will continue to challenge an entrepreneur in any future ventures. But the reality is that it all depends on why the business failed – whether in the United States, Europe or any other geographic region. Failing because of unpredictable market changes, new government regulation or other external factors is quite different from failing because of a gross error in managing the business and the causes of the failure – and how the failure was managed – will be a key determinant of whether an entrepreneurial team is able to raise finance in the future for a subsequent venture.

Some entrepreneurs suffer great mental anguish and emotional pain after a business failure, yet others are resilient and will pick themselves up, dust themselves down and go again. Resilience is one of the key words taught now in many business schools, but it is not a novel concept. You just have to be tough to be an entrepreneur and you must be able to pick yourself up and go again. The same may be said of VCs and other early-stage investors; they need to be used to failing, understand the reasons it happened but then move on with the business of backing early-stage, high-risk ventures. An insolvency followed by liquidation, and eventual dissolution of a company, is an exit but unfortunately it is an exit that does nothing to enhance the reputation of a VC. Again, the reasons for that failure matter. If the failure was due to some unforeseen event, then perhaps it is OK, but if the failure was due to a

Towards the Exit

fundamental flaw in the technology or business model – which could have been spotted during the due-diligence process – then this will go against the VC's track record.

For both entrepreneurs and VCs who serve on the board of directors of a company that goes bust, there is also the risk that they may be disqualified from acting in the role of a director in future companies. This occurs when it can be shown that the directors allowed the business to trade insolvently, in other words they carried on doing business when they knew there was no chance of repaying creditors to whom they owed money. In these cases, criminal proceedings may even arise. This is bad news for entrepreneurs who wish to go again, or VCs whose professional life involves investing in and joining the boards of start-ups. This happens very rarely, and most boards of directors take their fiduciary duties very seriously – with the right advice even a terrible exit can be handled successfully, minimising the financial harm to creditors and the reputational damage to the entrepreneurs and VCs behind the business.

Terrible exits happen but resilience and responsibility are key to handling them…

THE LIVING DEAD

Some VCs will argue that even worse than a company going bust is a company that goes on and on and on, surviving but never delivering an exit either. These companies, which are highly unlikely to deliver a great exit for the fund, continue to take up management time for the VC – they must be monitored, reported on and may lead to a substantial administrative burden. These companies are referred to in the venture capital industry as 'the living dead', companies that exist somewhere between life and death, never succeeding but never quite failing either. Some VCs will argue that insolvency at least provides a definitive end to a business and will allow them to move on. Sometimes the living dead companies can even prevent the closure (or completion) of a fund that is past its 10-year LP agreement, requiring the entire fund to either be extended or for special provisions to be made to hold the shares.

Living dead companies and the administrative burden they create for VCs are highly undesirable, and VCs will often seek to sell their shareholding in such a company through what is known as a secondary offering, in which they will sell their shares at a deep discount to other VCs who are prepared to take over the running of that business, perhaps investing more cash or seeking an exit in some other way. Secondary buyout funds are a specialised type of venture capital that focuses on buying baskets of shares from the portfolios of VCs who have either run out of time or money to take those businesses any further.

VCs avoid the living dead... like the plague!

THE EXIT: A PRACTICAL EXAMPLE

Just as in Chapter 8, the remainder of this current chapter is dedicated to a practical case study aimed at illustrating the reality of dealing with an exit. Exits are best experienced live and many of the lessons learned will only become clear when the reader is in the hot seat, but the Syntemix case study below provides a realistic insight into the decisions that must be made in a real-life exit. The nuances of how the board of directors must respond to and deal with an offer to buy their business is a core theme. The case study places the reader in the role of a recently appointed independent director to the board of a venture capital-backed business just as it is debating the strategic future of the company. Should Syntemix raise more money and continue independently, or should the board attempt to sell the business?

The case study explores how the board should behave and how conflicts of interest may arise and be resolved for investor directors present on the board. Questions of who should lead the negotiation and what the best outcome is for all shareholders are central to this case, and a model answer is provided at the end of the book. As with all business scenarios there is rarely a single correct answer, but there are principles the board must always observe.

Readers should examine this case and answer the questions provided before returning to the summary of Chapter 9.

Case Study

Syntemix: Engineering the Exit

Syntemix's revolutionary platform technology to produce industrial chemicals had promised much in the 7 years since its launch in 2007. The company had raised three rounds of investment from business angel groups and well-known VCs, valuing the company at $100 million post-money in 2014. But technical challenges since the Series B had led to problems in scaling the business and almost 2 years later investor patience was beginning to wear thin. With a year's worth of cash remaining, board meetings were dominated by one strategic question: should Syntemix attempt to raise a further round of finance (Series C) and continue to grow independently, or should the board seek a strategic buyer for the business, avoiding further dilution and providing a near-term exit for its fatigued investors?

You have recently been appointed as an independent non-executive director to the board of Syntemix. You were appointed because of your experience in serving on the boards of numerous venture capital-backed companies and some investors have quietly indicated that they see you replacing the current chair within a year.

Background

Syntemix was formed in 2007 at the beginning of an investment boom in green industrial processes. The science was developed at a well-known US university and the intellectual property surrounding the innovations was carefully protected at each step via a series of patents. Syntemix's platform technology used a pioneering 'green catalyst' process to enable the production of a wide range of industrial chemicals such as bulk fertilisers for agriculture, biofuels for the automobile industry and more specialised intermediates used in the pharmaceutical industry.

Having proven that the process worked on a small scale with a series of successful prototypes, the next key challenge facing the

The Exit: A Practical Example **269**

management team had been scaling the process to a commercially viable level and various trials with contract manufacturing services were underway. As with many venture-backed businesses, successful scaling of the business model was going to be the key to success.

The Shareholders

Following the launch of the business in 2007, the founders raised a $2 million seed round at an impressive pre-money valuation of $8 million. This investment was structured as ordinary shares consistent with the notion that founders, management and investors should be perfectly aligned in their motives to build value and deliver a fair exit for all. The key investors in the seed round were two angel groups: West Tech Angels (a group of former chemicals industry executives) and Dark Horse Angels (a group of high-net-worth investors supporting start-ups in their home state). Together, these groups brought substantial value to Syntemix through their industrial knowledge and connections to regional business networks.

In 2009, Syntemix completed its first venture capital-led round, a Series A round of $10 million at a $10 million pre-money valuation (i.e. a flat valuation compared to the seed round). The lead investor, Vertigon Ventures, was experienced in the sector and argued successfully that the seed round had been completed at too high a valuation and current market forces did not support a step up in share price, despite the progress Syntemix had made. Vertigon invested $8 million with a further $2 million from the West Tech Angels who had a strong appetite for deals in this sector. Dark Horse Angels were unable to participate in the Series A round and were content to hold onto their ordinary shares and board seat. The Series A round was structured in typical Vertigon fashion as Preferred Shares with an 8% cumulative dividend and 1× sale and liquidation preference (the classic 'double dip').

As the market for green industrial chemicals continued to gather pace, however, a Series B round was completed in 2012 with Syntemix raising $25 million at a $75 million pre-money valuation, a substantial increase that reflected growing investor interest in the sector. The round was led by Bob Meadows of Corsair Ventures, a respected figure in the chemicals industry who had recently raised his first venture capital fund alongside several co-founders. Corsair invested $12.5 million in the round, with $7.5 million from Vertigon and $5 million from Patriarch LP, a passive investment fund that followed Corsair's lead. Again, the round was structured as Preferred Shares with an 8% cumulative dividend and 1× sale and liquidation preference. Neither business angel group was able to invest further in the business, but the increased valuation minimised their dilution.

The Board

The first board meeting after the Series B financing round was supposed to be a moment of triumph as the board welcomed new directors: Bob Meadows and you, the experienced independent non-executive. But the look on Bob's face was priceless as Carol Presno unexpectedly presented a plan to raise a further $25 million Series C round within a year. You were familiar with the 'Oh Shit Board Meetings' that VCs often swapped stories about in the bar at industry conferences, but this one took first prize. Carol, perhaps buoyed by the success of the round and having taken a fresh look at the finances, had decided a further $25 million was required to secure success and developed a new plan accordingly. This had not been discussed with the board chair Daryll Harbakoff prior to the meeting and served as a source of embarrassment to the existing directors. It looked as if they had suckered Bob into a bottomless money pit but, as Sam Bassett explained to Bob during the coffee break, this was a surprise to him too and would need to be addressed.

This experience left a sour taste for Bob and unfortunately coloured his view of Carol going forward, something that would resurface every time there was a board debate about strategic issues. He had also begun to question board process and transparency and felt 'the jury was out' on the chair, Daryll Harbakoff. Your own experience told you that Daryll should have known this was coming. Had he not reviewed the agenda and board report prior to such an important meeting? Perhaps your elevation to the role of chair of the board would come sooner than you anticipated...

Syntemix board composition post-Series B

CEO:	Carol Presno
Series B Nominee Director:	Bob Meadows, Corsair Ventures
Series A Nominee Director:	Sam Bassett, Vertigon Ventures
Seed Round Nominee Director:	Steve Binder, West Tech Angel Group
Non-Executive Chair:	Daryll Harbakoff, industry expert and angel
Non-Executive Director:	*You (recently appointed)*
Observer:	Donald Jones, Dark Horse Angels

Note: Donald Jones was an observer but didn't 'just observe'. He was vocal, well respected and liked by everyone on the board.

The Strategic Debate

Over the course of several Syntemix board meetings, the debate about whether to raise a Series C or seek a buyer gathered pace. The company was not ready to deliver an exit at maximum valuation, but a Series C would likely be dilutive too. Bob and Sam both expressed concerns that it would be difficult to achieve a Series C valuation higher than the previous post-money unless serious progress was made on scale-up. Doubts about the CEO continued to linger, and directors were holding discussions outside board meetings about whether and when Carol could be replaced. Bob was pushing this. He had been told by a senior figure in the venture capital industry that 'the only role of the board is to fire the CEO' and he was sticking by this mantra.

The Offer

In early September 2014 Sam Bassett held a meeting in his office at Vertigon with Jenny Strathclyde. Jenny was a friend of Sam's and in the past had consulted for Vertigon on potential investments. Jenny was now a non-executive director of Swiss Precision Systems Inc. (SPS), a NASDAQ-listed engineering technology business that had carried out an IPO 7 years previously. SPS was urgently exploring how to bolster its flagging share price with a bolt-on acquisition. Jenny informed Sam that SPS was interested in a strategic deal with Syntemix and possibly an outright acquisition of the business. In fact, she had been mandated by the SPS board to use her connection with Vertigon to explore whether Syntemix would be open to a discussion.

Bassett could not believe his luck. As he showed Jenny to the door, he mulled over the prospect of a deal that could address his concerns about Syntemix. As a Series A shareholder, he knew that any deal would likely benefit Vertigon's fund more than others due to the great Series A valuation he had negotiated, meaning that this would require a delicate approach in the boardroom. This exit would likely push Vertigon's fund past the loan repayment point and into the carry zone. It meant a share of the carried interest for Sam, a welcome injection of cash as he and his wife were in the process of buying a house. It could also mean promotion within the firm to General Partner, giving him a role in raising the next fund and a bigger share of the carried interest.

Sam's first thought was to call Bob Meadows to share the news. After all, he knew Bob – as the latest investor – would have a strong opinion on the prospect of an exit. Bob cautiously welcomed the news (given his feelings about Carol and the possibility of a dilutive Series C round) and suggested bringing the rest of the board into the conversation. Sam called Daryll Harbakoff and asked him to schedule a call for the Syntemix board the next day. After a brief board debate, it was decided that Sam would deliver a message back to Jenny that the Syntemix board was open to an offer, but they expected the proposed deal to be communicated in a formal term sheet and only then would they seriously consider it.

A term sheet arrived in Sam's inbox from SPS's CEO 10 days later (see Annex I). It was light on detail and frankly a little disappointing from a company listed on the NASDAQ. The valuation of the offer meant that Syntemix was to be valued at only 25% of the market capitalisation of SPS (about $60 million) and the proposed transaction was to be an 'all share' deal – in other words, the Syntemix shareholders would be swapping their shares for SPS shares at an agreed ratio.

Importantly, it was immediately clear that not all Syntemix shareholders would benefit from this share swap equally. The Syntemix liquidation preference cascade meant that the Series A and Series B shareholders would be 'paid out' first, resulting in them taking $40 million worth of the SPS shares before the remainder were allocated according to percentage ownership in Syntemix. Notably the Series A shareholders (Vertigon and West Tech Angels) were going to be particularly well rewarded because of the relatively low Series A share price negotiated by Sam Bassett. A summary of the Syntemix capitalisation table and liquidation preferences can be found in Annex III.

The Response

As a recently appointed independent non-executive director of Syntemix, what advice would you offer to your board colleagues at this point?

- How can the board ensure they are getting the right price for Syntemix?
- What information should the board gather to support any decision?
- How should SPS shares be allocated to the Syntemix shareholders?
- Who should negotiate on behalf of Syntemix?
- What actions must the board undertake to ensure good governance?

The Surprise

The board listened to all your advice and gathered lots of information to guide their decision-making process. Following several lengthy meetings, the Syntemix board voted unanimously to sign the term sheet and proceed with negotiations. The directors felt that on balance, Syntemix shareholders would be better off holding shares in SPS, with its experienced management team and scope for growth. Despite the proposed lock-up period, they felt that the SPS share price could rise following the acquisition of Syntemix due to its valuable intellectual property, boosting the return for Syntemix shareholders.

Six weeks and many hours of negotiation later, the term sheet had been transformed into a final share purchase agreement (SPA) and a draft press release had been prepared in order to announce the deal to the stock market.

Five days prior to the scheduled completion date for the acquisition, however, the collapse of an investment bank in the United States led to turmoil on the US stock markets and although apparently unrelated to SPS, its share price took a 15% hit, significantly more than some other comparable companies.

The formula that had been devised for allocating SPS shares to Syntemix shareholders meant that the ordinary shareholders would now be impacted profoundly. Because of the $40 million liquidation preference, the deal was already skewed towards the VCs but following the SPS share price drop, the formula meant the preferred shareholders now took an even greater share of the SPS shares. Although the management team and founders of Syntemix held ordinary shares, they had negotiated very favourable employment agreements with SPS so were still prepared to go ahead. The Dark Horse Angels were, however, totally 'out of the money' – as it stood, they would receive nothing from the deal.

In a tense board call, Donald Jones made it clear that the Dark Horse Angels would not sign the shareholders agreement required to complete the transaction. Donald was well liked and respected by the board, and when he made it clear that the Dark Horse Angels, including himself, were prepared to let Syntemix fail rather than complete the transaction, they knew he was serious.

How would you advise the board to respond?

Annex I: Draft SPA Term Sheet Received 22nd September 2014

ACQUISITION OF SYNTEMIX INC. BY SPS INC.

Purchase Price/ Consideration:	46 million shares in SPS in return for 100% of the issued share capital of Syntemix Inc. (valuing Syntemix at approximately $60 million at the average share price of SPS over the previous 5 trading days prior to the signing of a definitive agreement).
Closing Adjustments:	Balance sheet to be delivered debt/cash-free.
Closing Balance Sheet Shares:	At close or within 30 days after closing, SPS will satisfy Syntemix's closing balance sheet obligations in cash. In order to fund these payments, SPS will hold back ordinary shares (equal to 1.2× the closing balance sheet obligations). These shares will be sold in the open market to generate the necessary cash to fulfil these obligations. Any excess cash from these sales will be returned to Syntemix.
Indemnity Holdback:	2.3 million shares held back for 18 months to support indemnification (survival period).
Lock-up Restrictions:	Syntemix shareholders will be bound by a lock-up period as follows: <ul><li>No sales for 30 days so as not to affect SPS's sales of shares to cover Syntemix balance sheet obligations.</li><li>Lock-up gradually released monthly over the next 11 months.</li></ul>
*IP Indemnification Cap:	40% of purchase price – Year 1 30% of purchase price – Year 2 20% of purchase price – Year 3 * In the event that Syntemix ownership of IP is challenged and/or invalidated, precise conditions to be agreed.
Other Conditions:	No litigation No material adverse events Employment agreement with Carol Presno and selected senior management to be agreed and signed.
Timeline to Completion:	2 months from the date of signing this term sheet.

Annex II: Financing History of Syntemix and SPS Inc.

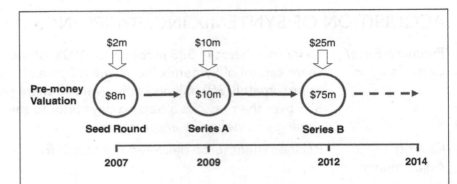

Syntemix Inc. financing history.
In private financing rounds valuation only changes when a new external lead investor prices the deal. Valuations are therefore 'sticky' and may not reflect current market conditions. The final investment round prior to the offer from SPS Inc in 2014 was the Corsair-led Series B in 2012 giving Syntemix a post-money valuation of $100m.

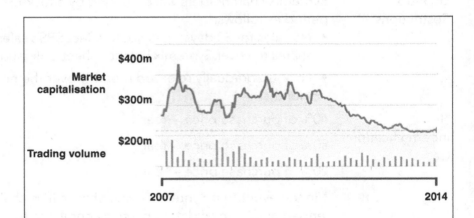

SPS Inc. financing history.
SPS had completed 4 VC investment rounds between 2001 and 2006 and had carried out its IPO in 2007, seeing an initial surge in share price resulting in a market capitalization of almost $400 million. Share performance has weakened from

Acquisition of Syntemix Inc. by SPS Inc. **277**

> 2010 onwards resulting in a market value of around $200 million on relatively low share trading volumes. The stock had failed to generate interest lately and in 2014 SPS's Board was seeking to trigger growth via an acquisition.

Annex III: Capitalisation Table and Liquidation Cascade for Syntemix as of 2014

Post-Series B capitalisation table

	Seed	Ser A	Ser B	Total	Fully Diluted Ownership (%)
Vertigon	-	9,000	2,100	11,100	39.6
Corsair	-	-	3,500	3,500	12.5
Patriarch	-	-	1,400	1,400	5.0
West Tech	1,000	1,000	-	2,000	7.1
Dark Horse	1,000	-	-	1,000	3.8
Founders	7,000	-	-	7,000	25.0
Option Pool	1,000	-	1,000	2,000	7.0
Shares Issued	10,000	10,000	8,000	-	
Total Shares	10,000	20,000	28,000	28,000	100.0

Total liquidation preference + cumulative dividend = $40m

Cap table and liquidation preferences.

At the time of the offer from SPS, Syntemix had completed three investment rounds issuing Ordinary Shares in the seed round and Preferred Shares with a 1× sales and liquidation preference and an 8% cumulative dividend in later rounds. At the time of the offer from SPS, the sales and liquidation preference was $35 million and the cumulative dividend was around $5 million. This meant that $40 million of liquidation preference had to be paid out to preferred shareholders in priority to ordinary shareholders.

SUMMARY OF CHAPTER 9

This chapter has examined what may be regarded as the most intricate stage of growing a new venture – the final stage known as the exit. Entrepreneurial teams raising equity finance from venture capital funds, angel investors, private equity funds or any other form of equity investor will need to deliver an exit for those investors at some point. The limited partnership structure adopted by most venture capital funds dictates that the exits must ordinarily arrive within a 10-year period at the very most. If a venture capital fund has invested in a business 4 years into the life of its fund, then that period may be reduced to 6 years and growing a business from start-up to exit over such a short space of time puts immense pressure on entrepreneurial teams.

The conflicts that arise between investors and entrepreneurial teams around the timing and type of exit are often some of the greatest conflicts that will occur during the growth of that venture, partly because of the different classes of share they may hold and how they are paid out at exit. Preference cascades or waterfalls will often exist and will exert a significant impact on the share proceeds from any exit that sometimes appears divorced from simple percentage equity shareholdings.

High-value exits usually dissipate the effects of preference cascades when preferred and preference shares behave almost the same as ordinary shares. The story is very different for poor exits, in which entrepreneurial teams and other ordinary shareholders may find themselves underwater and receiving little payout. In those cases, a management carve-out will have to be created to incentivise a management team to get the transaction across the finish line.

The vast majority of exits from venture capital-backed companies are via trade sales – acquisition by a larger corporate that buys the target company either in cash or shares or a mix of both, and sometimes through a series of payments, both upfront and deferred. Initial public offerings are usually reserved for the biggest and most successful new ventures, which are producing reliable, repeatable revenues that the public markets may evaluate using rational corporate finance metrics. This is the glamour end of the exit business, and the one that we read about in the media, but it is far less common than exits via M&A.

As the entrepreneurial financing journey reaches its conclusion, founders and entrepreneurial teams must consider the question – what next? Sometimes they are absorbed (at least for a period) in a new organisation, especially if the exit is via an earnout. What they do next varies – occasionally becoming business angels or serial entrepreneurs – and if they have delivered a very successful exit, they may find themselves being a spokesperson for the industry.

Like the Mesopotamian merchants of 5,000 years ago returning from a lengthy trading expedition to a foreign land, and sharing in the spoils of their success, they must decide whether they go again...

REFERENCE

Gompers, P.A. (1996). Grandstanding in the venture capital industry. *Journal of Financial Economics* 42(1): 133–156.

Chapter 10

Building Value: The Business of Venture Capital

This book began by asking a simple question: why do start-ups raise finance? This appeared to be a trivial question with a simple answer: of course, start-ups raise capital - that's what they do in the modern world. But it was not always this way and history has provided plenty of examples of global businesses that started on a shoestring and grew organically, ploughing profits back into the business slowly and over a long period of time. But venture capital has endowed entrepreneurs with the power of time travel, accelerating the growth and development and compressing the timelines required to reach the Promised Land.

This book has sought to examine this question in detail and consider the overarching theme of how start-ups use the capital they raise to build value, and consequently to liberate that value by delivering a high value exit.

281

CROSSING THE VALLEYS OF DEATH

At the simplest level startups raise finance to cross the Valley of Death, or to put it more accurately cross the multiple *Valleys* of Death they will face on an arduous journey to success. Unexpected adverse events reveal new, deeper and wider valleys as the venture grows, with unexpected crises both internal and external presenting new challenges. This makes the job of forecasting how much capital to raise difficult for entrepreneurial teams even if they obey the principles of asset parsimony outlined in Chapter 1.

Take money when you can get it, but respect asset parsimony.

Entrepreneurial teams attempting to go as far as they can on as few resource as possible are sometimes caught out by unexpected external shocks such as war, pandemics, financial crises or simply a competitor launching a rival product. Raising sufficient capital to cross the Valleys of Death with a buffer for unexpected delays is what they must do and paying constant attention to the near horizon and trying to anticipate what may happen is one of the core skills of successful CEOs.

Wise entrepreneurs raise more than they need in anticipation of setbacks that will almost certainly come...

MONEY PLUS AND REPUTATION

Crossing the Valleys of Death is not the only reason for start-ups to raise finance. Start-ups are often trapped in a credibility carousel, a vicious cycle in which they're unable to hire employees, attract customers, sign deals with suppliers or raise money. They need to find a way to break the carousel and money is usually the key. Raising money changes everything, and if they have raised money from highly reputable VC this does more than just funding operations. If a VC with a big reputation invests then suddenly everyone listens and wants to do business, as the start-up basks in the glow of its inherited reputation. The credibility, or legitimacy that start-ups gain via the reputation of a prestigious VC is worth something and entrepreneurial teams are prepared to accept investment at a lower valuation from reputable VCs just to benefit from this effect. Highly reputable VCs get to invest at lower prices thus enhancing their returns and adding to their reputation; it is complementary to the credibility carousel.

VC investment delivers more than just the money and we call this *money plus*. It comprises reputational advantages but also experience, networks, and other non-financial resources such as knowledge of industry sectors. Money plus is an intangible aspect of venture capital investments, and the same is true of investment from leading business angels: they can be worth their weight in gold if they deliver on their money plus promises. Venture capital backed businesses tend to grow faster and become more valuable than their non-VC-backed counterparts and academic researchers have at various times quantified this in a range of industries.

How much more equity entrepreneurial teams should surrender in return for money plus is a matter of debate and will vary from industry to industry and deal to deal. Since valuation of early-stage businesses is more art than science it is hard to provide guidelines on how much additional equity entrepreneurial teams should be prepared to surrender just to access money plus, but it is important to know that this should be part of the discussion. Most VCs, in their attempts to win a deal, will promise money plus in the form of additional help and advice both tangible and intangible and entrepreneurial teams should seek to confirm that these promises are based in truth; they should talk to the CEOs of companies the VC has already backed and understand what value they really deliver. It is important to make sure that money plus is unlikely to turn out to be *money minus*…

Entrepreneurial teams pay for affiliation with reputable VCs by surrendering more equity.

DILUTION AND CONTROL

When entrepreneurial teams sell equity in their business to raise the capital they need to build it they are not only surrendering a share of the economic spoils of success, they are also surrendering an element of control; they are no longer the sole owners of the business and they have a new business partner in the form of an equity investor. The dilution of their ownership means dilution of their control and new voices will now chime in to discussions about the strategic future of the business. Most of the time venture capital investors will appoint a director to the boards of the companies they back and investor directors will play an important role in charting the future course of the business.

Venture capital term sheets contain many clauses determining who controls the business from the appointment of directors to shareholder vetoes over certain activities. Who controls the business will change as it grows and raises more finance. A growing number of investors will join the company as it raises successive financing rounds and some of them will require an appointment of a director to the board. There will be a growing number of voices wanting to have a say and expressing their opinions in how the business should develop. All of these directors are bound by law to act in the interests of the company as a whole and not in their own interests or the interests of their fund, but the conflict of interests that investor directors must manage are substantial and are to be treated with great care.

Careful consideration should be given by entrepreneurial teams not only to the share of upside they are selling but also the control they are surrendering. It is no longer their company but is a company comprised of multiple shareholders many of whom will want a say.

MILESTONE-BASED FINANCE

Milestone based financing represents the very core of the entrepreneurial financing journey. It lies at the heart of the venture capital business model and will be a central component of how VCs evaluate an opportunity. They will ask the question: what value inflexion point will this company hit if I invest now? They are not seeking to back the company all the way across the Valleys of Death at this stage, but simply to provide enough capital to hit a value adding milestone so that the next time the company raises money it will do so at a higher share price and so on. VCs see the world as a series of financing rounds eventually arriving at an exit.

Hitting value adding milestones requires an understanding of what *value* really means and this is a central theme of this book. Building value does not necessarily mean generating revenue nor becoming profitable. Building value can mean generating intellectual property, generating proprietary data, building a brand, signing exclusive deals with suppliers or even gaining exclusive access to sell products or services in particular markets. All the above move the company closer to success, derisking potential investments and therefore encouraging investors to invest at a higher share price.

Building value means being needed by or feared by global corporations.

CAPITAL GAIN AND THE VENTURE FUND LOOP

Ultimately the venture capital business is about making money, but it depends on making money in a certain way, not by participating in long-term dividends or shares of revenue but by generating a *capital gain* over a set period. The venture capital business model is one of the oldest in the book: buy low and sell high, or more accurately buy very low and sell very high. The risks inherent in making venture capital investments are very high and VCs know that a proportion of their investments will fail and, therefore, the successes must be sufficiently large to pay for the failures. Every investment a VC makes must have the potential for very high returns so that even if the investment is only partially successful it is still a good one. The mindset of the venture capital industry is one of seeking the big wins and accepting that some will fail and fail big…

Since most venture capital funds are structured as 10-year limited partnerships, the time horizon for investing, growing and exiting from individual investments is necessarily less than 10 years. This time limit pushes VCs to back aggressive growth models that can deliver high performing exits within a limited period; a groundbreaking innovation that will come good in 20 years does not fit the venture capital business model and this has presented a challenge for entrepreneurs and VCs alike. There are some investors who describe themselves as *patient capital*, sometimes these are corporates and sometimes wealthy family offices and foundations which may have other reasons for investing such as strategic insights or semi philanthropic causes, meaning they are prepared to wait and are not necessarily tied to the 10-year loop.

However, the reality is that most VCs still follow the 10-year loop and have a business model that depends upon generating a capital gain. They are remunerated both via a management fee and a share of the profits of the fund termed carried interest. Almost universally carried interest schemes provide the VC fund managers with 20% of the profits once they have returned the entire fund including the management fee, and this 20% split seems to have survived through the ages certainly as far back as 19th century whaling agents and perhaps even earlier. Embarking upon a journey with a defined start point and a defined end point with profits to share out is essentially the same as backing a start-up and delivering an exit so it is perhaps unsurprising that the carried interest model remains the dominant form of reward despite the drawbacks of the 10-year LP agreement.

VALUATION AS ART

The valuation of start-ups and early-stage businesses is difficult. It is art not science because science requires variables that can be measured, and it is difficult to measure anything in a start-up. There will usually be very little in the way of revenues or other financial parameters which may be reliably counted. Valuation is what investors in private companies are prepared to pay: in other words, it is market driven and therefore dependent upon supply and demand. In this case supply is driven by the amount of venture capital seeking deals, and demand is driven by the number of entrepreneurial teams seeking venture capital investment. When these two are in balanced the global innovation engine roars on but when they are out of balance, we observe investment bubbles with greatly inflated valuations for even the simplest start-ups based on a business plan and a few founders. Alternatively, we may see the opposite: Stagnation in which good companies struggle to raise money because there is precious little venture capital available to invest.

The factors influencing the supply and demand of venture capital are varied and change frequently. Hot markets turn into nuclear winters very quickly and then reverse again. Venture capitalists and entrepreneurs are dealing with unpredictable financial markets and raising money for a start-up which may have been easy a month ago may now prove very difficult. Market forces determine valuations and entrepreneurial teams can only discover those market forces by talking to enough investors. They should never state a pre-money valuation in an investment pitch and should avoid naming their price at all costs. They should simply talk to as many investors as possible and a pattern will begin to develop in which investors will suggest or offer a range of valuations at which they are prepared to invest. Venture capitalists are a bit like real estate agents who know the price of a two-bedroom apartment in their patch of the city, they are immersed in the market, and they know how much they sell for. It is the similar for VCs: They see a lot of start-ups in their field, and they gain an idea of the range of prices for shares based on what they observe. Unfortunately, this means they sometimes get the valuation very wrong when the market changes rapidly and unpredictably. VCs make mistakes in valuations, and they mitigate the risk of these mistakes by structuring their deals in such a way as to protect them from falls in the market.

> *Entrepreneurial teams and VCs are afloat on a sea of unpredictable sentiment. Supply and demand for VC is in a constant ebb and flow and this will never change. Plan accordingly!*

PREFERENCE CASCADES

One of the important tools VCs use to protect themselves from the downside of risky investments is preferred or preference shares. These shares, which come in a variety of formats, combine some of the elements of a loan with some of the elements of an equity investment. These shares usually provide the VC with the right to receive their payout at exit in priority to any other shareholder and therefore protect them specifically in the event of poor exits when they are at risk of losing all or a portion of their investment.

When start-ups undertake the entrepreneurial financing journey, they are likely to encounter a series of investment rounds as they cross the Valleys of Death and each of these rounds will not only have different share prices but will also be comprised of different classes of preferred and preference shares, meaning that at the time of an exit the original founders and ordinary shareholders may sit below an entire cascade of preferences. The appropriately named returns waterfall needs to be calculated to illustrate exactly who gets paid what at different exit levels. This can be an illuminating process and is required to make sure that any ensuing debates about carve outs may be conducted in full command of the facts.

The harshest preferred shares with multiple liquidation preferences are observed in tough financial climates where few VCs have sufficient 'dry powder' (financial reserves) to invest, and they can therefore be very choosy about who to back and on what terms; there are bargains to be had and this can mean decreased valuations and increased preferences. The two must be weighed up hand-in-hand, and the impact of any agreements made now will also determine the trajectory or future financing rounds. Agreeing to a multiple liquidation preference now is unlikely to lead to the next round being on any more favourable terms for the entrepreneurial team. It is a slippery slope leading to a treacherous preference cascade and entrepreneurial teams need to assess their prospects before signing on the dotted line.

When the supply of venture capital is very high compared to demand from entrepreneurial start-ups the market will turn towards ordinary shares and entrepreneurial teams are in a good position to negotiate for investment via ordinary shares. In a utopian world this leads to perfect alignment between investors and entrepreneurs, everyone is pulling in the same direction at the same pace and will be rewarded proportionately upon exit according to their percentage ownership. Experienced entrepreneurs who have delivered exits previously have a better chance of negotiating these terms like this, but timing is probably the dominant factor and catching the market when there is a plentiful supply of venture capital is an entrepreneurial team's best chance.

VCs usually get their money back first and foremost in all scenarios.

THE ROLE OF THE BOARD

Crucial to navigating challenges such as preference cascades is the knowledge and experience of the board of directors in start-up. It is not obvious to founders and first-time entrepreneurs why they need a board, after all it is their company and who knows it better than they? But the role of the board is more than that, and it is about bringing to bear the collective wisdom around the table to plot the best course both strategically and from a financing perspective. Having a board full of VCs is less than ideal though, as they may focus on the financial game at the expense of everything else and occasionally will forget themselves and squabble about shareholder issues between their respective funds perhaps forgetting their fiduciary duty to the company. This is where a strong independent chair is really important and founders should think about this well in advance of raising money; a strong independent chair will be someone who listens, is constantly available between board meetings and carries sufficient gravitas to not only marshal the resources of the board but prevent disagreements becoming embedded and transforming into personal conflict. Anyone who has served on boards will confirm that conflict is necessary and is good because it leads to better decisions, but when conflict leads to baked in positions and rattled egos it can be destructive, and for small growing companies may prove to be fatal.

A strong independent chair should be supplemented with industry experts who know the sector the company is operating in, can utilise their networks to accelerate growth and can provide expert views on the dos and don'ts as the business goes forward. VCs will have seen a lot of challenges over their careers and having an experienced VC or two on the board is extremely valuable, but it is a balance and that is the watchword of a good board: balance.

290 Building Value: The Business of Venture Capital

This book cannot emphasise enough the importance of building a balanced board, the members of whom are engaged and proactive. They do not show up once a quarter to eat the biscuits and drink the coffee, they contribute and can make all the difference to potential success or failure.

THE DRAMA OF THE EXIT

When students think about venture capital, they mostly think about how to choose investments, but the venture capital business is far more than that. Experienced VCs spend more of their time solving people issues and confronting challenges faced by their portfolio companies than they ever bargained for, and one of those principal challenges is delivering the exit. Putting money into businesses is relatively easy compared to getting money out, and the timing and structure of exits can have a bigger impact on returns than negotiating valuations or preferred shares at the outset.

It may be surprising to learn, but in an M&A process negotiations between the shareholders within a target company can be as great as the negotiations with the potential acquirer. The price of the deal is one thing, but how that price is apportioned between shareholder groups is quite another and the equity agreements written in stone can sometimes be challenged by groups who believe they have not been adequately rewarded. Notable among these groups is the entrepreneurial team, those who must work hard to get the exit over the line, and if they believe there is not enough in the deal for them, they will negotiate to make sure their services are properly rewarded. For investors this can be frustrating, and they will remind the entrepreneurial team that this is the deal they signed up to and they should have thought about it carefully before they did so.

Hindsight is a wonderful thing, however, and whether teams did or did not know what they were signing up to may be irrelevant if the reality of 'now' is altogether different. They hold substantial bargaining chips, such as refusing to do the work to deliver the exit. Entrepreneurial teams should know that their key moment of leverage are right the beginning, when they can negotiate the best investment terms using competitive tension, and right at the end when they can negotiate based upon the leverage they have in delivering an exit. Investors need to understand this and be prepared to enter sensible conversations about what needs to be done to make the exit happen. Management carve outs are not uncommon and can be observed as both additional awards of equity and cash bonuses, whatever it takes to deliver that all important exit...

A FINAL WORD

The roots of the modern venture capital industry do not lie in 1970s Silicon Valley nor even in post–World War II Boston, they appear to go much deeper into the rich fertile lands of Mesopotamia around 5,000 years ago. It may be coincidence that the first recorded history of 'enterprise' occurred around the same time as the invention of the wheel and the minting of money as a means of exchange, but great leaps forward in innovation are often accompanied by the development of business models to exploit them. This type of confluence appears to have occurred time and again throughout history with the cycle of innovation growing ever faster and the finance industry for enabling it growing ever more sophisticated.

The goal for entrepreneurs and the investors who back them remains the same however: to build value via a journey with a defined start and a target end, and to make money from the completed journey. The venture capital industry and the start-ups it backs are not so different from the ancient merchants who set out on hazardous treks to distant lands, plotting the best course they could and meeting challenges along the way. The business model appears to be relatively well maintained between then and now and might suggest something about the fundamentals of human evolution and behaviour – dividing the spoils of a successful quest upon the heroic return is not unusual.

This book has sought to explain the business of venture capital for both entrepreneurial teams and those new to the VC industry with a simple goal: to enable start-ups and the investors who back them to build value by understanding each other's goals and the

Building Value: The Business of Venture Capital

business models by which they are rewarded. It is unlikely that conflict between venture capitalists and entrepreneurs will go away – there will always be (and should be) a tension existing in the investor-entrepreneur dyad as they seek to reach the right deal, but a solid understanding of their respective business models and the pressures they face can go a long way to smoothing the path to success.

Case Study Solutions

Nanomachines: CREATING VALUE THROUGH MILESTONES

As with all things in business, there is rarely a single solution to questions. We can see from the Nanomachines chart below that the first true measurable milestone is when results from the first prototype are obtained. Prior to that the achievements are useful, but nothing more than the activities expected from any good management team – they do not de-risk the business by any substantial measure. We can see from the cash flow that it costs about £4,500,000 to achieve results from the first prototype. Assuming these results are positive, the management team then needs time to go out to VCs with a new business plan to raise the next round of finance before their cash runs out. There is no point raising just enough to hit a milestone and then immediately running out of money. Allowing for delays, this might suggest that at the outset they should raise let's say £6,000,000 to allow them to hit the first prototype results – allowing for delays and the time then required to raise a new round.

The new round should then be sufficient to allow the company to launch its product, as that is the next tangible milestone. Allowing for a cash buffer to account for delays, this amount could be approximately £5,000,000.

So, a total of £11,000,000 has been raised in two rounds to cross a Valley of Death in which the maximum negative cash balance is

Case Study Solutions

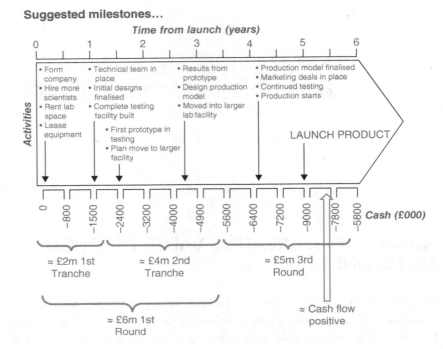

£9,000,000. This seems like a sensible amount, allowing a £2,000,000 (just over 20%) buffer for delays.

But how willing would VCs be to invest £6,000,000 upfront? This is where tranches come in. VCs may well decide that sending £6,000,000 to the bank account of a start-up is just too risky and will release the investment in stages (tranches) that themselves depend on mini milestones within the round. In this example, the VCs may argue that the company does not need £6,000,000 immediately and they will release the second part of the first round of funding after some basic achievements (like putting the technical team in place and hiring premises) within 1 year from the first investment, thereby splitting the round into two tranches of £2,000,000 followed by £4,000,000.

Gabriel.AI: RAISING THE FIRST ROUND

This case study is intended to explore the terms of venture capital investments and the process of evaluating the terms, negotiating and making choices from the perspective of an entrepreneurial team.

The first point to note is that term sheets are a useful tool for both the investor and the entrepreneurial team – aligning the commercial principles of an investment before beginning the expensive legal process of producing a legally binding shareholders agreement. The term sheet must be viewed holistically. The entire offer from VCs must be evaluated by balancing the pros and cons of the offer outlined in the term sheet. In other words, the VCs may have offered a good valuation, but other aspects of the term sheet may be unduly harsh. How do these factors interact and how should decisions be made?

It is important to recognise the core negotiating points in a VC term sheet versus clauses that are 'standard venture capital terms' and not worth expending too much energy on – such as certain veto rights, information rights, drag rights, tag rights, warranties, etc. It is difficult if not impossible to remove these 'must haves' for the VCs, although details such as the cap on warranties could be negotiated down.

The goal is to shift the deal in favour of the entrepreneurial team, guided by the key points highlighted below.

Pre-money and Post-money Valuation

In the case study, the stated pre-money valuation is £2,000,000 but it is made clear that this represents a 'fully diluted' valuation and is to include a stock option pool. VCs will also want to ensure a stock option pool is in place, but they are usually not willing to pay for it. Their assumption is that the founders should have put one in place and therefore must pay for it from their share of the equity. In the case study, a 10% stock option pool (if fully issued and therefore 'fully diluting' the shareholders of the company) would be 10% of the post-money valuation of £5,000,000 (i.e. valued at £500,000).

Therefore, the 'true' pre-money valuation is £2,000,000 – £500,000 = £1,500,000. Consequently, the founders will own £1,500,000 of stock in a business valued at £5,000,000 on a fully diluted basis. The founders will own **30%** of the equity in the business, not 40% as may be suggested by first glance at the term sheet. The stock option pool 'owns' 10% and the VCs will own the remaining 60%.

To be entirely correct in understanding how much equity the founders will own, it is important to consider the valuation in tandem with the vesting schedule for founders' shares. At the moment when the third tranche of the investment is completed (the second anniversary of the initial completion), the vesting schedule of the founders' shares states that they will own 75% of the equity that is due to them (see clause in term sheet on vesting). In other words, they will own 75% of their 30% equity, which is 22.5%. Not until the third anniversary of the initial completion will they own their full 30%. This is not a form of deception by the VCs, but an important tool to ensure that the founders they have backed remain in place and do not leave.

Phases (Tranches) of the Proposed Investment and Milestones

The term sheet contains three tranches, which would typically be regarded as too many, and appears to represent a 'drip-feeding' approach to the investment (akin to micromanaging) – giving considerable power to the VC.

The first target in negotiating on behalf of the founders would be to get rid of the tranches entirely, as they only benefit the VC and shift the balance of power substantially. The VC could argue that the milestones have not been met and withhold the tranche or renegotiate the terms of the investment in the second and third tranches (see above).

The next best solution would be to combine tranches two and three to create a more manageable two-tranche investment of £1,000,000 at initial completion and £2,000,000 on the first anniversary. It could be argued by the founders that if the VCs can't make up their minds to fully commit to Gabriel.AI after 12 months, then there is a problem in their own selection procedure. The general principle is that it is in the interests of the company to have the committed funds in the bank and 'risk-free' as soon as possible.

Some of the milestones are followed with the phrase 'acceptable to PVII LP', which means that the power to decide whether milestones have been reached is solely in the hands of ProVenture managers – they could decide whatever they want. Note that the power to decide is not even in the hands of the ProVenture appointed directors, who would be bound by their fiduciary duty to the company to act in its best interests. A possible 'win' in a negotiation with them is to change the approval of the milestones to 'the board', as it must act in the interests of the company and the other directors could out-vote the ProVenture directors if needed. ProVenture would likely counter that the board decision must include the support of the ProVenture director and that is the likely solution in these situations, balancing the outcome.

It is always best for the founders to shift decision-making and the power of veto from shareholder level to board level, as the board must act in the interests of the company, whereas the shareholders need only act in their own self-interest.

Milestones Should Be Objective and Measurable

- The recruitment of a CEO (often seen as a negative by founders) should **not** be viewed as such. Recruiting a new CEO can improve the chances and the value of the company in the long run for the founders.
- The last milestone regarding the investment round *'Identification of additional investors acceptable to PVII LP who have expressed an interest in leading a Series B financing round of at least £5,000,000'* is completely out of the control of the company – they are at the mercy of ProVenture as the lead investor, and again this must at least be in the hands of the **board**.
- In the final sentence of the milestones clause, it states: *'The Investors may agree to defer or delay any Milestone deadline, or to waive any Milestone in their absolute discretion.'* This means in the unusual event that an exit occurs prior to all of the tranches being invested (e.g. if a major corporate offers to buy the company for maybe £100,000,000 before the second tranche is invested), PVII LP would only own a third of its equity (20% of the issued share capital) at that point. By waiving the milestones, it could force the company to accept the additional £2,000,000 investment immediately before the acquisition occurs, therefore maximising the funds ownership to 60% – even though the

investment is not needed. This would effectively hand a sub-stantially larger return to PVII LP virtually risk-free. The founders should delete this clause or make the clause subject to the approval of the board to stop this activity.

Share Classes

- It is important to identify that PVII LP is investing in preferred shares. In this case, the shares are participating preferred shares, which means that the shares act as a combination of loan and equity. In any sale or liquidation of the company (i.e. in any exit), the investors first receive their principal and dividends (similar to interest) of 8% per year like a loan, and then these shares simul-taneously convert to the equivalent of ordinary shares so that they can claim 60% of the remaining value in the equity. Note that the dividends are not paid out annually but accumulate on the balance sheet ready to be paid out as a priority on exit.

- It is important to note that these are not simply participating shares but contain a 2× liquidation preference, meaning the VCs receive their cumulative 8% interest and 2× their principal investment back (i.e. interest plus investment). This puts the founders under a significant liquidation burden – often referred to as a **waterfall** or **preference cascade**.

- It is important to contrast participating preferred shares with ordinary shares and ideally illustrate how, in general, the impact of the preferred shares on the founders is higher at low exit valu-ations. Examples could show how an exit from Gabriel.AI would flow to the VCs and founders at different exit prices given the 2× liquidation preference.

- It is important to discuss how the preferred shares interact with the valuation and note that it is important to consider them **together rather than separately**. In this case, the ideal goal is to remove all mention of preferred shares and have the VCs invest in ordinary shares. The argument here is that in an early-stage venture such as this it is very important to align the inter-ests of the investors and founders, and this is best done via holding the same class of shares.

The next best position is to propose that the VCs invest in **non-participating** preferred shares, in which the investors first receive their principal and dividends **or** convert their shares to ordinary shares prior to an exit to claim 60% of the value in the equity. This is another common investment instrument in the venture capital industry and is often used when market conditions are in favour of entrepreneurial venture. This way, the VCs have to make a choice at exit – loan or equity, not both. There will be an exit valuation above which it is better for the investors to convert to ordinary shares and simply participate on the same basis as the founders. Only when the exit is poor will they choose to receive their investment plus interest (as if it were a loan).

The next best position is simply to remove the '2×' from the liquidation preference (a straight 1×) and decrease the (%) interest rate on the cumulative dividend, or even put an expiry date on it...

The Role of the Board

It is important to discuss the role of the board of directors generally, and in a start-up in particular. This should include a discussion and critique of the value-added element of a venture capital investment – the so-called 'money plus' aspect – and a discussion of whether VCs really deliver the money plus they promise. There is substantial academic literature to draw from on this topic, and students should highlight this.

The board is to be comprised of five persons according to the term sheet. The right to nominate directors appears balanced with the founders appointing one, PVII LP appointing another. The remaining appointees are nominated and/or approved by a combination of the founders and PVII LP.

One notable issue it that there is one board position for the founders not two, which may present a difficulty for them. Which one of them should be appointed? Or should they argue for both to be appointed initially – perhaps in board seat number (4) 'One director appointed by the founders and approved by the PVII LP director', but this would have to be approved by PVII LP's director.

A good response here would be to talk to PVII LP and understand their reasoning behind the proposed board structure.

It appears that the board is balanced and does not suggest that PVII LP wants to dominate decision-making. The fund also wants the right to appoint a non-voting observer to attend the board meetings. This is often the case, as it allows an associate at ProVenture to attend with the partner and pick up action items to assist the company. It is not a bad idea to agree to this proposal, but it could be leveraged to therefore appoint the remaining founder as an observer – to add symmetry to the board appointments. This would likely be agreeable to the VCs.

Additional Terms and Clauses That May Be Commented On Briefly

'The Company is expected to remunerate directors/observers appointed by investors and reimburse expenses incurred in the normal course of attending board meetings.' Why should the company be expected to **pay** the VCs for attending and doing their job? After all, it is they who asked for the board seat and likely promised how much value they would deliver via their role. This would be a strong point to make, as the entrepreneurs will argue that all of the investment should go to **building value in the company**, not paying the VCs!

Veto and Information Rights

Several clauses in the term sheet are 'boiler plate', such as veto rights and information rights. Perhaps 'details' could be negotiated, such as the spending levels that require approval, but these rights are standard and will not be removed in VC deals.

Preconditions to Completion

There is nothing of note in this clause. It is reasonable that the VCs should want to review the IP and do other basic due diligence. Although there is a requirement to produce a short list of software partners, and this is 'to the satisfaction of PVII LP', this is acceptable as everything must be acceptable to PVII LP before the investment is made!

Legal Fees, Timing and Exclusivity

ProVenture states that Gabriel.AI will pay not only its own legal bill for completing this investment but also ProVenture's legal bill. This will seem outrageous to founders, and to some extent it is, but this is standard practice in the venture capital industry when investments are made. Why is this so? Venture capital firms like ProVenture use this approach to charge legal fees for transactions to the fund on top of the 2% management fee they charge for the everyday running of the fund. It is a way of capitalising their legal costs for investment in the investment itself and preserving the management fee for other costs.

In the case there is a (maximum) £50,000 legal bill payable by the company for ProVenture's legal costs, Distinction-level students might point out that this is acceptable if the investment is completed – but what if it fails part way through because the preconditions to investment are not met. If ProVenture pulls out of the investment, Gabriel.AI is left not only with its own extensive legal bills but also (apparently) ProVenture's. The preconditions to investment are at least in part 'to the satisfaction of PVII LP' and therefore this is a risk.

Often the negotiated solution here is that the legal bills fall where they fall and in a failed (aborted) deal, each party deals with its own legal bills. This approach decreases the risk for Gabriel.AI substantially and prevents a mounting legal bill acting as leverage for the venture capital firm to prevent Gabriel.AI pulling out of the deal for reasons that it does not regard as 'reasonable'.

What Information Should the Founders Find Out About ProVenture Before Signing the Term Sheet?

The key point to recognise is that **due diligence is a two-way street**. Just as the VCs want to know everything about Gabriel.AI, then so too should Gabriel.AI know everything about the fund that is buying part of the company. After all, they are going to be shareholders and partners in the business. Are they the right investors for the business and are the founders going to be able to work with them through the challenges that undoubtedly lie ahead? Of course, most start-ups do not have the luxury of choosing their investors – there may be only one choice – but in any case, the

302   Case Study Solutions

founders should go into this with their eyes open and with maximum knowledge about who they are getting into business with.

We are aware that this is ProVenture's second fund 'PVII LP'. It is important to understand the track record of Fund I and the status of Fund II.

- What kind of investments (and how many) were made by Fund I? What exits were achieved and when? Were the companies 'sold too soon' to create a track record to raise Fund II (known in the literature as grandstanding).
- When was Fund II raised (and is it actually raised or are they still in fundraising)? Sometimes VCs hunt for deals even before they have raised their fund in order to help with the marketing of the fund to potential investors (LPs), as it demonstrates ready-made deal flow. This is important, as it essentially answers the question of whether the funding is available immediately, or is this the reason for the three tranches – they just don't have all the money?
- What is the size of Fund II and what is its age at the time of this investment? As venture capital funds are typically structured as 10-year Limited Partnerships, it is very important to know whether Fund II is in year 1 of the LP agreement or year 4 (and therefore close to the end of the 5-year investment period). The latter would mean there is only 6 years to deliver an exit from Gabriel.AI, as opposed to 9 years if the Fund is in year 1. This puts a very different timeline on the exit horizon and therefore will influence the VCs' approach to strategy within Gabriel.AI. Are they really building for the long-term value of the business or is this more of a 'quick flip' and reserves for further investment in Gabriel.AI's future rounds? The principle of VCs investing pro rata in their investments, to continue to support them and signal this tangibly, is important and is a fundamental aspect of maintaining the perceived valuation/share price of the company in the eyes of potential future investors. A VC who is unable or unwilling to make its pro-rata investment in future rounds leaves the company vulnerable to an attack on its valuation by opportunistic investors, who sense the weakness of the existing investors via their inability to invest further funds.

- Who will be the PVII LP-nominated board director and what 'money plus' value will they bring?
- What experience do they have in Gabriel.AI's industry space and how will they leverage their network?
- What reputation do they have with other VCs and within the software industry? How will they help Gabriel.AI raise the next round of finance when that is required?

Some of this information, such as the age of the fund and the investments made by Fund I, will be obtainable via the fund's website and press releases. In the case of 'money plus', the founders could request to **speak to the CEOs/founders** of businesses that PVII LP backed previously, either in Fund I or Fund II. Most VCs will be willing to have prospective new management teams speak to their existing portfolio – they view it as a family and see the benefit of teams interacting with each other.

If the founders asked you to take the lead on negotiating with ProVenture, what approach would you take to get the best deal?

The optimal approach to negotiating with VCs is to have other options. This means creating competition and signalling that the founders have alternatives. This does not mean bluffing by creating fictitious alternatives, but it may mean following up quickly with other potential investors who may have expressed interest in Gabriel.AI and informing them that the company now has a term sheet from a leading VC with the intention of prompting them into issuing a rival term sheet. Note: it is important that students recognise that they cannot send rival VCs ProVenture's term sheet or tell other VCs that it is ProVenture that has issued a term sheet; the venture capital industry is a small community and word gets around, what was intended to create competition may end up doing the opposite – the VCs get together! This is a subtle point but is crucial in creating competitive tension: maximise the perception of competition without lying or revealing names.

If a competing term sheet is extracted from a rival VC, then the best approach for students is to negotiate both term sheets in parallel **before signing** either of them. Once a term sheet is signed,

Gabriel.AI will be bound by the exclusivity clause and cannot speak to other investors.

By playing off one term sheet against the other, eventually a point will arrive where it is clear that there is no further movement from the VCs and at that point a choice has to be made...

SolidEx: RAISING CAPITAL TO GROW

Comparing Term Sheets

The rival Skappa and Hippogriff term sheets are similar in form and contain many identical terms common across the venture industry, so they serve as good examples of typical term sheets. They are, however, different in a number of important ways that make these investment proposals very different in nature, with different potential outcomes for the various stakeholders. The areas of difference highlight the various important levers VCs will pull within deal structures to achieve their goals.

Readers may wish to create comparison tables to examine the important differences in the two term sheets on offer.

Amount and Form of Investment

The Investor Syndicate and Aggregate Amount of Financing

It is typical in venture capital deals for the incoming lead investor to state what portion of the round it requires the existing investors to contribute. This is a balance between the new investors **wanting** to see financial commitment to the deal from the existing investors versus wanting to invest the maximum they can to buy as much of the company as they can whilst it is still (in their opinion) cheap. The existing investors being willing to invest in the new round is an important signal that they also believe the new valuation placed on the business by the new investors is the right one. Refusing to invest may signal to the new investors that the price is too high and desiring to invest more may signal the opposite. It is a delicate dance...

Case Study Solutions   **305**

In this case both Skappa and Hippogriff have carved out a portion of the round that they expect to come from the existing investors.

1. The Hippogriff syndicate structure suggests that the fund is biting off a little more than it can chew with the SolidEx deal. Hippogriff is proposing a £40,000,000 round but requires £12,000,000 (30% of the round) from the existing investors and a £16,000,000 investment (40% of the round) from as yet unidentified additional investors. The capitalisation table shows that collectively, Vertigon and Circadian own 32.7% of the company at the time of the case. We know that the University Seed Fund has reached its maximum commitment to the company and the contribution from the angel investors and founders in the Series B is likely to be beyond their means and therefore minimal. Vertigon and Circadian will, therefore, need to invest all of this £12,000,000 between them, probably according to the ratio of their holdings (55% for Vertigon, i.e. £6,600,000).

    *   Can Vivien Smith persuade her investment committee to invest this amount, and would that be wise from a portfolio perspective? Is SolidEx really such a potential outperformer in the Vertigon portfolio that she should stick her neck out for it?

    *   Can Calvin Hughes persuade the Circadian investment committee to raise its official ceiling on investments to invest £5,400,000 and would that be wise? Investment limits are there for a reason and are usually written into the LP agreement as a safety measure.

    *   Perhaps Vertigon and Circadian can persuade Hippogriff that less investment from the existing investors is appropriate. There is a risk that if existing investors cannot invest pro rata then this sends a negative signal, but in this case they are being asked to invest far more. It will probably be OK to signal that the university and the angel investors/founders are unable to participate (this is not unusual beyond Series A).

2. The composition of the proposed Skappa syndicate is very different. It shouts 'domination!'. Skappa is proposing a £60,000,000 round with only £10,000,000 to come from the existing SolidEx investors. This may be helpful (and therefore

attractive) to the already thinly stretched existing SolidEx investors who are close to their maximum commitments to the investment. It will be troubling too, because Skappa will become the largest shareholder and therefore will have a lot of control.

- The obvious point here is that the £60,000,000 proposed round from Skappa is not what SolidEx requested. The business plan called for £40,000,000 and Skappa have proposed investing £20,000,000 more.
- The simplest solution for the SolidEx board is to push back on the size of the investment and restate that they only wish to raise £40,000,000 and that the entire £40,000,000 is due on completion of the round. An ideal outcome for SolidEx is to raise the £40,000,000 all at completion.

Valuation

Most entrepreneurs look first at the pre-money valuation, but all is not what it seems, and valuations sometimes are not directly comparable. The precise form of share specified in the term sheet will make a significant impact on the returns to shareholders at exit.

Share Rights

Compare the following extracts from the term sheets, particularly the underlined phrases:

Skappa

'... upon the liquidation (or other return of capital) or <u>sale of the Company</u>, the holders of the Preferred B shares will first be entitled to receive an amount equal to all arrears of dividends on the Preferred B shares and <u>2.0× the subscription price for its Preferred B shares together with an amount equal to 8% per annum</u> on the subscription price of the Preferred B shares compounded monthly in priority to any distribution to holders of any other class of shares. Any balance shall then be distributed firstly to the holders of the Preferred A shares who shall be entitled to receive the subscription price for the Preferred A shares (together with any accrued or unpaid dividends) and <u>thereafter equally between all shareholders (pro rata to shareholdings and on an as-if converted basis)</u>'.

Case Study Solutions **307**

Hippogriff

'A mechanism will be included to ensure that upon the liquidation (or other return of capital) or sale of the Company, the holders of the B Preference shares will first be entitled to receive an amount equal to all arrears of dividends on the B Preference shares and the subscription price for its B Preference shares together with an amount equal to 6% per annum on the subscription price of the B Preference shares compounded monthly in priority to any distribution to holders of any other class of shares. Any balance shall then be distributed to the Ordinary shareholders in proportion to their shareholding.

Under any sale (exit) scenario, Skappa and other Series B investors will first receive 2.0× their investment (£120 million) plus 8% per annum. Then, after the Series A shareholders have received all of their investment capital and interest (or have converted to ordinary shares), everyone shares in the remainder of the proceeds according to their shareholding – including the Series B investors who will receive £120 million + 8% interest per annum + their (%) equity share of anything left over.

This is called the double dip or more formally the **participating preferred convertible share**. The result is that the VC gets paid twice. This may seem inherently unfair, but it is a common mechanism used in the venture capital industry. It is seen as more (or less) depending on market conditions and serves to protect the downside risk for VCs and maximise their return in 'modest' (i.e. poorly performing) exits. The argument VCs provide is that it rewards entrepreneurs only for outstanding performance and disproportionately taxes them in mediocre exits, since that is not what was pitched to the VCs when they got into the deal. The unusual feature here is that Skappa is not just proposing to receive its investment back first. They want 2.0× their investment. This is more unusual and indicates a very aggressive stance by the VCs.

The Hippogriff proposal does not contain a double dip. Under Hippogriff's deal we can see that the Series B investors also receive their investment + 6% cumulative dividend, but then the remainder is shared proportionately by ordinary shareholders alone. That does not mean the Series B shareholders cannot benefit from the

308   Case Study Solutions

equity – they can choose to convert all their preference shares to ordinary shares but they cannot have both! They have to make a choice, and this choice will depend on the valuation of the exit – either they opt for receiving their investment amount + 6% per annum (like a loan) or they choose to convert to ordinary shares and simply receive their percentage of the proceeds. This decision will be a purely numerical one and there will be a crossover point as the exit price increases, whereby it is more favourable for the Series B to convert to ordinary shares than remain as preferred shares. The Series B shares here are **non-participating converti-ble preference shares**. This appears a fairer approach to the exit.

- *The Skappa term sheet demands money + interest **AND** equity.*
- *The Hippogriff term sheet demands money + interest **OR** equity.*

The Hippogriff approach follows the same preference rights that the Series A shares had in place, but note that there is an additional subtle twist to the proposals that may serve to split the board... Whereas Skappa's share rights may be unpalatable, they also leave in place the existing preferred mechanism for the Series A shareholders. In the Hippogriff proposal, all existing preferred rights are swept away as the term sheet only refers to ordinary shares and specifies in the preconditions to completion that all existing share classes are converted to ordinary shares prior to the Series B. It is not uncommon for new investors to insist that all previous existing preferred shares are converted to ordinary shares. It is a more aggressive approach to existing investors and likely to be seen if those investors are not able to invest further in the company and may be in a weak position.

This is an aspect that the existing investors in SolidEx may want to negotiate (i.e. the reinsertion of their preferred rights). This is not, however, a discussion for the board as it is not in the interests of the broader company and the ordinary shareholders. Again, note the split between board and shareholders and different directors on the board...

Skappa's term sheet may appeal slightly more to those directors on the SolidEx board who are investor nominee directors and perhaps thinking of their own fund's returns. The Hippogriff term sheet may appeal more to the directors nominated by founders and management. There is apparently a conflict of interest for two groups of directors on the board of SolidEx, all of whom are supposed to act in the interests of the company. This is a common situation, where differences in the terms of an investment can appeal more or less to different investors 'represented' on the board.

Milestones

A major difference between the two investment proposals is the use of milestones. With the Hippogriff deal, SolidEx will receive the full £40 million investment on the day of completion – the money is secured, and the deal is done. With the Skappa deal, the £60 million investment is split into two tranches (portions), only the first £30 million of which is certain. The remaining £30 million investment is dependent on the company achieving several demanding milestones:

1. SolidEx to demonstrate a commercially viable prototype battery to the satisfaction of SKVIV LP within 12 months from the initial completion.

2. SolidEx to have established a commercial partnership with an automobile manufacturer generating at least £5,000,000 in revenue via upfront payments within 12 months from the initial completion.

3. The board to have appointed an experienced CEO to the satisfaction of SKVIV LP within 12 months from the initial completion.

Note that the first and third milestones are only achieved when the Skappa director is satisfied, so this effectively hands power to Skappa to decide whether it wants to trigger the investment of the second £30 million. So, is the Skappa deal really a £60 million investment or is it a £30 million investment with an option for Skappa to do what they want after that? What happens if Skappa refuses to trigger the second £30 million? They have the right to do so or to renegotiate the terms, presumably to a lower valuation.

Importantly, and this is a subtle point, Skappa also has the right to waive the milestones. Why is this important? The answer lies in the fact that if a major corporate came along and offered to buy SolidEx within the first year for a huge sum, Skappa could force the company to accept the second tranche and walk away with double the proceeds compared to if it had invested the first tranche only.

	Pre-money valuation	Amount invested	Post-money valuation	Type of share	Milestones
Skappa	£80,000,000	£60,000,000	£140,000,000	2× Preferred	Yes
Hippogriff	£60,000,000	£40,000,000	£100,000,000	1× Preference	No

The Board

The proposals from Skappa and Hippogriff for board structure could not be more different and hint at the motivations and philosophy of each investor – dominance versus collaboration. Under the Skappa deal there is one place for Series A investors and none for the seed investors nor the university, not to mention the newcomer Sarah Klein and Roger Agan who has invested considerable personal wealth.

This highlights the personal conflict of interest that directors may face – trying to act in the interests of the company but faced with decisions that may have them leaving the board. For those who are trying to build a career, for whom income or reputation matters the most, there is an issue. Even if they believe Skappa to be the best venture capital firm to take this company forward, they are effectively voting each other out of a job. It is no surprise that the board composition is usually one of the most heavily negotiated aspects of a term sheet.

Preconditions to Completion

Both term sheets impose a set of preconditions to completion that must be completed to the satisfaction of either Skappa or Hippogriff. This is normal and is difficult to negotiate away. The Hippogriff preconditions are onerous, however – they are very specific and extend into activities that would be better undertaken once the money is in the bank. There may be no time to achieve these milestones prior to the company running out of cash, and they will need to be negotiated significantly.

Costs

It is normal for an investee company to pay the costs of the incoming investors, but Hippogriff's costs seem abnormally high and surely can be negotiated.

Timing

Hippogriff's expected timeline to completion (July 2023) is too long and extends to the point where SolidEx's cash will run out. This would be a very dangerous position to be in. SolidEx's board must negotiate a shorter timeline to completion to avoid a cash crisis near the end of the process, which would put them in a very weak negotiating position.

All in all, Skappa's term sheet is better in terms of 'getting the deal done' – they have the money and their timeline to completion is rapid. But what will they be like when they get hold of the business? Will this be a rocket ship to the stars or a burden that will crush the company?

SUMMARY

This case study is meant to illustrate the challenges faced by the board of a growing business raising capital under time pressure. The good news is that they have two term sheets to review at the same time, which is as good as it gets for most businesses raising capital. The bad news is that, of course, neither term sheet is perfect and the differences between them are subtle. The only correct course of action for the board is to seek to negotiate both in parallel – edging both closer to a better deal for the existing SolidEx shareholders. At a certain point, negotiations will have been pushed as far as possible and a choice will have to be made... there is no ideal solution, just the best choice at the time.

Syntemix: ENGINEERING THE EXIT

Synopsis

This case study explores the issues surrounding exits from venture capital investments and the role of the board of directors in navigating the complexities of the M&A process and ensuring it acts in the interests of all shareholders. The challenges of managing conflicts of interest for directors appointed by venture capital funds runs throughout the case, and the interaction between shareholders holding different classes of shares bought at different prices is a major theme. The negotiations between shareholders *within* the target company can be as great as the negotiations with the *buyer*, and the case considers how the board should approach this challenge and ensure it is seen to be behaving appropriately.

> *As a recently appointed independent non-executive director of Syntemix, what advice would you offer to your board colleagues at this point?*

We focus on the following themes:

- How can the board ensure it is getting the right price for Syntemix?
- What information should the board gather to support any decision?
- How should SPS shares be allocated to the Syntemix shareholders?
- Who should negotiate on behalf of Syntemix?
- What actions must the board undertake to ensure good governance?

The key principle running throughout the case is that the board must act in the interests of all shareholders, and importantly must be seen to be doing so.

Ensuring the Right Price for the Deal

As with all exits via M&A, the only way to ensure that the price for Syntemix is the best price is to test the market and seek alternative offers for the business – in other words, to establish a market-based valuation. The challenge facing the board is to deliver alternatives whilst under time pressure to respond to SPS. Readers should consider what tactics the board may use to delay signing the SPS term sheet whilst developing competing offers quickly.

We are told in this case that the term sheet provided by SPS is lacking in detail, so one idea the board may use is to ask for a more detailed set of terms to provide it with the time required to seek alternatives. The board should 'go around the table' and ask its individual members for connections among SPS's competitors to generate competing offers.

The best way for the board to demonstrate to shareholders that it has properly tested the market is for it to appoint a reputable investment bank/corporate advisor who can go out to potential buyers and seek a buyer who can move quickly. The optimal solution is to have competing offers moving along at the same pace, so that one can be traded off against the other.

Key message: The board must always attempt to generate competition by seeking alternative bidders who can progress the transaction in the same time frame.

Comparing Valuations of Private (VC-Backed) Companies with Publicly Traded Corporations

Syntemix has raised three private rounds, the first from angel investors and the next two led by VCs, as illustrated below. The most recent valuation event for Syntemix was a 2012 investment round led by Corsair Ventures, giving it a post-money valuation of $100 million. We are told in the case that progress has been challenging since the last round, and the VCs express doubts that any new financing could be concluded at an increased valuation from the last round. We may conclude therefore that the valuation is now difficult to defend.

The valuation of SPS, on the other hand, is set daily by the market based on buyers and sellers for the stock. The current $240 million market capitalisation reflects a decline in SPS share price. The key question for students is how to compare the relative valuations of a private company versus a public company. Ultimately, this reduces

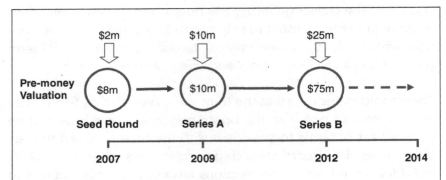

Syntemix Inc. financing history.
In private financing rounds, valuation only changes when a new external investor prices the deal. Valuations are therefore 'sticky' and may not reflect current market conditions. The final investment round prior to the offer from SPS Inc. in 2014 was the Corsair-led Series B in 2012, giving Syntemix a post-money valuation of $100 m.

to a question of ratio of ownership between Syntemix and original SPS shareholders in SPS stock after the transaction.

What proportion of SPS should Syntemix shareholders own immediately after the transaction? If the relative valuations of the two are taken as read, then Syntemix shareholders would own roughly

$$\frac{\$100 \text{ million}}{\$100 \text{ million} + \$240 \text{ million}} = 29.4\%$$

SPS has offered 45 million shares, which we are told is equivalent to $60 million in SPS shares at the time of the offer. Applying the same principle as above gives

$$\frac{\$60 \text{ million}}{\$60 \text{ million} + \$240 \text{ million}} = 20.0\%$$

This is roughly two-thirds of what Syntemix shareholders might expect to own post-transaction if the $100 million in 2012 is valid.

However, we know that market conditions have altered since the 2012 venture capital round and progress has stalled, so perhaps this is not an unreasonable offer. SPS will argue that the absolute valuations are irrelevant as their stock is liquid/tradeable and therefore commands a 'liquidity premium' compared to SPS stock.

What we do not know, however, is the prospect for SPS shares to grow in value. We can see from the stock chart that the share price has been flagging and the motivation for SPS in seeking to acquire Syntemix is to seek growth in its share price. It is incumbent on the Syntemix board to evaluate SPS as if it were making an investment in the business as below. Only by evaluating and carrying out due diligence can the board decide whether this is an appropriate investment to make. It must seek to address questions such as: How is the SPS share price likely to behave post-transaction? How liquid is SPS stock and can it be sold?

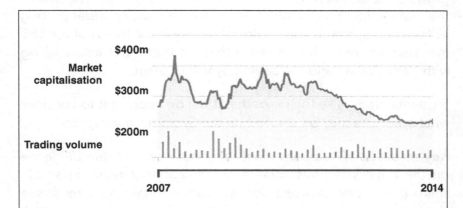

SPS Inc. financing history.
SPS had completed four venture capital investment rounds between 2001 and 2006, followed by its IPO in 2007. Share performance had weakened from 2010 onwards, resulting in a market cap of around $200 million on relatively low share trading volumes. The SPS board had decided that a strategic bolt-on acquisition was needed to breathe life into the company's share performance.

316   Case Study Solutions

Key message: Venture capital valuations are 'sticky' and do not move between rounds or financial transactions. The board must appreciate the 'liquidity premium' that private shareholders must 'pay' to exchange illiquid privately held shares for fungible public stocks.

What Information Should the Board Gather?

This is an all-share transaction; no cash is changing hands and Syntemix shareholders will become SPS shareholders, effectively exchanging the cash invested and value created within Syntemix for SPS shares.

Therefore, full due diligence needs to be carried out as if the Syntemix shareholders were making a cash investment into SPS shares. The board must ensure it is preserving the value of Syntemix in the transition to SPS shares. It must evaluate the SPS business plan, including the size of its market, competition, prospects for growth, intellectual property, financial projections and importantly – the management team. After all, the board must consider putting its faith and Syntemix shareholders' money in the hands of the SPS management team. It must ask if that is a better bet than sticking with Carol Presno and the current Syntemix team.

Students often raise the point that it will be important to consider what synergies may be created via the Syntemix transaction.

Key message: The board must carry out detailed due diligence on the buyer's business plan and management team. In an all-share transaction, shareholders in the target company must see the transaction as an investment, just as if it were making a cash investment in a company. A transaction such as this is not a one-way street.

How Are Shares Allocated to the Syntemix Shareholders?

The case presents the reader with a capitalisation table outlining Syntemix share ownership. Importantly, students are told that the Series A and Series B rounds were invested in preferred shares, with a 'double dip' and an 8% cumulative dividend. This means that in any sale or liquidation event (i.e. exit), the preferred

Case Study Solutions   **317**

shareholders first receive their initial investment and dividend before then receiving their proportionate share of the proceeds according to their equity ownership. In class we teach that preferred shares such as this are commonly used by VCs. This approach is observed depending on market conditions and serves to protect the downside risk for VCs and maximise their return in 'modest' (i.e. poorly performing) exits. The argument VCs provide is that it rewards entrepreneurs only for outstanding performance and penalises them in mediocre exits, since that is not what was pitched to the VCs when they invested.

Most examples illustrate this concept using cash-based exits; it is easy to grasp that the first $40 million of cash goes to the preferred shareholders but it is less obvious with an all-share transaction. The key learning here is that just because this is an all-share transaction does not mean the preferred return goes away – the first $40 million of value in SPS shares necessarily goes to the Syntemix preferred shareholders to satisfy the liquidation preference as dictated by the shareholders agreement. The remaining shares are allocated according to the equity ownership (%) in the cap table (hence the double dip). In this case the preferred shareholders would receive

1. $40 million of the $60 million worth of SPS shares according to the preference.

2. A further number of SPS shares according to the following ratio of the remaining $20 million of value:

$$\frac{18{,}000 \text{ preference shares}}{28{,}000 \text{ total issued shares}} = 64.2\% \text{ of } \$20 \text{ million}$$

$$= \$12.86 \text{ million}$$

In total, (1) and (2) provide the preferred shareholders with $52.86 million of $60 million of value (88%) in SPS shares, leaving 12% for the remaining ordinary shareholders.

The usual response is that this 'isn't fair' but from the perspective of the board it is doing nothing wrong and cannot be held

318 Case Study Solutions

accountable by shareholders if it obeys the shareholders agreement and has fully tested all other reasonable options for the company. If this is the best deal on the table for the Syntemix shareholders as a whole, then the board should proceed. In fact, issues may arise if the board departed from the shareholders agreement. Conflict between share classes in venture capital-backed businesses can be intense at exit for these reasons. The board may expend as much energy managing this internal negotiation as it does negotiating with the buyer of the business.

Key message: The preference cascade dictates the allocation of value in an exit, even in an all-share transaction.

Key message: The board has a duty to ensure that the shareholders agreement is enforced however unfair it may seem. As we see later, the board may have to depart from this for commercial reasons if it believes doing so is in the interests of shareholders.

This aspect of the case also highlights the personal conflict of interest that directors may face – trying to act in the interests of the company but faced with decisions that may lead to preferential returns for their own investment fund if they are investor-directors. For those who are trying to build a career, for whom income or reputation matters the most, that may be a particular issue. In this case, Sam Bassett appears conflicted as his fund Vertigon Ventures stands to benefit disproportionately from what is ultimately a modest transaction for the ordinary shareholders.

Board Process

How the board responds to SPS's offer is a key aspect of this case. The first question the board should ask is whether this offer is genuine, or is SPS simply fishing for information? This is a tough question to answer but there are several ways to gather more information. First, asking the CEO of SPS for a meeting to walk through the offer should give some insight into the level of seriousness of this offer. Sometimes larger companies will 'shake the tree' to explore which opportunities represent the 'lowest-hanging fruit' and a face-to-face meeting adds an important dimension to the level of engagement.

Case Study Solutions **319**

The next step may be signing a mutual non-disclosure agreement (NDA) in which the parties both commit to maintaining confidentiality with regard to the discussions. Although this if often difficult to enforce and is no guarantee that the offer is genuine, it represents a next step in terms of commitment – it forces the CEO of SPS to sign a legal document and that is not a step taken lightly by public companies.

A final note on board process is whether to form an 'Exit Committee' – a subset of the Syntemix board who will form the negotiating team for the SPS deal. The question of who is on it is an important one. There are several apparently conflicted individuals on the Syntemix board and one or two whose competence is being questioned. In this case, it looks as if **you (the recently appointed non-executive director)** may have to step in alongside the chair and CEO, both of whom lack credibility with the shareholders… This is far from ideal but the Series A and Series B nominee directors appear conflicted as a result of the preferred shares held by their funds.

The Surprise

The sudden and unexpected decline in SPS's share price creates a significant polarisation of returns to the Syntemix shareholders, depending on the class of shares they hold. The decreased share price means that the preferred shareholders take even more of the value as a proportion of the deal, so much so that the ordinary shareholders are 'out of the money'. The management team are prepared to continue with the deal, having secured lucrative employment packages with SPS (perhaps they sensed that they were living on borrowed time with the existing Syntemix board), but the Dark Horse Angels are not prepared to sign a deal that delivers nothing for them, and rightly so!

It might be argued that their hand could be forced by the drag-along provisions in most venture capital-backed shareholders agreements and articles, but many acquiring companies will not accept this – they don't want to be liable for any potential lawsuit from small shareholders and will not accept the risk – and they will insist on 100% of the Syntemix shareholders signing up to the deal.

320 Case Study Solutions

What are the options for the Syntemix board? They could try to raise the issue with SPS and claim that they need a better deal, but SPS will push back, stating that they are not responsible for the Syntemix preference waterfall. After all, they are likely aware that Syntemix is under time pressure and will soon run out of cash. They know that Syntemix needs this deal and that this is their problem to solve...

Another option for the Syntemix board to consider is delaying the deal to see what happens to the SPS share price but as is often said in the world of M&A, 'time kills deals'. This is not the time to play a waiting game to see what happens.

Ultimately, the board is faced with negotiating a carve out for the Dark Horse Angels. This is the only rational option. Why else would the Dark Horse Angels sign the deal if not for money? Their representative is not a board director and arguably does not have fiduciary responsibility to the company (although this point could be debated...), so they can play the ultimate hardball. We do not know from the case what 'the deal' needs to be but we know there needs to be one to get this transaction over the line...

Key message: Flexibility is the key to getting deals completed. The board needs to bring all parties together to strike a deal that works for everyone. Sticking to the rigid formula dictated by shareholders agreements does not work if one party is 'out of the money', if their agreement is required...

SUMMARY

This case study is meant to illustrate the challenges faced by the board of a growing business faced with an exit opportunity under time pressure. The good news is that they have a term sheet to review at a time of stress in the business. The bad news is that, of course, the term sheet is far from perfect. The correct course of action for the board is to seek an alternative, if possible, to obtain a better deal for the Syntemix shareholders. In the absence of a better alternative, the board must negotiate the best deal it can and must be seen to have done so without fear of conflicts of interest being raised in a lawsuit after the deal is completed. The flexibility required in creating a carve out for the Dark Horse Angels is a key aspect of this case. As with most cases, there is no ideal solution, just the best choice at the time.

Index

2 and 20 model 69, 84–85
2009 financial crisis 54–55

A

ABC Ventures 118–119, 129–143, 159, 163–187, 197–198
accelerators 16, 20–21, 26
acceptance aspects 28–30, 118–121, 207
acquisitions 55, 60, 104, 252–253, 262, 272–278, 297, 315
adverse events 7, 204–205, 275, 282
agency 61–62, 79–80, 84, 286
AI (artificial intelligence) 187–199, 294–304
ancient history 43–45, 49, 51, 279, 291
angels *see* business angels
appointments to the board 22, 62, 149, 158, 174–182, 194–200, 215–216, 227, 235, 255–257, 268, 284, 299
ARDC (American Research and Development Corporation) 47–50
asset parsimony 3–5, 7, 12, 282

B

banks
  business models 62–66, 78
  deal flow 86–87
  deals and term sheets 184
  equity 14, 19, 31
  exit delivery 255–256, 262, 274, 313
  historical perspectives 47, 49–50, 55–56
  raising capital 240–241
  valuations 118, 125, 134
Bell, Alexander Graham 49
biotechnology 36–37, 53–54, 202
board and control
  see also appointments to the board
  business models 62–65, 69, 78
  deal flow 108–109
  deals and term sheets 149–151, 158–159, 164, 168–169, 173–184, 187–190, 194–200, 212–213, 220–242, 257, 272–275, 284, 295–313, 320
  equity 22–23, 35
  exit delivery 28–29, 245, 249–250, 254–277, 312–320
  milestone-based finance 24, 28–29, 35, 297–298, 309
  raising capital 201–243, 297–300, 303, 306–311
  role of 258–259, 289–290, 299–304, 312–320
  valuations 119, 125–126, 131, 144
bridge rounds 210

Index

324

bubbles, investment 11, 54–57, 88–89, 96, 111–112, 246, 286–287
building value, definitions 36–38
business angels 16–21, 31–34, 283
  business models 61
  exit delivery 259–260, 268–274, 277–279, 319–321
  historical perspectives 49–50
  negotiations 187–188
  raising the next round 213, 216, 305
  valuations 112, 123–124, 146, 313
business models 2–3, 10, 59–84, 103, 284–286, 291–292
  see also venture capital business model
  deal flow 87–89, 91, 94, 103, 106–107
  equity 13–21, 26–28, 33, 40–41
  exit delivery 246, 266, 269
  historical perspectives 44, 47, 52–53, 57–58
  inside the deal 154–156, 159–160
  milestone-based finance 26–28, 33, 40–41, 284
  valuation 113, 116
business plans 5
  agency 61–63
  deal flow 89, 91–92, 99, 107, 109
  dynamic allocation of capital 73
  equity and milestones 32, 35, 37, 293
  exit delivery 249, 259, 316
  fund deployment 71
  historical perspectives 53
  inside the deal 186, 189, 195
  raising capital 219, 228–229, 236, 306
  valuation 131, 134–135, 287
business-to-business (B2B) 53
business-to-consumer (B2C) 52–53
buy-in, buyout 15–17, 152, 267

C

capital gain 26–29, 45, 59–61, 82–83, 247, 285–286

capitalisation tables 124, 273, 277, 305, 316
carried interest 65–69, 72–73, 77–79, 131–132, 246, 260–261, 272
carve-out 117, 136, 141, 261–263, 278, 288–291, 320–321
cash-flow 293–294, 316–317
  business plans 91
  deals and term sheets 184–185, 199
  equity 14–17, 21–22, 26, 37–40
  exit delivery 245–257, 262–263, 267–268, 272, 275, 278–279, 316–317
  fund structures 63–65, 66
  historical perspectives 56
  milestone-based finance 26, 29, 35–41, 293–294
  raising capital 1, 5–7, 203–209, 214–215, 219–221, 226, 234, 241–242, 311
  valuation 113, 116–118, 122–125, 128, 144
Circadian Capital 215–220, 234, 305
collusion aspects 95–97
competition
  business models 68, 80
  deal flow 85, 91, 95–96, 100–103, 107–108
  deals and term sheets 151–154, 160–164, 181, 186, 195–199
  exit delivery 255, 259, 291, 313, 316
  raising capital 10, 202–204, 221, 228, 236, 239, 303
  valuation 123–126, 132, 144
completion preconditions 106, 175, 182, 196, 229, 237, 300, 310–311
compulsory transfer 173, 179, 193, 225–226, 233–234
conferences 86, 202, 216, 241, 270
confidentiality 182, 196, 230, 237
connections/contacts 19–20, 47, 85–95, 108–109, 161

conversions 120, 139–141, 178, 180, 192, 211, 224, 226, 232, 234
convertible loans 120, 124, 209–212, 241–242
convertible shares 127–143, 146, 170–171, 261–264, 269, 307–308, 316–317
corporate finance advisors 255–256, 279
corporate venture capital 32, 80–84
Corsair Ventures 269–271, 276–277, 313–314
costs 73
  deal flow 88, 98, 103
  deals and term sheets 182–185, 195–197, 229, 237, 311
  milestone-based financing 293
  raising capital 205, 221, 229–230, 236–238, 301, 311
COVID-19 pandemic 11, 55–56
credibility 8–9, 80–83, 126–127, 144–146, 160–163, 207, 282–283
credit crunch 54–55
crowdfunding 16, 18

D

Dark Horse Angels 269–271, 274, 277, 319–321
A Day in the Life 85–109
deal carry 68–69
deal flow 10, 85–109, 207, 302
deal management 20, 151, 175–186
deals and term sheets 149–200, 212–215, 220–243, 257–259, 272–275, 295–320
  deal flow 105
  exit delivery 257–259, 272–275, 312–320
  raising capital 207, 212–215, 220–243, 295–311
  valuation 142, 145–147
debts
  equity 15–17, 34–35, 40
  exit delivery 264, 275

historical perspectives 45
  valuation 118, 129
DEC (Digital Equipment Company) 48–49, 50
decision making
  business models 60–64, 68, 71–73, 78–84
  deal flow 93–95, 99–100, 104–106, 108–109
  deals and term sheets 149–152, 156–163, 174–175, 181, 186–188, 194
  equity 22–24, 35
  exit delivery 251, 254, 267, 273–274, 312, 318
  raising capital 209, 212, 219–221, 227, 235, 239, 295, 297, 300, 308–310
  valuation 120–122, 131
deferred payments 246–249
demand, supply balance 10–12, 88–91, 111–112, 286–287
dilution 283–284
  business models 71–72
  deals and term sheets 172–173, 176, 180–182, 190–195, 234
  equity and milestones 22, 25–26, 31, 35–36
  exit delivery 268–272, 277
  raising capital 5, 7, 211, 217–218, 222, 228, 231, 234, 236, 295
  valuation 114, 145–146
dividends 285
  deals and term sheets 170–171, 177–178, 192
  equity and milestones 27–28
  exit delivery 269–270, 277, 316–317
  raising capital 224, 231–232, 298–299, 306–307
  valuation 128–129
Doriot, Georges F. 47–48, 50
dotcom boom 11, 20, 52–54, 56, 88
double-dipping preferred share 127–143, 146, 170–171, 261–264, 269, 307–308, 316–317

326 Index

down rounds 29–30, 180,
193, 226, 234
drag-along 172, 256–258, 263
drag rights 179, 193, 225, 233, 295
drawdown notice 64–65, 131
due diligence
    deal flow 98–100, 104–105, 119
    deals and term sheets 150–154, 160,
        172, 175, 182, 190, 196
    exit delivery 253–254, 266,
        315–316
    raising capital 222, 229–231,
        237–238, 300–301
    valuation 128
dynamic capital allocation 72–74

E

earnouts 249, 259–260, 279
ecosystems 8, 31–32, 57, 70, 80, 109
elevator pitch 93
equality in shares 127–129
equity 13–27, 30–35, 40–41, 283–284,
    287–288
    business models 68–69,
        71–73, 76, 81–83
    deals and term sheets 149,
        153–157, 165–167, 173, 182,
        189–190, 195, 198
    exit delivery 246–247, 252–254,
        258–263, 278, 290–291, 317
    historical perspectives 48–51
    pie 14–15, 24, 114–117
    raising capital 210–211, 215, 219,
        222, 228, 231, 236, 295–299,
        307–308
    selling 14, 22–24, 69, 114–123,
        126–146
    valuation 111–123, 126–146
evergreen approach 80–84
exclusivity 285
    deals and term sheets 153–154, 160,
        164, 175, 182–184,
        196–197
    raising capital 203–204, 229–230,
        237–238, 301, 304

exit delivery 103–104, 245–279, 281,
    285–292, 312–321
    business models 59–66, 69,
        72–81, 83–84
    deals and term sheets 149–157,
        165–166, 170–173, 198,
        245–279, 297–302, 306–308,
        312–321
    equity and milestones 16, 23–32,
        35, 41, 1923
    historical perspectives 44, 54–55
    raising capital 204, 211, 239–243,
        297–299, 302, 306–308
    taxonomy of 248–250
    valuation 115–124, 128–147,
        166–167, 248–258, 268–276,
        295–296, 313–319
    venture capital business model
        27–28, 41, 59–66, 69,
        72–84, 246
exotic exits 252–253

F

Fairchild Semiconductor 51
family investments 16–17, 21, 31,
    49–50, 124, 157, 178, 225, 233
fees 65–67, 286, 290
    business models 65–69, 75–79, 82
    deals and term sheets 158–159,
        184–185
    equity and milestones 21, 25,
        32–34
    exit delivery 262
    historical perspectives 44
    raising capital 301
    valuation 131
financial crisis of 2009 54–55
fire sales 264
first round capital raising 187–199,
    294–304
flat rounds 30
food chains 31, 61
fools and angels 17–20, 49–50
forced sales 256–258
Ford, Henry (Motor Company) 2

Index **327**

founders 287–289, 295–305
  business models 67, 69
  deal flow 101–102, 106–107,
    115, 119
  deals and term sheets 156–158,
    165–167, 173–183, 186–196
  equity and milestones 14, 22–24, 26,
    28, 32, 41
  exit delivery 246, 259–262,
    269–270, 277–279
  historical perspectives 50
  raising capital 205, 215–220,
    225–229, 233–240, 295–305, 309
  role of the board 289, 299–300
  valuation 128–136, 138,
    143, 287–288
friends investments 16–17, 21, 24, 31,
  49–50, 124
fund carry 68–69
funding gap evolution 33–34
fund structures 62–67, 78–82, 85, 109

G

Gabriel.AI 187–199, 294–304
General Partner 66–68, 183, 272
global credit crunch 54–55
governing law 183–185, 197,
  230, 238, 301
grandstanding 64, 256–258, 302
growing ventures
  business models 61, 81–83
  connections 85–88, 95
  deal flow 86–88
  deals and term sheets 150–151, 155,
    166, 201–243, 304–311
  equity and milestones 16, 28,
    35, 40
  exit delivery 242, 245–279
  milestones 28, 35–36
  raising capital 201–243
  valuation 112–114, 120–125

H

Hippogriff Ventures 213, 221,
  231–241, 304–311

history 43–57, 124–125, 276–277,
  291–292, 314–315

I

incubators 16, 20–21
indemnities 183, 186, 195, 228–229,
  236, 275
information asymmetry
  business models 62, 84–85
  deals and term sheets 156, 198
  equity 18, 22
  valuation 128–131, 134–135,
    139–140, 144–147
information flow 253–254,
  312, 316–318
information rights 181, 195,
  228, 235
initial public offerings (IPO) 60,
  122, 225, 233
  deals and term sheets 179,
    192–193
  equity and milestones 26–32
  exit delivery 246–247, 250–252, 256,
    270, 272, 276–278, 315
  historical perspectives 48, 53–55
innovation 46–52, 64, 80–82, 88–91, 94,
  101, 108–109
insolvency 126, 135, 257, 264–266
institutional memory 106
intellectual property 36–38, 104–105,
  195–196, 202–205, 268
intermediaries 14, 53, 61–63,
  83, 85
internal rate of return (IRR) 65, 82
internet 18, 52–54
investing pro rata 30
  business models 71–74, 81
  deals and term sheets 155–156, 171,
    177–178, 192, 197
  raising capital 208–209, 215, 220,
    224, 302, 305–306
  valuation 119, 125
investment amount and form
    165–167, 176–178, 190–197,
    222–223, 231, 304–309

Index

IPO *see* initial public offerings
IRR *see* internal rate of return

J

J.H. Whitney & Co 50

L

law/legal aspects 158–159, 183–186, 197, 230, 238, 301
lead investors 19–20, 70, 150–153, 161–164, 197, 269, 276, 297, 304
legitimacy 8, 282
leveraged buyouts 16–17
lifecycles 27, 239
Limited Partnership Agreement (LPA) 62–67, 74–75, 80–85, 99, 101
Limited Partners (LP) 10, 33, 286
  business models 63–71, 75–79, 82–84
  connections and reputation 95, 99
  deal flow 89–90, 95, 99
  deals and term sheets 158–159, 166, 176–183, 190–197
  exit delivery 27–28, 250–251, 261, 266, 270
  historical perspectives 44–45
  raising capital 216, 217, 222–240, 243, 296–303, 305, 309
  supply and demand 89–90
  valuation 123, 131–132, 135
liquidation cascades 277
liquidation preference 43, 288
  deals and term sheets 171, 177, 181, 192–194, 224, 232
  exit delivery 269–270, 273–274, 277–278, 317
  raising capital 298–299
  valuation 139–142
liquidity 26, 246, 249–252, 264–265, 315–316
living dead companies 74, 266–267
loan repayment points 67–69, 78, 260–261, 272

LP *see* Limited Partners
LPA *see* Limited Partnership Agreement

M

M&A trade sales 122, 170, 246–250, 255–260, 278–279, 290, 312–313, 320
makeup, syndicates 161–164
management/managers
  carve-out 117, 136, 141, 261–263, 278, 288–291, 320–321
  deals and term sheets 156–158, 165–167, 173–183, 186–196, 228, 236, 301–304
  exit delivery 246, 259–262, 269–270, 274, 277–279
  raising capital 205, 215–220, 225–229, 233–240
  valuation 121, 125–128, 132–136, 141–144, 147
market conditions 30
  deals and term sheets 189, 199
  exit delivery 256, 276, 314–317
  raising capital 211, 299, 307
  valuations 121–124, 136–139, 144–146
market-driven negotiation 123–124
Mesopotamia 43–45, 279, 291
milestone-based financing 24–41, 71–79, 284–285, 293–304
  deals and term sheets 151–153, 165–170, 174–177, 190–191, 196, 223, 296–298
  examples 39–40, 293–294
  exit delivery 245–249
  Nanomachines 39–40, 293–294
  raising capital 202–203, 208–210, 223–224, 229, 309–311
  valuation 118, 125, 143, 146
money plus 8–12, 19, 22, 56, 282–284, 299, 303
  business models 66, 69–71, 80

deal flow 95–96, 107–108
deals and term sheets 151,
    158–161, 184, 189, 303
exit delivery 248, 255
historical perspectives 47–48, 56
raising capital 207–209, 213
valuation 126
multiple fund management 68, 76–79
multiple liquidation preference
    139–142, 288
mutual non-disclosure
    agreements 319

N

Nanomachines 39–40, 293–294
NASDAQ 10–11, 56, 109,
    114, 271–273
NDA see non-disclosure agreements
negotiation 267–277, 312–321
    business models 66–71
    deal flow 96
    deals and term sheets 105–107,
        114–119, 149–154, 159–164,
        168–175, 182–199
    exit delivery 253–256, 260, 267,
        272–274, 290–291, 312,
        318–320
    preference shares 288–289
    raising capital 206–213, 217,
        222–223, 230, 238, 242,
        294–297, 300–304, 308–311
    valuation 123–130, 141–147
networking events 19–20, 47, 86–87,
    91–95, 108–109, 150–151,
    202, 207, 289
non-completion aspects 185–186, 301
non-disclosure agreements (NDA)
    99–100, 319
non-monetary value 9
non-participating preferred shares
    136–142, 146, 170, 211,
    217–218, 264, 299, 308
nuclear winter 53, 287

O

offers 118–121, 271–273
    see also initial public offerings
    deal flow 106
    deals and term sheets 150–151,
        162–164, 170–172, 178–179,
        188, 192
    equity and milestones 19–21, 28,
        35–36
    exit delivery 249–255, 267, 271–278,
        312–315, 318–319
    raising capital 4, 207, 211–213,
        220–221, 224–225, 232–233,
        241–242, 295–297, 304, 310
    valuation 118–121, 122, 145–146
one-line pitch 92–93
option pools
    deals and term sheets 165–167,
        176–178, 182, 190–192,
        195, 236, 295
    exit delivery 277
    raising capital 217–219, 222, 225,
        228, 231–232, 236, 242
    valuation 130–135, 138–143, 295
ordinary shareholders
    deals and term sheets 170–171
    exit delivery 261–262, 274, 277–278,
        307–308, 317–319
    raising capital 218, 232, 288
    valuation 137, 143–144
ordinary shares 288
    deals and term sheets 177–178,
        192, 198
    exit delivery 262, 269, 274,
        277–278, 317–319
    raising capital 216–218, 224,
        231–232, 237, 298–299,
        307–308
    valuation 127–144
outcome hierarchies 68,
    142–143, 170
overlapping fund management
    16, 21, 75–79

Index

P

participating preferred convertible shares 127–143, 146, 170–171, 261–264, 269, 307–308, 316–317
paying for association 9
penalties 64, 156–157, 172–173, 186
pension funds 51, 62–63, 66, 78
phases *see* tranches
piracy 78–79
pitching strategies
  business models 61–63, 71, 77–79
  deal flow 89–100, 104, 159–160
  equity 19, 40
  exit delivery 245, 317
  raising capital 5, 187–188, 202–203, 207–209, 307
  valuation 144, 287
portfolio proactive design 90–91
post-money valuation 117–121, 124, 129–137, 166–167, 176, 189, 268, 271, 295–296, 310
pre-emptive rights 171, 178, 192, 225, 232
preference cascades 143–144, 246–247, 261–265, 273, 278, 287–289, 298–299, 318–320
preference shares; preferred shares 287–290
  deals and term sheets 149, 154–156, 165–166, 170–180, 190–193, 198–199
  equity 16, 22
  exit delivery 246–247, 261–265, 269–278, 290, 316–320
  raising capital 206, 213, 217–218, 222–226, 231–237, 298–299, 306–310
  valuation 127–149
preferred convertible shares 127–143, 146, 170–171, 261–264, 269, 307–308, 316–317
pre-money valuation 117–121, 124–130, 144, 163–167, 176, 189–190, 206–207, 217, 231, 269–270, 276, 295–297

private company valuations 313–316
private equity 15–17, 31–32, 49–51, 153, 252–253, 278
proactive strategies 69, 90–91, 97–98, 108–109, 290
profit share *see* carried interest
Promised Land 6–7, 25–26, 40, 53, 59, 121, 203, 207, 247, 281
protected value creation 102–103
ProVenture 187–199, 296–304
public equity 15, 31–32
publicly traded corporation valuations 313–316

Q

qualified leads 86, 94–97, 109

R

R&D 5, 49, 103
raising capital 1–12, 118–121, 187–199, 201–243, 294–311
real pitch 93
redemptions 127, 171, 177–178
reinvest 1, 18, 30–31, 63, 66, 71–76, 156, 171, 197–198, 220
rejection aspects 97–98, 106–107, 109
reputation
  deal flow 96–97, 107–108
  deals and term sheets 160–164, 188–189
  equity 14, 19–20
  exit delivery 258, 265–266, 318
  money plus 282–283
  raising capital 8–9, 207, 239–241, 303, 310, 313
  valuation 121, 126–127, 146
reserve funds 47, 73–74, 125, 161, 214, 288
restart 1
return on investment (ROI) 3, 88, 139

S

sale of companies 117, 122, 135, 138

sale preference 171, 177, 181, 192–194

Sand Hill Road 45, 51–52

seed funding/investors
  business models 72
  equity and milestones 21, 31–34
  exit delivery 269–271, 276–277, 314
  raising capital example 213–220, 305, 310
  valuation 112, 124

Series A financing 32–34, 72, 190, 215–220, 262, 269–276, 305–310, 314–316

Series B financing 32–34, 72–73, 213–215, 220–222, 262, 268–273, 276–277, 305–308, 314–316

Series C financing 61, 72–73, 262, 268–272

shareholders
  see also ordinary shareholders
  business models 62, 64, 73, 81
  deal flow 107
  deals and term sheets 149–151, 155–159, 170–181, 192–193, 198–200
  dilution and control 284
  equity 20, 22–24
  exit delivery 245–253, 257–278, 290, 307–308, 312–320
  milestone-based financing 26–32, 35, 41
  raising capital 10, 201–202, 205–206, 210–218, 221–228, 232–242, 288, 295–297, 301, 306–308, 311
  role of the board 289
  valuation 116–120, 124, 127–137, 143–146

share purchase agreements (SPA) 274–275

shares 283–290
  see also ordinary shares

business models 59–60, 65–69, 72–73

classes 298–299

deal flow 95–96, 100, 107–108

deals and term sheets 149–167, 170–182, 189–200, 298–299

equality 127–129

equity 14–17, 22–24

exit delivery 245–253, 257–278, 312–320

historical perspectives 43–45

issues 172–173, 178–182, 192–193, 225–226, 232–234

milestone-based financing 24–32, 35, 40–41, 285, 297

prices 114–123, 165–166, 172–173, 201–204, 217–218, 250–252, 269–276, 313–320

raising capital 9, 201–243, 295–299, 301–302, 306–311

rights 151, 170–171, 177–178, 192–193, 224, 231–232, 306

transfers 172–173, 179–180, 225–226, 232–234

valuation 114–124, 127–147

signing term sheets 105, 183, 230, 238, 301–304

Silicon Valley 43–45, 49–52, 291

single term sheets 162–163

Skappa Ventures 213, 221–230, 239–240, 304–311

social capital 86–87

SolidEx 212–243, 304–311

sourcing deal flow 85–108

special purpose acquisition companies (SPAC) 252–253

speeches 93–94

spinout 20–21, 214–219

SPS see Swiss Precision Systems Inc.

stagflation 51

stakeholders 253, 304

stakes
  business models 71–74, 83
  deal flow 104, 115
  deals and term sheets 155–156

332 Index

stakes (*continued*)
  equity and milestones 16, 22, 25, 27, 30
  exit delivery 253, 259
  maintenance 155–156
  raising capital 208, 215, 304
  valuation 123
start-ups 281–282, 286–289, 291–292
  business models 59–64, 67–71, 78–83
  deal flow 86–109
  deals and term sheets 150, 155–157, 163–165, 168–169, 173–175, 184–189, 197–198
  equity 13–41
  exit delivery 245–247, 257, 264–269, 278
  historical perspectives 44–47, 50–52, 55
  milestone-based financing 13–41
  money plus and reputation 282–283
  raising capital 1–12, 201–243, 299, 301
  role of the board 289, 299
  valleys of death 282, 288
  valuation 111–117, 121–126, 129–130, 135, 143–146, 286–287
strategic debates 271
subsequent funding rounds 118–121, 201–243, 304–311
successive funds 74–79, 201–243
sunk costs 73
supply and demand 10–12, 88–91, 111–112, 286–287
Swiss Precision Systems Inc. (SPS) 271–277, 312–320
syndicate deals 95–96, 150–153, 161–164, 190, 222, 231, 240, 304–305
Syntemix 267–277, 312–321

T

tag rights 179, 192, 225, 233, 295
terminology aspects 23, 32–33, 117–118, 136–137, 198, 248–250

term sheets 149–200, 212–215, 220–243, 257–259, 272–275, 284, 295–320
  deal flow 105
  exit delivery 257–259, 272–275, 312–320
  raising capital 207, 212–215, 220–243, 295–311
  valuation 142, 145–147
time frames 125–128, 182–185, 196, 229, 237, 254–256, 301, 311
top-rate teams 101–102
tradeable 32, 315
trade sales via M&A 122, 170, 246–250, 255–260, 278–279, 290, 312–313, 320
tranches 166–170, 174, 178, 189, 205, 294–297, 302, 309–310
transfers 172–173, 178–182, 192–193, 225–226, 232–234

U

Uber 112
underutilised assets 87
University Seed Funds 215–217, 305

V

Valleys of Death 282–284, 288
  adverse events 7, 204–205, 282
  business models 59–61, 71–73
  deal flow 89–91, 103
  equity and milestones 25–26, 35
  exit delivery 247, 256
  milestones 25–26, 35, 284, 293–294
  raising capital 5–11, 201, 204–205
  valuation 113–118, 121, 143
valuation 111–147
  see also post-money valuation; pre-money valuation
  as art 286–287
  business models 72, 75
  cash-flow 113, 116–118, 122–125, 128, 144
  deal flow 88, 95–98, 101, 108–109

deals and term sheets 149–153, 160,
163–173, 176, 189–190,
197–199
equity 14–15, 22, 27–31, 36, 39
exit delivery 27–29, 115–124,
128–147, 166–167, 251,
254–258, 269–272, 276, 290,
295–296, 298–299, 313–320
historical perspectives 55, 58
milestone-based financing
27–31, 36, 39
money plus and reputation 283
preference cascades 288
raising capital 202–213, 216–218,
222–231, 242, 295–296,
298–299, 302–310
value
-adding milestones 25–29, 35, 40,
118, 203, 205–206, 208,
245, 284–285
business models 59–60, 64–66, 81
creating through milestones
39–40, 293–294
creation escalators/stairways
38–39
deal flow 95, 102–103, 107–108
deals and term sheets 157–158,
161, 165–167, 173–174,
181, 185, 188–189, 194
definitions 36–38, 41, 113–114
equity 16, 19, 22–24
exit delivery 41, 281, 285–292,
297–302, 306–308, 312–320
historical perspectives 46–47,
52–53
inflexion points 25–29, 35, 40,
205–206, 245, 284–285
protected 102–103
raising capital 3, 6, 9–11, 202–204,
227, 235, 239
valuation 112–122, 130–132, 141
venture capital business model 19, 44,
55, 60–61, 83–84, 284–286
capital gain 285–286
deal flow 88, 94

deals and term sheets 155–156, 159
exit delivery 27–28, 41, 59–66, 69,
72–84, 246, 290
milestone-based financing
284–285
venture fund loop 285–286
venture capitalists (VC) 1–3, 7–11
business models 60–84, 103
connections/contacts 85–87,
91–95, 108–109
deal flow 85–109
deals and term sheets 147,
149–168, 175, 184–200
equity 15–24
exit delivery 245–279, 285–292,
297–302, 307–308, 313–320
fund deployment 71–79
historical perspectives 44–45, 51–58
milestone-based financing 25–41
raising capital 202–243
valuation 112–123, 126–131,
139–147
venture capital valuation method
122–123, 316
venture debt 34–35, 40
venture fund loops 77–79,
84, 285–286
Vertigon Ventures 216–220, 234,
269–273, 277, 305, 318
veto rights
deals and term sheets 149,
158–159, 174–175, 181,
194–195, 198, 284,
295–297, 300
milestone-based finance 24, 28
raising capital 227, 235
selling equity 22–23
voting rights
deal flow 178, 180, 192, 194, 198
exit delivery 273
milestone-based financing 297
raising capital 224, 227, 232, 235,
297, 300, 310
selling equity 22
share equality 127

334 Index

W

warm contacts 86–87, 94–97, 202–203, 207–209

warranties 35, 183, 186, 195, 228, 236, 295

waterfalls 143–144, 261–265, 278, 288, 298, 320

West Tech Angels 269–273, 277

World War II 46–48, 50–51, 291